TECHNOLOGY AND SOCIETY

TECHNOLOGY AND SOCIETY

Advisory Editor
DANIEL J. BOORSTIN, author of
The Americans and Director of
The National Museum of History
and Technology, Smithsonian Institution

FORD METHODS

AND THE

FORD SHOPS

BY
HORACE LUCIEN ARNOLD
AND
FAY LEONE FAUROTE

ARNO PRESS
A NEW YORK TIMES COMPANY
New York • 1972

Reprint Edition 1972 by Arno Press Inc.

Reprinted from a copy in The University
of Illinois Library

Technology and Society
ISBN for complete set: 0-405-04680-4
See last pages of this volume for titles.

Manufactured in the United States of America

————————————

Library of Congress Cataloging in Publication Data

Arnold, Horace Lucien, d. 1915.
  Ford methods and the Ford shops.

  (Technology and society)
  Reprint of the 1915 ed., issued in series: Works
management library.
  1. Ford Motor Company. I. Faurote, Fay Leone, d.
1938, joint author. II. Title. III. Series.
IV. Series: Works management library.
TL215.F7A7 1972   629.2'34   72-5029
ISBN 0-405-04682-0

WORKS MANAGEMENT LIBRARY

FORD METHODS

AND THE

FORD SHOPS

BY

HORACE LUCIEN ARNOLD

AND

FAY LEONE FAUROTE

NEW YORK
THE ENGINEERING MAGAZINE COMPANY
1915

Press of
J. J. Little & Ives Co.
New York

PREFACE

FORD'S success has startled the country, almost the world, financially, industrially, mechanically. It exhibits in higher degree than most persons would have thought possible the seemingly contradictory requirements of true efficiency, which are: constant increase of quality, great increase of pay to the workers, repeated reductions in cost to the consumer. And with these appears, as at once cause and effect, an absolutely incredible enlargement of output reaching something like one hundred fold in less than ten years, and an enormous profit to the manufacturer.

What is the personality behind these startling results? What are the ideals worked out in them? What are the conditions and methods in the shops where they have been secured in regular every-day operation?

The story is told completely, practically, and graphically in the pages of this book. It was begun at the direct suggestion of the editors of *The Engineering Magazine* by Horace Lucien Arnold, who has never been surpassed for clear vision of shop matters and clear description of the things that are of value therein. Upon his death, with the story still unfinished, in January, 1915, the work was taken up and completed by Fay Leone Faurote, who carried it out loyally in the spirit of its inception. Both authors worked with the direct co-operation of Henry Ford himself and of the Ford engineers. They had full access to the most intimate data of every department, and unstinted assistance in the preparation of illustrations and the compilation of figures. In the volume now presented the pages are re-arranged in sequence slightly different from that of their appearance as a series in *The Engineering Magazine*, so that the work of the two authors is to a certain extent interleaved, chapters IX on sheet-metal work, XII on special machines and fixtures, XIV on body finishing, painting and upholstering, and XVI on safeguarding the workmen being from the pen of Mr. Faurote, while the rest of the book is Arnold's. Notwithstanding this divided authorship, the work as a whole was carried out with unity of purpose and singleness of viewpoint, the re-arrangement serving merely to present the entire study in a somewhat more logical order of development.

To the manufacturer, manager, or engineer confronted by the problems of mechanical production this exposition will excel in interest and value anything of the kind heretofore attempted, not only by the intrinsic quality of the text and illustrations, but by their exposition of what is up to now the final word in efficient, standardized, repetitive production. The Ford product represents the limit of specialization in a single type, of which each part has been evolved from practically unlimited service tests. But while it thus deals with the production of interchangeable components, embodied, so far as manufacture is concerned, in semi-automatic machinery, and turned out by progressive processing and gang assembling with specialized transportation, it has very wide application in other lines where similar practice can be adopted in whole or in part, with similar advantages to purchaser, worker, and consumer. Wherever standard articles are manufactured, some part, and perhaps the most important part, of the Ford policies will be found applicable. The manufacturing world is indebted to the great manufacturer who gave his methods and policies so freely to public description, and to the knowledge and conscientious care of the authors who have realized so fully the opportunity afforded them.

CHARLES BUXTON GOING.

New York, October, 1915.

CONTENTS

The three principles underlying Ford cost-reducing practice are: (1) placing men and tools in operation sequence, (2) installing work-slides, (3) using moving assembly lines. Their operations illustrated by the front-axle job. Description of the part and the work done on it. The original machine tools and operations devised to handle them. Suggestions for radical improvements in the machining work. The many components of the front axle illustrated and described. Lists of the operations on each, with the tools and men employed, and the times taken. Diagram of the front-axle machining department, showing every machine tool to exact scale. The time tickets and production records, and how they are used. Organization of the assembling department; the foremen employed and their duties. Descriptive list of the assembling operations and their sequence. The unique tools and operations devised to meet special problems of the work. Former and present assembling practice compared. Data of the time savings effected, showing how a time of 150 minutes was cut down to 26½ minutes.

Concise description of these parts as made in the Ford shops. Special problems of Ford crank-shaft construction. Illustrated description of the operations employed: four heat treatments; four hand jobs; twenty-nine machine operations, with machine tools, men, and times taken for each. Characteristics of the Ford piston, contrasted with general practice. The seven machining operations fully described. The Ford piston packing rings; peculiar difficulties imposed by adherence to the use of eccentric snap rings. The piston-ring "pots"; enormous weight of metal cut into chips. The machining operations described in detail. Ring inspection. The testing machine used, and how it operates.

A description of the commutator, with plate showing the components and complete assembly. How the commutator operates. The daily production; times and costs. How the men on the commutator job are organized. The workmen's routine. The form blanks and their use. Special machine tools employed. How a foundry is installed in the machine department to promote efficiency of production. The progressive finishing operations described in detail, with machine tools used, men employed, and times taken. Construction drawings and explanations of special fixtures. Description and illustration of cost-reducing devices. Commutator dis-assembling. A summary explaining how the Ford shops make a complete commutator in sixteen minutes and twenty-seven seconds of one man's time. Eight principles of time-saving practice clearly enunciated. Diagram and explanation of tool placing in the commutator department.

How the Ford foundries shatter the traditions of foundry costs. Of the 1,450 men employed, only 5 per cent are skilled foundrymen. Pay conditions that make the workmen absolutely docile. Novel policies of employment and discipline. How other foundries can reach Ford costs. Description of the general foundry buildings, and the introduction of novel Ford features. The endless-chain-driven mold carriers. The unique core-sand gallery and mixing stage. The labor equipment of each mechanically driven mold-carrying circuit. Details of the power-driven mold carriers, with diagram of old and new foundry arrangement. The core dryers and core ovens. Particulars of the new endless-chain core-oven construction. The foundry cranes. The brass and aluminum floors. Analysis of the iron used and details of cupola charging. Table showing production per square foot of foundry floor. Cost of iron in the ladle. The core-sand-mixing stage. Summary of Ford foundry equipment. Description of cylinder molding, and organization of molding gangs. Foundry officials. The foundry shifts and their working hours.

Ford painting practice upsets all supposed standards of space, time, and skilled labor requirements. How the endless-chain conveyor is adapted to body finishing. Description of the body-painting and upholstering process line in the new buildings. An interior transportation system with its main line, side tracks, stations and terminals. The first priming operation and the giant atomizer by which it is done. The operations of drying, sanding, and second priming. Drip tanks and catch tanks by which surplus paint is returned to the paint-supply system. How color varnishing is effected by similar methods. Rubbing the bodies on a traveling rubbing deck. Upholstering by gangs who walk or travel slowly with the body as it moves on its endless conveyor. Flowing on the finishing varnish. The drying room. Putting on the wind-shield and top. Fitting the side curtains. How the body grows to perfection under processes similar to the spectacular chassis finishing. How the cushions are made. How the bows are made. How the wheels are painted by dipping and centrifugal drying. How the wind-shield and fenders are enameled and dried by continuous travel through heated rooms. How the rear-axle assembly is painted.

Factors usually controlling factory design. Space conditions and production requirements forced the Ford engineers to bold flights of invention. Description of the new buildings in which rough stores are received on the top story, descending by gravity to final assembly on the lowest floor. Novel features of hollow-column air distribution. The time and cost history of the new Ford factory additions. General specifications of the new plant. The roofs and skylights. The doors and windows. The elevators, stairways, and

FORD METHODS AND THE FORD SHOPS

CHAPTER I

THE GENIUS OF THE PLANT

BEYOND all doubt or question, the Ford Motor Company's plant at Highland Park, Detroit, Michigan, U. S. A., at the time of this writing is the most interesting metal-working establishment in the world—because of its size (something over 15,000 names on the payroll); because it produces one single article only (the Ford motor car) for sale; because the Ford Motor Company is paying very large profits (something like $15,000,000 a year); and because, with no strike and no demand for pay increase from its day-wage earners, the Ford Company made voluntary and wholly unexpected announcement January 5, 1914, that it would very greatly increase day-pay wage and would at the same time reduce the day-work hours from nine to eight.

The Ford Motor Company is under one-man control, Henry Ford, head of the company, holding 58½ per cent of the $2,000,000 capital stock; and it was Mr. Ford's own initiatory proposal to augment day-pay largely while reducing work-day hours from nine to eight, with an entire disregard of the commercial features of the situation—simply and solely with a view to the increased happiness and self-respect of his workmen, and in the face of Ford Company dividend reductions made "Ford bonus" announcement, as first published in the Detroit afternoon papers of Monday, January 5, 1914.

1

Henry Ford, Master of Affairs

Character students will be interested in comparing this profile with the full face shown on page 17

Employers of labor the world over burst into a torrid eruption of denunciatory comment over the Ford bonus as soon as it became generally known, giving no heed whatever to its stated cause—a desire to better the condition of day-pay earners by wage increase, and to augment the number of day-pay workers by shortening the work day from

Looking East Down the Middle of the Plant

The view is taken from John R Street, and shows the new six-story buildings on the right. The loading docks are in the center, the foundry to the left

nine hours to eight hours, all as given out by the company at the time of first announcement. The Ford Motor Company turns out one thousand automobiles per day at its Highland Park plant; two other plants, one at Ford, Ont., Canada, and one at Manchester, England, bring the total Ford car-producing capacity to at least 1,200 cars per day, and the company has a world-wide selling and service organization which ensures the sale of its cars up to production capacity limit.

The volume and growth of the business are most strikingly shown by a simple tabulation of the company's gross sales for the past eight years, the figures below being for the fiscal year which ends October 1.

1906	$1,491,626.16	1910	$16,711,290.45
1907	5,773,851.38	1911	24,656,767.75
1908	4,701,298.42	1912	42,477,677.22
1909	9,041,290.55	1913	89,108,884.56

1907 was a panic year. The sales from October 1, 1913, to February 1, 1914, were $26,814,842.12, an increase of $8,034,601.33 over the same period twelve months ago. The expansion has followed closely the placing of more sales agents in the same territory, giving each agent less territory to cover. From these figures of astounding growth, better per-

The Highland Park Plant, from the Corner of Woodward Ave. and Manchester St.

The new buildings may be faintly seen down Manchester Street, which is at the right of the picture

Power House, with 5,000 Horse-Power Gas Engine
The man standing half way back on the right gives an idea of scale

haps than any other form of statement, one may realize the problems
the shops have had to meet to fill output demands.

Besides these altogether unusual industrial and commercial features,
the Ford company has gone into thermo-dynamics on original lines by
installing a 5,000 horse-power gas engine, the largest yet shown, of its
own design, to drive the Highland Park plant. This large engine, and a
smaller gas engine, of the same general design as the large engine but
only 1,500 horse power, driving an 850-kilowatt dynamo and a 2,000 cubic-
foot air compressor, now occupy the floor of the present power house,
single floor and basement, as will be shown fully in later chapters. But
not content with this impressive gas-engine exhibit, the Ford company
is now actively engaged in enlarging the power-house ground plan and
giving it two additional floors to make room for no less than seven
motors with gas producers, "regenerators" and steam boilers, all
based on an entirely novel scheme of heat saving, original with
this company.

The top floor of the enlarged and remodeled power house will carry
30,000 horse power of gas producers and 6,000 horse power of steam
boilers, connected by "regenerators," which are entirely new elements
in heat-saving; the second floor, 10-foot ceiling, serves for ash-handling,
while the main floor will carry seven engines, the present small gas
engines of 1,500 horse power, to drive the present 850-kilowatt dynamo
and 2,000 cubic-foot air compressor, and, in addition, five combined
steam and gas-engine units, of 6,000 brake horse power each. The idea
of combining steam cylinders with gas-engine cylinders for heat saving
is entirely new, so far as now known to the Ford engineers. The dimensions and arrangement of these five new combined steam and gas engines,
all alike, are, gas-engine side, two 4-cycle, water-cooled cylinders, tan-
dem, pistons 42 inches diameter by 72 inches stroke; steam side, tandem-
compound, high-pressure pistons, 36 inches diameter by 72 inches stroke,
low-pressure pistons 68 inches diameter by 72 inches stroke, both sides

to work on the one crank-shaft, each combined gas and steam unit to show 6,000 brake horse power.

The gas-producer-regenerator-steam-boiler combination and working scheme are confidently expected to form, when completed, the most economical heat-engine plant ever shown.

The entire cost of these Highland Park power-plant changes and

Drilling Screw Holes in a Cylinder Casting from Four Sides at Once—Forty-Nine Holes in One Operation

An excellent example of Ford practice—special semi-automatic machinery, served by semi-skilled "one-job" tool tenders

additions, including everything, will be something like a million and a half of dollars, showing conclusively that the Ford company does not hesitate to follow its own convictions as to what is the correct thing in the way of plant-driving engines.

Again, in the matter of low labor-cost production, the Ford company elects to pay day-wages instead of working its men at piece rates or on

Looking down One Side of Tool-Making Department
The Ford plant was working 247 tool-makers when this picture was taken, February, 1914

the premium plan; and, as the Ford plant profits are large while the cars are low-priced, the labor recompense is of much interest.

The Highland Park plant has a gray-iron foundry believed to be better equipped for time saving and low-cost production than any other foundry in the world, and has developed a machine-shop system of sub-dividing workmen's duties which effects very large labor-cost savings. It has applied team work to the fullest extent, and by this feature in conjunction with the arrangement of successive operations in the closest proximity, so as to minimize transportation and to maximize the pres-

Team Assembling and Mechanical Transportation of Front Board and Steering Gear

The boards travel toward us down the long line seen in the lower picture growing in completeness as they move, each "team", working simultaneously on opposite sides of the board, adding some step to the assembly. As the finished board comes off the end of the line it is taken away by the wire-rope conveyor shown above, counting itself and recording its own number as it passes out.

7

sure of flow of work, it succeeds in maintaining speed without obtrusive foremanship. It works on a single unit assembly for sale and on only one production order per year, keeping the stock of components constantly between close limits through the use of "shortage chasers" reporting at two-hour intervals—all as will be explained fully in a following chapter. It has a machine-tool plant, largely of specialized construction, which cost $2,800,000, works about 240 tool-makers and 50 special tool-and-fixture draftsmen in its tool and fixture-making department, and today employs 40 wood-pattern makers and 65 metal-pattern makers in improving its own shop facilities. It has installed shop lines of overhead transportation in various forms not equaled elsewhere, and is improving its already superlatively excellent metal-working plant so rapidly that Ford-factory methods are more than likely to be changed before the description is published. Lastly, and quite the most notably of all, the Ford company is willing to have any part of its commercial, managerial or mechanical practice given full and unrestricted publicity in print. Therefore these disclosures of Ford company means and methods for production-cost reduction and profit ensuring will be read with deep interest by all students of metal-working economies the world over.

The Ford Highland Park plant is the direct result of the thoughts and desires and fancies of Henry Ford's own mind and the work of Henry Ford's own hands; hence a brief sketch of Henry Ford's life is not only the most befitting introduction to these revelations of Ford plant practice, but is absolutely indispensable to a full understanding of the Ford Highland Park plant—the establishment, its efficiency, and its colossal commercial success.

Henry Ford's Own Story

William Ford, of English ancestry though born near the town of Brandon, Ireland, and bred a farmer, emigrated to America in the year 1847 at the age of twenty years, bought forty acres of the two hundred and forty acre Litogot farm in Greenfield township, eight miles west of Detroit, Michigan, and began as farmer of his own estate. He found favor in the eyes of Mary Litogot, married her in his thirty-fifth year, and later fell heir to the Litogot farm. Six children, three boys and three girls, were born to the Fords before the untimely death of their mother at the early age of thirty-five years, and of these six children the eldest was Henry Ford, born July 30, 1863, who grew to be a slender lad, unlike either parent, with a passion for mechanical construction.

The boy Henry learned to read and write at home, and began to attend school in the town of Springwells, a division of the original township of Greenfield, when between seven and eight years of age, walking the two and a half miles between the Ford farm and the schoolhouse twice a day through the winter school terms and working on the farm (which he detested) through the summer times.

Henry Ford's mind and fancy both drove him to things mechanical, while his father wished him to become a farmer, the result being that

Springwells Township School House
Henry Ford attended this school from his seventh to his seventeenth year

the boy decided for himself that his schooling was completed at the age of sixteen, and that he would not be a farmer and would be a mechanic. Following the bent of his irresistible inclination towards things mechanical, the boy Henry left the farm, against his father's commands, went to Detroit, eight miles eastward, and entered Flower Brothers' machine shop at apprentice wages, and at the same time began to do night work with a watch and jewelry repairer, McGill, who had a little place at Baker and Twentieth streets. On the farm, before leaving for Detroit, the boy Henry had a shop of his own gathering together and building, in which he had a vise, a bow-string driven lathe, and some sort of a forge, and he made himself a competent country-side repairer in general of everything which came in his way, so that he fell easily into his night work at McGill's, as he did into his apprentice duties at the shops. Flower Brothers were general machinists and steam-engine builders, working about 30 or 40 men, and here young Ford served for about nine months only, leaving this first machine-shop job to enter the employ of the Dry Dock Engine Company, Detroit, Lake marine engineers, building steam engines exclusively. They worked 206 hands and had the largest machine shop at that time in Detroit.

At the end of his two years of Dry Dock Company service Henry Ford, aged nineteen, felt himself master of the machinist's trade as practiced at those shops, and he left his job there and took service with John Cheeny, State agent for the Westinghouse portable steam engines, built at Schenectady, New York. His position was that of "road expert," going out to set up new engines of 10 to 20 horse power, to give instructions to purchasers, and to make repairs. This was a summer job; and Henry Ford, never idle for a minute, put in the two winters of his two years with John Cheeny in his old shop on the farm in Greenfield, where he had a forge, vise, and upright driller, and a hand-lathe, foot-power driven, together with a varied kit of hand tools that enabled him to build almost any small-size machine that interested his adventurous mind. During these two winters Henry Ford, twenty and twenty-one years of age, worked most of the time on a farm locomotive, mounted on mowing-machine cast-iron wheels and driven by a single-cylinder steam engine, piston about 4 inches diameter with 4-inch stroke, with gear reduction to the rear drivers. It was not designed for any especial service, the idea being to make it serve as a general farm tractor. The gauge was somewhere about 48 inches, wheel-base about 72 inches. It had a fire-tube vertical boiler, and the machine ran well and pulled well and taught its youthful constructor many lessons that can be learned only from the experience of a young mechanic directing the labor of his own hands in constructing new machines of his own devising. During this period he also made many experiments with electric machines.

At the end of two years' work for Cheeny, Henry Ford's father, seeking to win his son from the degradation of things mechanical, made him a present of 40 acres of land in Dearborn township, two miles west of Greenfield. This 40 acres of land was largely forest—maple, beech, oak and basswood—and young Ford bought a circular saw mill, rented a 12-horse-power portable engine to drive it, went to work for the Buckeye Harvester Company setting up and repairing "Eclipse" portable farm engines in the summers, and ran his saw mill and sold lumber winters for two years. At the end of his twenty-fourth year, Henry Ford, being now a landed proprietor and a lumber manufacturer, happily married Miss Clara J. Bryant, born and raised in the township of Greenfield, Michigan, but not a schoolmate of her husband. The issue of this marriage was an only child, a son, Edsel Bryant Ford, born November 6, 1893. Immediately following his marriage, Mr. Ford, feeling the need of a home, used lumber of his own sawing to construct a house, 31 feet square and a story and a half high, on the Dearborn 40-acre farm, moved into it with his bride, and also moved his private machine shop from his father's farm to the Dearborn farm; he sawed lumber and sold it, did some farming, and began building a steam road-carriage to fill in his leisure moments.

For the chassis of this, the first Ford passenger car to run on common roads, an ordinary buggy was taken, and equipped with a single-cylinder steam engine, piston 2-inch diameter and 2-inch stroke. The speed reduction was double, a belt from the motor crank-shaft to a sprocket shaft and chain from the first sprocket to the differential-gear sprocket, with divided axles to which the rear driving wheels were fixed. The gauge was 56 inches and the wheel base about 60 inches. The steam boiler for this road carriage was the same puzzle to Henry Ford that it has been to every common-roads steam-carriage builder from the days of Cugnot, 1769, to the present time. Boiler after boiler was built—water-tube and fire-tube and flash designs, all with high pressures, from 250 to 400 pounds. None of them was entirely satisfactory to their designer, who finally concluded that the steam engine was not the best driver for a common-roads passenger vehicle, and abandoned this, his first and only steam-car, uncompleted, when he was twenty-six years old. At the same time he gave up his life as a farmer and lumber manufacturer on the Dearborn 40-acre homestead, obtained employment as night-shift engineer for the Detroit Edison Illuminating Company (twelve hours out of the twenty-four, from 6 p. m. to 6 a. m., at $45 per month), rented a house at 58 Bagley Street, only two squares from the Edison plant, and began living there with his wife, bringing his machine shop from the Dearborn farm and setting up his tools in the barn of the Bagley-street residence. At the end of three months the Edison Company began to recognize the value of the new engineer and raised his pay to $75, and at the end of nine months promoted Henry Ford, who had in the meantime showed much ready skill in making some emergency repairs, to the position of chief engineer of its main plant at $100 per month, which was soon increased to $125 per month, the limit wage. This chief engineer Ford drew for the seven years he held the position; he lived in the Bagley-street house, was supposed to be on duty during the entire twenty-four hours of every day in the year, and put in his days at the Edison engine room and his nights at the Bagley-street house and his private machine shop in the Bagley-street barn.

In that barn shop he built the first Ford gas-engine-driven passenger car.

In his own narrative of this seven years, which took him to the age of thirty-three, Mr. Ford did not specify his hours for sleep; he simply said that he was in good health and did not sleep very much during those seven years of double duty.

The Bagley-street Ford car motor was two 4-cycle gas-engine cylinders, placed horizontally side by side, water-cooled, pistons $2^9/_{16}$ diameter by 6-inch stroke, make-and-break spark ignition, with poppet valves, $1/_2$-inch diameter intake and $7/_8$-inch diameter exhaust. The wheels were wire spoke, 28-inch diameter front and rear, with rubber tires, 42-inch gauge and 60-inch wheel base. This motor was cooled by thermal circulation between the cylinder jackets and an open-top water tank. This first Ford car was placed on the road in the early part of 1893, ran well, and could do 25 or 30 miles per hour.

In 1895 Henry Ford began his second gas-engine-driven car, 52-inch

The Bagley Street Barn Where Ford Built His First Car
This was not the car which is the basis of the present industry, but a predecessor

Henry Ford's First Gas Engine—Piston 1 Inch Diameter by 5 Inches Stroke
It is lying on the drawing board in Edsel Bryant Ford's room, opening off Henry Ford's private office

gauge, 84-inch wheel base, wire wheels with rubber tires, motor two cylinders opposed, pistons 4-inch diameter with 4-inch stroke, water-cooled, 4-cycle, with a lever and ratchet hand-start from the driver's seat. This was placed on the road in 1898. In the same year Mr. Ford left the Edison company service and the Detroit Automobile Company was organized to exploit this opposed-cylinder car. It had $50,000 capital stock, of which Henry Ford held one-sixth and his salary was $100 per month as engineer in charge; $10,000 cash was paid in and two or three cars were built.

Henry Ford left the Detroit Automobile Company (which afterwards became the Cadillac Automobile Company) in 1901, bought a shop building at 81 Park Place, north of Grand River Avenue, moved the tools from his own shop to this new place, and at once began the construction of a new motor car, cylinders 4 by 4 inches opposed, 28-inch diameter wire wheels, gauge 56 inches, and 90-inch wheel base; this was on the road in 1902. Mr. Ford built this car without assistance, having money enough of his own to finance the construction, and promptly organized the Ford Motor Company, capital stock $100,000, of which he held 25½ per cent and in which he held the position of chief engineer with $2,400 yearly pay. Twenty-eight thousand dollars cash was paid in, and the commercial model, the first "Ford car" known to the world at large, was placed on the road in June, 1903; the first Ford car was sold to a purchaser in the following month, July, of the same year. The Ford Motor Company was highly successful, paying dividends from the beginning of commercial operations.

In 1906 Mr. Ford realized that he could not carry out his own clearly defined policies without absolutely free control, and, the Ford-car reputation and sales being well established, he had no difficulty in obtaining money to pay $175,000 for enough stock to bring his personal holdings up to 51 per cent of the entire company shares, which gave him a free hand. Later, he paid seven for one for enough more shares to bring his personal holdings up to 58½ per cent of the present $2,000,000-capital Ford Motor Company organization, which 58½ per cent is now the sole and undivided property of Henry Ford himself.

Here, to those who can read between the lines of this briefly sketched biography, is the whole story—the farm-born and bred boy with an irresistible natural inclination towards mechanical construction, gathering a shop together on the farm. His first metal-cutting tool, fashioned from one of his mother's steel knitting needles, broken in two, shaped to a cutting edge, hardened by heating red hot and plunging it into a cake of soap, and furnished with a roughly whittled wooden handle, was exhibited by Mr. Ford while giving these items of personal history, as he sat at his table in his room at the present Ford factory, working 15,000 hands, with a machine-tool equipment valued at $2,800,000; the farm boy and schoolboy becoming at the age of sixteen a skilled repairer of everything that came his way, from watches to farm machinery, and all this (much to his father's disapproval) without pay, for the mere love of doing things; the home-leaving for the drudgery of a machine-shop apprentice; the quick changes of employment as soon as one shop had no more lessons to teach him; and, through it all, his ownership of his own workshop, from earliest boyhood to this day—the self-urging to work day and night—and also through it all the constantly appearing passion for mechanically propelled vehicles, from the boy-built farm locomotive to a thousand Ford cars a day at the Highland Park shops. Always his own master, no matter what his service to others might be. Obsession? Fate? Luck? Genius? Whatever the word may be, certainly a life to one end, and a supreme success resulting from an existence of supreme effort.

Above, Ford's Private Office.   Below, His Secretary's Room, to Which for a Time
after the Bonus Plan Was Announced, a Thousand Letters Asking
for Positions or Financial Aid Came Daily

HENRY FORD: A CHARACTER STUDY

Henry Ford's character is extremely simple, and extremely easy to read; he is perfectly frank, is wholly self-reliant, is extremely affectionate and confiding by nature, is absolutely sure he is right in every wish, impulse and fancy, places no value whatever on money, and has a passion for working in metals and particularly for devising and building mechanically driven wagons to run on the ground or on common roads. His sense of humor is keen and he is ready to touch with his hands the men whom he likes. He has no sense of personal importance, meets his factory heads on terms of absolute and even deferential comradeship, and because he had, up to about his thirty-fifth year, an intimate personal knowledge of day-wage life, his strong natural impulse to aid his workmen and bring some chance of happiness into their lives takes the form of increasing day-pay and shortening labor-hours of his own motion, without waiting to be stimulated by demand from others for such action on his part.

Mr. Ford is by nature a comrade; and this, together with his sense of humor, leads him to smile often and much and to enjoy a laugh at his own expense, and he is rather inclined to under-rate his own abilities and his own achievements. Socially, he likes men, especially young men and boys, and has a deep affection for wild animals and birds and flowers growing, which leads him to dislike to see animals or birds in captivity, and to dislike to see flowers cut from their roots.

War, battle, killing, and bodily mutilation are all alike abhorrent to Henry Ford, who lives a live of absolute freedom himself, following his own desires, fancies, and impulses with utter and absolute disregard of the opinions of others, as do all artists and originators and men of achievement.

As to literature, Mr. Ford may be said to have no literary tastes or inclinations whatever. He cares nothing for fiction, nothing for poetry, nothing for history and very little for scientific works, but has a strong liking for epigram, for short sayings which say much and include sharp contrasts. He abhors letters, and will not read a two-page letter through if he can possibly avoid it.

Henry Ford was the first-born child of two ardent lovers of mature age, both children of the soil. He was a child of great and absolutely faithful and constant love, and is therefore what he is, a strict monogamist by nature, strongly interested in homeless young boys, of whom he cares for a considerable number at Dearborn. He follows his own self-imposed tasks without one thought of looking back, unconscious of

Henry Ford. A Character Study

obstacles in his chosen path and careless of reward at the end of his labors, so that he but follow his ideal and reach the goal he has set for himself.

In person Henry Ford is full medium height, spare, active, goes bare-headed, perfectly healthy; he is wholly self-reliant, a law and a gospel

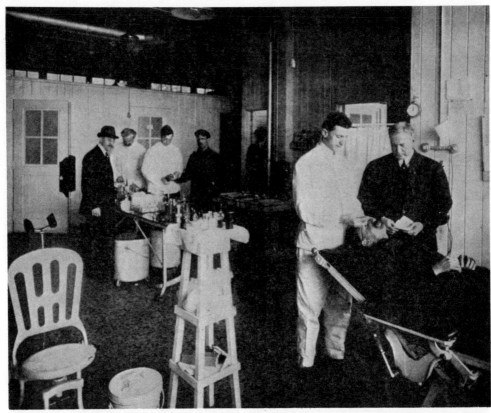

Main Hospital, Ford Works. Dr. Mead, Surgeon-in-Chief, at the Extreme Right

to himself, a man of incredible capacity for work with his own hands, and governed in his social life by a deep sympathy for all free living things and especially for young things.

Henry Ford's rightful Coat of Arms is a file and hammer crossed, with a glowing heart above and the motto "I love," "I build," and "I give," in the side and bottom space.

Being what he is here said to be, what his biographical sketch shows him to be, and what his birth inexorably determined he should be, Henry Ford is an inventor, a creator, a master mind with a vivid imagination whose dictates he follows relentlessly; a generous comrade, making strong friends and willing servants of those whom he takes into his confidence, quick to praise the young men who are his factory aids and who are constantly encouraged by him in their strongly individualized and highly successful efforts towards bringing the Highland Park plant to that condition of Ideal Efficiency which is the never-to-be-fully-attained ambition of the competent factory manager at large.

Mr. Ford, having perfect health and digestion, cares nothing for food, is never fatigued, does not use tobacco in any form, has no liking for any stimulant, and eats but two meals a day; apparently never knows fatigue, listens willingly to others, decides quickly, and of two mechanical devices chooses intuitively that which best suits the desired end, be it of his own suggestion or another's.

HENRY FORD AS A FACTORY MANAGER

Save in the broadest sense, Mr. Ford has never been the manager of the Ford Motor Company's plant at Highland Park. From the very first showing of the second car, 1902, up to the present day, Mr. Ford's energies and those of his immediate assistants have been directed wholly to three principal objects: first to the production of enough cars to meet purchasers' demands; second, to making car improvements; and third, to means for distributing cars and instructing and assisting Ford car

Assembling the Flywheel Magneto. A Characteristic Example of Team Work
The work is moving toward the back of the picture, approaching completion by successive operations as it passes from team to team

buyers and users in the proper care and management of their new vehicles. The general scheme of the Ford Motor Company's operations has been largely of Mr. Ford's origination, but the details of organization have been carried out by others. So far as a close observer can discover, Ford himself had no premeditations, but acts wholly upon inspiration. In reply to a direct question he disclaimed any systematic theory of organization or administration, or any dependence upon scientific management, and seemed to lay emphasis wholly upon the personal equation. As he put it, "I know what kind of help I want and I look around until I find the man I am sure will give it." He has thus built up about himself not so much an organization as a staff of aides—all ranking as equals, none in command of any one department, all ranking any titular departmental head, each eager both to meet any suggestion Ford advances or to volunteer suggestions for his decision, each as likely as the other to be put in charge of any shop-betterment idea Ford may conceive, because he observes no discrimination in lines of service. This alone makes the Ford establishment unusual, to say the least, in its direction. It also makes the establishment his own absolutely throughout, though, as he said, leisurely looking out of his office window, "I have no job here— nothing to do."

The Basis of Ford's Success—The Ford Car

The whole vast expansion of the Ford plant, which has evolved the methods and policies to be set forth in these chapters, rests upon one broad, simple foundation—the commercial success of the Ford car. Some survey of the scope and reason for this success is therefore essential to any full understanding of the mechanical and physical features of the business built upon it.

From the first, Ford's motor-car designing ran towards a small, low-cost automobile, to meet all-round service requirements of the average man at a price which the average man could afford to pay. The 1914 "Model T" Ford car is 56-inch gauge, 100-inch wheel base, has wood-spoke wheels, a half-elliptic spring in front and a half-elliptic spring in the rear, is driven by a four-cylinder, 4-cycle water-cooled motor of about 20 brake horse power, pistons $3\frac{3}{4}$-inch diameter with 4-inch stroke, and a planetary speed change, two forward speeds and a reverse with one universal joint to the propeller shaft and bevel gear and balance gear to the rear axles. It can show about 35 to 40 miles an hour on good roads, making about 18 to 20 miles to the gallon of gasoline.

The distinctive feature of the Ford-car chassis design is the triangular

Girl Workers Making Fields for Fly-Wheel Magnetos

bracing of both front and rear axles, with a globe-joint triangle apex attachment to the chassis frame, which gives an absolutely free vertical wheel position and adjustment to each one of the four wheels independently, to suit road surface level variations. The Model T chassis frame is supported front and rear the same, at the middle of the end cross members.

Ford's experience in connection with farm steam engines made him fully aware from the very first of what must be done for the buyer to make him a fully satisfied purchaser—how the buyer must be coached and taught, and supplied with low-cost repairs and replacements; and he saw to it that every owner of a Ford car was taught and helped in every way towards satisfactory service.

The small price, small weight and general suitability for both business and pleasure requirements of the average man and average family, combined with the inherent desire of humanity at large for rapid translation, and with methods of placing Ford cars in easy reach of prospective buyers, and the careful attention to the needs of car buyers and users, taken together, fully account for the spectacular financial success of the Ford Motor Company Highland Park plant, where a new-born car pushes the doors open itself and glides out into the world under its own power, a thousand times during each working day of the year.

Expert analysis does not show any one point of such commanding merit in the Ford car as to compel the intending buyer to prefer it to any other. The Ford car is good at all points, but it has only one point of radical departure in design from many other small cars; the Ford ignition is by a flywheel magneto instead of by a wholly distinct magneto, gear-driven from the crank shaft, as is common practice; but this one point of notable difference is not enough to account for the Ford car sales preponderance, because the ordinary separate magneto gives a good and satisfactory ignition; hence the real cause of the Ford car sales volume must be looked for elsewhere.

Every man takes the easiest way to do what he wishes to be done. The Ford selling system details make it easier for the man who desires a motor car to buy a Ford car than to buy any other car whatever, simply because the vast multitude of selling agencies places the Ford car in easiest reach of the intending buyer, who is thus made certain to consider the Ford before buying; and when made fully acquainted with the Ford car and fully informed as to the small fuel consumption, the low price of replacements (which are listed at bare cost) and taught by the willing salesman to handle the car on the road, the inquirer is almost certain to purchase because of the low price.

Thus the commercial serpent of Ford car trade is seen to have its tail in its mouth, making the circle complete and endless, and, so far as can now be seen, impregnable. The Ford cars are bought by everybody because they are low-cost, good, and everywhere present; and they are low-cost, good and everywhere present because the large sales enable the Ford company to produce cars cheaply, to make them good, and to support thousands of selling agencies scattered over the entire habitable face of the world. The astounding results expressed briefly in figures are given on page 3.

The Highland Park Plant

The Ford Motor Company factory is located in the village of Highland Park, adjoining the north boundary of the city of Detroit, Michigan, U. S. A. Highland Park has at the date of this writing (Feb. 14, 1914), a cosmopolitan population of about 20,000, including Hungarians, Poles, Servians, Armenians, Bohemians, Russians, Jews, Roumanians, Bulgarians, Slavs, Italians, Croatians, Swedes, Norwegians, Austrians,

Negroes, Irish, Scotch, English, Dutch, French, Germans, Danish, Welch, Spanish, Japanese, Greeks and Mexicans. The greater part of these representatives of the diverse nations of the world have been added to the Highland Park population because of the Ford-plant location in that village.

The Ford Motor Company's realty extends 56 rods north of Manchester Avenue, on Woodward Avenue, 180 rods east on Manchester Avenue, 56 rods north to the Detroit Terminal Railway Company's right of way, and thence the north boundary line extends 180 rods west to Woodward Avenue. The Detroit Terminal Railway is a belt line, connected with every railway entering Detroit, giving the Ford spur tracks direct railway communication to all railway stations in North America. An outline ground plan is shown on the folding insert facing page 24, and plans of the separate floors are given on the reverse side. Full descriptions of the shop and foundry and other buildings and of their equipment and operation are found in later chapters.

This Highland Park realty holding was purchased in 1907, at a cost of $62,000, and the first Ford factory building on this plot was erected in 1908. Additions to the plant buildings have been and yet are under continuous erection, and this story will be obsolete before it is printed because of the very large additions now under construction.

At the present time there are three buildings four stories high, the total factory floor-space, including the machine shop, covering 28.29 acres, with an additional 2.12 acres of floor area in the Administration building. The two six-story buildings under construction will add 14.85 acres, making a total of 45.26 acres of floor space.

The superstructures of all buildings except those of one story are reinforced concrete. The one-story buildings, which comprise the machine shops, heat-treatment building, foundry, auto shed, engine house and boiler house, are structural steel with concrete foundations and brick or concrete side walls.

Floors in machine shop are of wood over tar rock or cinders, on a six-inch concrete bottom. In the heat-treatment building floors are of brick except directly under the machines, where they are of concrete. In the foundry a greater portion of the floor is dirt-filled, with some patches of concrete and brick. Throughout the factory proper, most of the floors are of concrete, though the upper three floors of the four-story building facing Woodward Avenue are of one-inch maple on a cinder fill, and a few maple floors are laid in other parts of the plant.

Roofs are generally of reinforced concrete covered with built-up roofing, flat except on the machine shop and foundry, which are saw-toothed. The exterior walls of all factory buildings show about 75 per cent of glass, double strength, in steel sash. The roofs of two of the four crane-ways and of the auto shed are nearly 100 per cent ribbed wire glass.

Heating of the old buildings is by indirect system on the first floors and by direct hot-water radiation on the upper stories. The new buildings will be heated entirely by indirect system, the apparatus being placed on the roof and the air forced down through hollow interior columns.

Highland Park lies 58 feet above Detroit River watermark, is nearly

Endless Belt Conveyor between Two Rows of Punch Presses
It carries the product from one operation to the next and finally to sorters who put the various pieces into their separate boxes

Another Example of Special Tools with Semi-Skilled Tenders
Stepped three-spindle lathes for a steel axle job

level, and has about 3 feet of sandy loam overlying a deep blue-clay bed, with limestone below. The water supply for manufacturing purposes comes from three artesian wells, and is slightly salt. Drinking water is taken from city mains, and is excellent.

The cash cost of the Ford plant buildings, tanks, and fixtures totaled $3,575,000, February 10, 1914. The first building was erected in 1908, and additions have been in constant progress ever since. The machine-tool equipment has cost about $2,800,000, to February 10, and is constantly being increased. Very large six-story buildings are now (April, 1915) in progress of erection on each side of the railway tracks, each track served by a traveling crane which will load and unload cars by crane transfer direct to seventeen different landings on each floor of these new buildings, and the entire space between the foundry and Manchester Street will be roofed over when the new buildings are completed. Handling of materials and work in progress of finishing is now the principal problem of motor-car cost-reduction, as the machine tools and the assembling processes and methods are now highly specialized; but the factory, as now arranged, employs somewhere from 800 to 1,000 truck-men, pullers and shovers, most of whom will be needless when the new buildings are completed and traveling-crane service is given fullest possible employment. The present machine shop will be transferred to the new buildings, and the present machine-tool floors will be used for storage only. In the new shops the foundry will occupy the top floor of one building and rough stores and the machine tools demanding most light will occupy the other top floors; work in progress will descend in

Monorail Trolley Hauling a Truck from Railroad Platform to Factory

natural course of operations until it reaches the train-loading platforms in completed condition, ready for instant shipment. This will be more fully shown and described later.

The lightest Ford car, 1914, weighs 1,400 pounds, and as 1,000 cars are turned out per day this gives 1,400,000 pounds of materials to be handled many times over in the course of each day's work, thus making transportation improvements the principal factor of future Ford car flat-cost reduction. The importance of shop transportation was very early recognized in the Ford machine shop, and is answered as far as may be by placing the needful tools and fixtures, no matter what they are, in the line of work-finishing travel, rather than in groups of similar tools, as in the ordinary machine-shop practice. The present shop transportation is by a gantry crane serving the foundry, three traveling cranes serving the stock and heavier work machine-shop floor, and by a monorail line, equipped with electric locomotives, which makes a belt line about the shop, with a direct line from the foundry past the heat-treating building, to the machine shop. But in addition to these means of mechanical load-carrying there is yet a very large volume of muscular lifting, hauling, pushing and dragging done in the Ford shops, much of which can be saved in the new six-floor buildings, with crane service

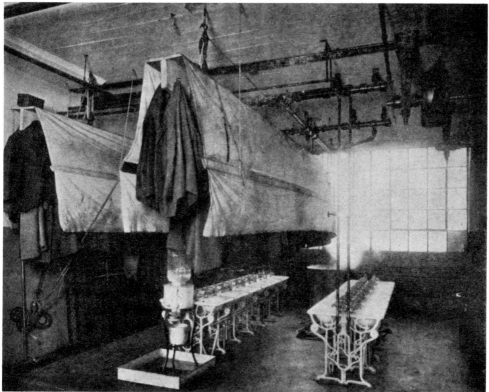

A departmental lavatory, with individual basins, water bottle, and canvas-covered coat hangers raised by rope and pulleys

direct from the railway tracks to seventeen separate landing points for each of the floors of each building and with the foundry on the top floor.

The American manufacture of the third model (the Ford car of today) was no sooner established than the organization of the Canadian Ford Company, Limited, capital stock $1,000,000, was undertaken and carried out by Mr. Ford and his associates, the Canadian stockholders furnishing about one-third of the capital invested. The company was chartered in August, 1904, to supply the English provincial demand, the territory to be covered comprising Canada, Australia, New Zealand, South Africa, and India.

Tool Crib Surmounted by Closets

Stairways to the urinals are seen to right and left of the tool window. These department cribs and closets minimizing the workmen's travel are a characteristic feature of the Ford shops

The Canadian company began commercial operations by building 110 cars in 1905, increased this output to 11,589 cars in 1913, at the end of which year they had built a total of 29,000 cars and were in a highly prosperous condition. The new Canadian plant, located 1½ miles in a northerly direction from the custom house, Windsor, Ontario, Canada, was begun in 1910, and the buildings have now a floor area of 300,000 square feet and are being enlarged.

The Canadian Ford Company, Ltd., at the time of this writing, February 25, 1914, carries 1,510 names on the pay roll and is working up to about maximum capacity in turning out 110 cars per day, identical in every particular with the American Ford cars. The Canadian factory plant is the same, save in size, as that at Highland Park, and the works are driven by a pair of Hamilton-Gray engines, 750 horse-power each, 1,500 horse-power combined, similar in design to the big engines at Highland Park.

The Ford company is by no means builder of the entire Ford car.

The bodies, wheels, tires, coil-box units, carburetors, lamps, 90 per cent of the car painting, all drop-forgings, all roller and ball bearings, grease cups, spark plugs, electric conductors, gaskets, hose connections and hose clips, the horn, the fan belt, the muffler pipe, and a considerable part of the bolts and nuts, are purchased from outside sources of supply. There is about $11,000,000 value of drop forgings made yearly in the United States, and of this the Ford company buys about $5,000,000 worth, or nearly one-half. The body making is another very large item, which employs several thousand men in five entirely separate and distinct factories.

To shorten as much as may be the lines of travel of materials and components in the shop, the machine tools are placed much closer together on the floor than is usual, so that there is but barely room for the workman to make his needful movements; and to simplify each individual's task as much as possible, team work is employed very largely,

Applicants for Work crowded into Manchester Avenue on Rumors of the Ford Bonus

Shifts start and stop at various hours in different departments as the flow of work requires. Thus the employees pass in and out by groups—not all together

the work sliding along on pipe ways as assembling progresses. A direct necessity for successful team-work is ready closet access, and the closets are therefore placed over the tool-cribs, one or more for each assembling job, so that team workers may lose as little time in necessary absences as possible. The arrangement is illustrated on page 28.

The foregoing brief particularizing of the peculiar shop conditions, brought about by mere works magnitude, will enable the attentive reader to follow some detailed examples of Ford shop practice intelligently, although the Ford production routine involves some altogether novel agencies, among which the "shortage chaser" is the most unusual as well as the most indispensable feature, all, as will be shown in the immediately following chapter, describing some of the more notable features of Ford machine-shop practice.

CHAPTER II

THE FORD STOCK SYSTEM AND EMPLOYMENT METHODS

I T is absolutely correct to say that the Ford Highland Park shops are unique. The place certainly stands alone in three vital particulars, which dominate the practice at every point:—

First, the company has but one solitary item of commercial product, the Ford motor car, made in one form only, because the differing body forms do not in any way modify the single chassis.

Second, the entire human race desires to ride, and to ride fast and cheaply, and the Ford car meets these conditions of human desire more suitably than any other automobile meets them, and hence is truly and in every sense a certain money maker.

Third, the Ford car holds so closely to the one unchanged model that it becomes commercially possible to equip the shops with every special tool, great or small, simple or complex, cheap or costly, which can be made to reduce production labor-costs.

The Ford shop production has never yet met the purchase demand for cars. There has never yet been a year in the history of the Ford Motor Company in which it did not refuse "immediate delivery" spring and summer orders. The Ford factory product is always over-sold; no car is ever stored at the Highland Park plant for one single day, because this plant has absolutely no place to store its product save in railway cars, and 90 per cent of the automobiles shipped from Highland Park carry with them cash-on-delivery bills of lading. The remaining 10 per cent of the Highland production is shipped to the various Ford "branches," which are, in fact, merely removed members of the Highland Park plant, owned by the Ford Motor Company, and operated by men paid by the Ford Motor Company, who sell this 10 per cent of the plant production at retail, to supply the branch local demand. This branch handling capacity, equaling 10 per cent of the total production, is the reservoir which takes care of the difference between day-by-day actual sales and the total output. The fact that 10 per cent of the total production provides a sufficient storage volume for cash-sales fluctuations shows the unparalleled steadiness of the increase in the demand for the Ford Motor Company's one and only automobile.

These three points of generic distinction—first, that the factory produces but a single article for sale; second, that it is an article of universal human desire, sold for cash to within 10 per cent of the total volume of production the moment it is completed; third, that being exempt from commercial demand for change of form, this article can be built through special machine-tool equipment of enormous cost—these three extraordinary characteristics place the Ford shops in a class by themselves for their certainty of money-making and exemption from rivalry with their product or competition for their gains.

These are not merely unconsidered assertions made in the interests of the Ford Motor Company. On the contrary they are the carefully matured conclusions of a widely inclusive search for the ultimate causes of the profits which compel a steady flow of vast sums of money through the Ford treasury, day in and day out, the whole year round.

The motor car had its epoch of opportunity, and Henry Ford was fortunate enough to make the car best fitted of all cars of its date to seize this opportunity, and to give this car sufficient vitality and stamina to enable it to hold what it grasped. He who best supplies a universally existent human desire has Fortune at his feet, as all students of commercial success are well aware. Mankind at large will surely purchase whatever meets its desires, and the lower the price the wider the field of sale. That is the foundation of trade at large, and what is here said of the true cause of the Ford car success cannot possibly be controverted.

The Ford factory holding thus, as it certainly does, a position commercially unique, may be safely expected to show very marked features of factory practice, wholly unlike the practice of any other existing factory, because the practice of every factory must be dominated by commercial conditions solely, if it is to continue in active existence, and the Ford factory does not disappoint those who expect to find its practice unique at vital points.

Maximum Production the Objective

The urgent demand for maximum production is the dominant condition which governs every activity of the Highland Park shops. It is true that the automobile trade at large has its dull trade season of the year, that the spring and summer sales of motor cars vastly exceed those of the fall and winter, so far as the purchases of actual car-users are concerned; but nothing of this season-of-the-year-governed call for cars is ever felt in the Ford shops to the extent of giving the factory a slack period. The Ford system of branches and local sales agents acts as a reservoir of production; so that, because the maximum yearly production of the Ford car-building shops has never yet equaled the prospective demand for cars in the near future, the Highland Park shops are always worked to full capacity.

The Highland Park shops are very far from manufacturing the entire Ford car. A long list of components, both rough and finished, are purchased from outside suppliers, who produce and sell to the Ford Company the bodies, wheels, tires, coil-box units, carburetors, lamps, 90 per cent of the car-body painting, all drop forgings, all roller and ball bearings, grease cups, spark-plugs, electrical conductors, gaskets, hose connections and clips, horn, fan-belt, muffler pipe, and part of the bolts. It is the policy of the company to deal with several suppliers of the same component, to ensure supply by drawing from several sources (which certainty of supply could not be had from any single producer) and also to make possible avail of competitive advantages not to be had if the total orders were placed with a single producer only.

Because the Ford Motor Company has but one production unit, the Ford car, and because the commercial demand for these cars has been, from the very first up to now, in excess of the plant production supply, the Ford production order is largely a matter of form and anticipatory surmise, based, as to quantity, on the "best judgment" of the sales department.

This commercial condition of being always over-sold must, of course, dominate the Ford factory activities in all directions, and does, in point of fact, make the fixing of a production limit by an inflexible production order an impossibility.

The Ford fiscal year begins and ends October 1, and inventory is taken at that time, by actual count and survey. The Ford shops are minutely systematized, and all accounts are carefully and accurately kept; no purchase order is issued without what amounts to a complete inventory of the component under replenishment, so that, save to discover theft, the Ford shops might dispense with the costly function of "inventory by count and survey" altogether, so far as fixing purchase order quantities is concerned.

Prior to October 1 of each year a consultation between the sales-department heads and the manufacturing department is held, and the estimate of the number of cars to be turned out during each individual month of the year to come is marked in the twelve month-spaces on a large sheet of section-lined paper, ten spaces to the inch. This monthly car-production number is communicated to the factory heads, and is used as a basis for the purchase-order department; but the original numbers of cars to be produced in any month to come may be changed on advices from the sales department.

As the fiscal year goes on, the factory superintendent plots a "production curve" on the large sheet of section-ruled paper headed by the twelve spaces filled with the car-production quantities of the individual months, and thus obtains a diagram which shows the factory car output in detail and in total, at a glance, as the months progress.

Meantime, the factory departments are producing finished components to meet the requirements of the production-order schedule, and it would seem that, with an accurately compiled record of finished stores produced, checked by an accurate record of complete cars, complete assembled units, and finished components shipped from the Highland Park plant, there should never be a moment's doubt or question as to the individual finished-component stores on hand and ready for use by the assemblers, so that all prospective shortages of components would be accurately known and replenished to the safety mark long before the prospective shortages became a present actual condition; but such is not the fact.

LOCATION AND ARRANGEMENT OF OFFICES

The offices of those departmental heads directly instrumental in machine-shop supply and working are located on the west side of the machine shop, begin at an east-and-west line through the middle of the Administration building, and extend northward, in the following order:

First and second, anteroom and office of the machine-shop superintendent, who has one assistant, the two working together in such absolute harmony that I was informed that they were of equal rank, which appears to be the truth in practice, though not in accordance with the register of officials; third, inspector-in-chief; fourth, buildings maintenance; fifth, the clearing house, which is also the stock-superintendent's office, and sixth, the shortage-chaser's desk, shared with the clearing-house chief clerk. Close at hand the clerks working under orders from the clearing-house chief clerk, who keeps board and book records of all components produced, are stationed, all in an unenclosed space.

Interior of Machine-Shop Superintendent's Office and Group of the Principal Officials of the Machine Shop

THE STOCK SUPERINTENDENT

The Ford Company's purchase routine is very full and elaborate, so elaborate, indeed, that no short story of it can be made adequate and it must be reserved for a supplementary chapter.

Requisitions are based upon the production volume determined upon at the first of the year, in connection with the data of a remarkable continual inventory of components on hand in the main and branch establishments. Contracts are not generally made for the entire season's need, but in larger or smaller lots, following the indications of the market.

When a delivery has been ordered on a purchase contract, the purchasing agent turns over the particulars of the transaction to a "follow-up" assistant, who keeps after it continuously until shipment is made. As soon as he has details of shipment date, car numbers, and routing, the supervision of the movement passes to the traffic department, who keep in touch with the consignment until the goods arrive at the unloading platform. They then enter into the custody of the material department,

Shop Transportation. Sprague Monorail System Passing through the Ford Plant

by whom they are routed to the exact point of use in the shops. A system of sectional letters and numbers, conspicuously painted on columns and girders, guides even the uneducated foreign labor used for handling and trucking to the correct destination. In case of over-accumulation of stock at any point, the routing clerk is notified by telephone and directs a new place of delivery until the stock has been reduced at the point of congestion. Wherever possible, purchase orders provide for shipment in packages of exact count size, thus greatly facilitating inspection for quantity. All material is strictly charged and credited from department to department, according to the quantity that passes inspection. Rejections are charged, billed, and shipped back to sellers.

The stock receiving is in charge of one individual, the stock superintendent, who has an office between that of the machine superintendent and that of the shortage chaser, with one principal office assistant and six office clerks. He has besides 1,285 men outside of the office—department stock keepers, checkers, counters, and weighmasters, with a horde of stock handlers and truckers, who go where he says go, and come as bidden. Besides this considerable manual force, the stock superintendent has control of all traveling cranes and the electric monorail service.

The machine-shop traveling crane-way extends through the shop on north and south lines and covers a railway siding. The monorail lines surround the machine-shop floor and extend from the factory building line on John R Street to the eastern end of the foundry. besides having various other lines of travel inside the machine shop.

The Ford shops receive by rail about seventy carloads per day of freight from outside suppliers, and send out about one hundred and seventy-five cars loaded with Ford automobiles, daily.

Test pieces from rail shipments of pig-iron and bar-steel go to the chemist for analysis before unloading begins, and if the analysis is not to specifications the car is side-tracked; such instances have been known but are, of course, extremely rare. The analysis is satisfactory as a rule, and the checkers and counters and weighers are set to unloading the car as soon as may be after the chemist's report is in hand. Sheet steel is taken in without analysis and the stock received may go anywhere on the premises, but is usually sent to one of the many regular stock-receiving departments. Drop forgings, of which the Ford Company uses about $5,000,000 value yearly, are unloaded on the platform south of the smithy and foundry, which presents a very busy scene during work hours.

THE FORD SHOP TRANSPORTATION

One of the principal problems placed before the Ford engineers is that of transportation within the factory walls. The lightest complete Ford car weighs about 1,400 pounds, and if a thousand cars a day are turned out at least 1,400,000 pounds of materials must be moved daily, not once only, but many, many times over, each day, in the course of construction. Hence the traveling cranes, hence the many monorail lines, and hence the great numbers of truckers, and pullers and pushers and roustabouts in general, everywhere visible in the Ford shops during working hours. The unrelenting push of sales orders has forced the management to work for constantly expanding production capacity, regardless of everything else. At the time of this writing the first two of a series of new six-story buildings, each floor having seventeen landing stages served by an overhead traveling crane, are approaching completion; and with this great increase of floor area, supplemented by efficient traveling-crane service, much of the present hand trucking and roustabout work will be eliminated.

The Ford pay-roll is split about evenly between direct and indirect production labor, and the stock general superintendent's item of 1,285 men outside of his own office gives something of an idea of what the mere handling and placing of the 1,000-cars-per-day construction-materials cost. Not only is the fullest possible use made of the traveling cranes and the monorail system, but endless-belt and endless-chain transportation is established in many locations. Most of all, however, the Ford engineers have taxed the convolutions of their brain surfaces to shorten the lines of natural work-travel on the factory floors, first by crowding machine-tools together far closer than I have elsewhere seen machine-tools placed, and next by first finding the shortest possible lines of production travel of every car component, integral or assembled, and then placing every production agent needed either directly in that shortest line, or as near that line as possible, to the extent of placing even the brazing fires where most travel-saving advantage demands.

It is of record that in the old Piquette Street days, previous to the time when any attempts at Ford shops systematizing were made and chaos reigned supreme, the first systematizer found that the Ford *en-bloc* four-cylinders casting traveled no less than 4,000 feet in course of finishing, a distance now reduced to about 334 feet.

At first sight the Ford close tool-placing seems to be carried even

Shop Transportation. Hand-Truckers Moving Filled Component Receptacles

Illustrating the Close Placing of Machine Tools in the Ford Machine Shop

beyond the limit of economical application in labor-cost reducing; but a somewhat extended observation of the more congested areas of Ford machine-shop floor space failed to find a single instance in which the workmen did not have all the room necessary for economical action. It is true that the wanderer in the Ford shops is forced to keep to main lines of travel, where much care is needful to avoid a mishap through the monorail trains overhead or by way of the never-pausing hand-truck traffic on the floor level, but I am forced to the conclusion that even the closest spacing of machine tools in the New England manufacturing machine shops is still prodigal of floor space. Every factory economist well knows that every square foot of floor space carries the same tax of overhead costs, which cannot be recouped save by placing a profit-earning load thereupon. Yet the traditions of the Elders yet carry weight in spite of the missionary labors of Mr. Taylor and his disciples, and perhaps the Ford shops are doing an unguessed cost-reducing service in showing how closely even the larger of the small machine tools may be placed with no loss of per-hour efficiency.

Of course, after what has been here said, the visitor will not expect to find in the Ford shops any examples of orthodox machine-tool placing in generic groups, lathes together in one place, drilling machines, milling machines and planing machines each in a group by themselves.

The automatic screw machines, which are great floor-space consumers unless placed diagonally, force segregation, and obtain it. The large drawing-presses which produce the pressed-steel crank-box are also in a line by themselves, since labor saving and transportation saving both demand the grouping, and two long lines of Bliss presses producing many different articles in sheet metal are placed back to back to enable one long horizontal belt traveling between them to carry all the work

National-Acme Automatic Screw Machines, Showing Diagonal Mode of Placement

produced to the eastern end, where two men stand and sort the products, each into a receptacle of its own kind.

The gear cutters, both spur and bevel, are placed in bunches where their finished product can be built into the appropriate assembly with least transportation, and a long line of Potter and Johnson automatic lathes are the first machine tools to meet the eye of one entering the machine floor from the Administration building, because these tools work on single pieces and can economize floor space by close end-to-end placing.

But when it comes to brazing furnaces, which are usually regarded as unthinkable on a machine-shop floor, and are relegated to separate and despised quarters, often far out of the natural line of component travel, the Ford engineers have no hesitation in placing them as nearly as may be in the natural production line of travel, and brazing fires are seen in many unexpected places in the Ford shops.

The Ford Workers

Having shown the factory buildings, and stocked the department, rather hurriedly it must be confessed, the place is now ready to hire in men. Molders? Core makers? Smiths? Machinists? Not in numbers to notice. The foundry superintendent asserts that if an immigrant, who has never even seen the inside of a foundry before, cannot be made a first-class molder of one piece only in three days, he can never be any use on the floor; and two days is held to be ample time to make a first-class core maker of a man who has never before seen a core-molding bench in his life.

Tool-Makers, Experimental-Room Hands and Draftsmen

These constitute the aristocracy of every shop. They must be good, they must be experienced, and the better they are and the bigger wage they can earn the more valuable they are to the shop. The Ford shops work about 250 tool makers and 20 men or so in the experimental room, and a large force of metal-pattern makers in the foundry pattern shop, all of whom must be first-class mechanics. The Ford management asserts that its tool makers are as good as can be found in the world, although they are nearly all of western growth, and what tool-making jobs I have noticed in the tool-making department were certainly being well done. The Ford Company has a large quantity of shop special-tool work constantly in progress, and all special tools at work in the machine shop so far as noticed showed as good design and construction as need be. Nothing is scamped or hurried in the Ford shops tool-making, as might be assumed without writing the assertion in so many words, because economy in tool-making is always rank extravagance on the balance sheet. The general appearance of the tool room and its equipment is shown in the illustration on page 6 of the preceding chapter, in which the large installation of Hendey lathes is especially noticeable.

As to machinists, old-time, all-round men, perish the thought! The Ford Company has no use for experience, in the working ranks, anyway. It desires and prefers machine-tool operators who have nothing to unlearn, who have no theories of correct surface speeds for metal finishing, and will simply do what they are told to do, over and over again, from bell-time to bell-time. The Ford help need not even be able-bodied.

I had been told that all applicants for Ford jobs must be up to grade under a "military examination" by the Ford surgeons. Nothing could be farther from the truth. The employment agent, who looks applicants over before sending them to the surgeon for examination, said to me that so long as it seemed to him that a man could do work enough to pay overhead charges on the floor space he would occupy, he sent him to the examining surgeon. He quoted Henry Ford as saying "We must all live. If a man can make himself of any use at all, put him on, give him his chance, and if he tries to do the right thing we can find a living for him, anyway."

This Ford labor policy must have given hope, most valuable of all human possessions, to many and many a despairing brain.

Pursuing the work-applicants-examination story, Dr. Meade said: "No, the examination is not 'military' in any degree. We might accept a man with but one eye, or one hand, or one foot. The applicant must have no contagious disease, or if he has such a disease he may receive hospital treatment gratis if he shows a disposition to take care of himself until he has passed the condition of possible disease-communication. Chronic contagious disease is cause for peremptory rejection."

The Ford Company does not demand physical perfection in its workers; it simply takes such precautionary steps in hiring workmen as are, from the standpoint of the wise factory manager, necessary to give a fair prospect of that mutually profitable interdependence of the employer and the employed, which is the only satisfactory and altogether just embodiment of the working relations of capital and labor.

It is of vital importance to successful factory management that workmen should be steady in their habits, and dependable in the point of continuous service. Of course, there are occasions which fully justify the worker's absence from his place during work hours, and by making statement to his foreman the Ford shop hand can obtain leave of absence for such time as may be needful. Absence without previous notice is rigidly disapproved, and upon return from unpermitted absence the worker is at once taken to the watchman's office, a form is filled out, with excuse for absence fully detailed, and signed by the workman, who is then taken to the physician's office and "investigated." Should the medical staff find the excuse valid, the workman is permitted to resume his duties, in good standing. If the workman's excuses are not deemed satisfactory he may be either discharged outright, suspended, or "admonished" by his superiors with a view to his own good, before beginning work anew.

And in general, the Ford Company claims that it is best for all concerned that it should stand in an advisory position as to the conduct of each of its workmen, and should assist, lead, and guide him in the right direction to make such use of his natural powers and abilities as will best conduce to his own value to himself as a man, and to the Ford Company as an employee.

Of course, the man who begins to act as conscience to another man has a long road before him, as such a course can easily be made to end in paternalism carried to a degree of inclusiveness commonly looked for only in the most rigidly self-righteous of New England households.

Let not the reader hasten to conclusions based on meager information. All economists are agreed that the only reason why any one man works for another man is because the hired man does not know enough to be the director of his own labor. And, incontrovertibly, the employer being wiser than the employed, the wisdom of the employer should be applied to the benefit of the employed, to some extent at least.

So far, the Ford Company's efforts to be of real service to its toilers has been productive of absolutely nothing but good, with no qualifying addendum whatever.

HIRING FORD HANDS

Eleven form blanks of prime importance are used in hiring, working, and discharging hands, and keeping needful workmen's records. There are, of course, a vast number of other form blanks relating directly to labor in use in the Ford shops, where at least one-half of the clerical labor goes to prevent carelessness and dishonesty, but the eleven here specified are vitally needful.

THE EMPLOYMENT OFFICE

The employment office is in charge of one head, who has one assistant, one interpreter, one record keeper, and one typist. The special feature of the office furniture is the workmen's record-envelope filing cabinets, in charge of the records keeper, who at this date, March 26, 1914, has about 108,000 hired, discharged, quit and laid-off records on file, the records being complete, and containing one envelope for each

workman employed by the Ford Company since the time of record establishment.

The minor equipments of the employment office include a board on
which hang rubber stamps designating factory departments, a vertical
wall-file of trades, to be displayed on the Manchester Avenue door as
occasion demands, and chairs for waiting employment applicants.,

The Ford badge, here shown full size, is a piece of sheet German-
silver stamping, with a spring safety pin and catch fixed on its back.
The high numerals, four-places, are 9,999 and prefaced letters separate

The Ford Badge

the badges into series; any desirable number of these
badges, always with the same serial letter, may be
assigned to any one department, and the same serial
letter numbers may cover several departments, each
department having assigned to it as its own belonging, numbers in serial rotations, as, say, C-1 to C-
400, for one department, followed by C-401 to C-800
for some other department. All Ford employees paid
from the time-keeper's office must wear this badge
(which bears the same number as the time-clock
ticket), must pass the time-clock when entering or leaving, and are
known by the badge number only on the Ford time-keeping and wage-
paying records.

PAY-DAY

Every day is pay-day for some part of the Ford working force, and
the entire time-keeping and pay-roll routine is ordinary practice. The
pay is made up once in two weeks.

ADVANCE PAY

A private membership association, in which no subscriber is permitted to invest more than $2 per month, membership open to all,
advances money to workers in need, at the rate of 10 cents for the use
of $5 for from one to thirteen days, all loans charged against pay-roll
credits and paid next pay day. This makes the membership borrower
his own loan-shark, as the profits from advances go wholly to the association subscribers. Of course, the fore-handed subscriber who never
asks advances is the greater gainer, but it is far better for the man who is
forced to solicit a loan to apply to an association of which he himself is a
member than to go to an outside Shylock for assistance.

The Employment Department. Individual Records Are Kept in the Cabinets in the Background

EMPLOYMENT-DEPARTMENT RECORDS

These are kept in envelopes, which are filed in index boxes, and have an alphabetical index based on the first three letters of the surname of the worker, past or present.

The employment office receives and files a very large number of employment-requesting letters, and upon requisition for labor first refers to this applicants' letter file, and if it does not obtain men enough therefrom, next makes application to the Manufacturers' Association of Detroit, of which the Ford Motor Company is a member, and so commonly fills all demands for labor promptly.

FACTORY LABOR REQUISITIONS ON THE EMPLOYMENT DEPARTMENT

Formerly, any department foreman could make direct requisition on the employment department for more men. This practice has been changed, the department foreman being now required to forward labor requisitions to the machine-shop heads, who then notify the employment department of the department foreman's requisition, thus placing responsibility on the machine-shop heads, instead of on the department foremen.

FOREMEN

March 9, 1914, the Ford machine-shop superintendents had under their direction 11 department foremen, 62 job foremen, 84 assistant foremen, and 98 sub-foremen, 255 men in all above the rank of ordinary workmen, and all having the power of discharging workmen at will. The sub-foreman is also known in the Ford shops as the "straw boss."

DISCHARGE PROTEST

Until within the last twelve months discharge by any foreman was absolute and final. The "straw boss," one grade above the ordinary workman, seems to have been inclined to accentuate his slight elevation by "personal feeling" discharge of his subordinates. This was before the bonus day, when men were not clinging to their Ford jobs as they are now, and the straw boss's arbitrary discharge brought about such a condition of labor affairs that at one time the Ford Motor Company was hiring about 500 new men per day to maintain a working force of about 15,000.

The straw boss had to have the right of discharge to give him authority, and, indeed, it is one of the traditions of labor employment that discharge by any superior is final as against the workmen. But the discharge of old hands and hiring in of new men to replace the discharged, at the rate of 500 per day, is a costly affair, and it was finally decided to give the discharged workman a right of appeal to an impartial tribunal. This innovation showed its working value by an immediate reduction of the foremen's labor requisitions on the employment department. The discharged workmen fought the discharge, the discharging foreman had to show good cause for his act, and of course, became very careful to be sure of cause before acting, all with the highly desirable result of reducing the daily average number of hands now, March, 1914, discharged or taken on, to about five or six per day each way, in or out.

This whole matter of the straw boss is of much importance to the factory manager who wishes to cheapen component production in repetitions by the use of specialized laborers, and at the same time desires to pay the specialized laborer skilled-labor wage. The monotony of repetitive production can be alleviated only by a satisfactory wage-rate, and is, perhaps, much more easily endured by immigrants, whose home wage stood somewhere about 60 cents for 10 hours' work, than by native-born Americans. The straw boss is indispensable where the immigrant is the principal worker.

The high mark of the Ford employment department was 526 men hired. This number fell off 200 almost immediately after the discharge appeal was inaugurated, and has now dropped to what appears to be about the legitimate normal. Evidently the straw boss, sure of the finality of his discharge, became a malevolent despot, but at once came to his senses when he was forced to show good grounds for discharge.

I cannot forbear here repeating my statement that the successful results of the Ford Company's unprecedented methods of utilizing unskilled labor in skilled repetition-production are of the highest interest, and should be fully detailed for careful study by all large employers of repetition workers.

FORD PAY ROLLS

There are two Ford Company pay rolls, the administration building pay roll and the factory pay roll. The factory pay roll is made up in the factory time office, from factory time-clock ticket records. The administration pay roll is made up from administration building time-clock tickets, by the administration building paymaster.

The administration building time clocks are placed in the basement, the men entering to south of main entrance and the women to north of

Ford Motor Company Employment Record.

No............................

Name ....

Present Address ....

Home Address ....

Age ....Married ....

Children .... English ....

Dependent on you..

To what extent...

Have you ever worked for Ford Motor Co.?................

Last employed ....

Sight ....Hearing ....

Have you any disease or permanent disability or have you ever undergone any surgical operation, broken bones, etc.?

....

I declare and Warrant that the answers made herein are correct and true, and that they shall form the basis and become part of my contract of employment and that any untrue answers will render the contract null and void, and I hereby elect to become subject to the provisions of Act No. 10 of Public Acts, Extra Session of 1912, of Michigan.

Signature ....

Department .... Occupation ....

Rate { Skill........................ Foreman ....

{ Hourly........................ Hired by ....

Date Started ....Time Started.............

Memo. ....

Employment Record

Ford Motor Company

PAY CHECK

No. **C-9199**

PAY ENDING *April 5th 1914*

RECEIVED PAYMENT

Form No. 732.

PAY ENDING *April 5th 1914*

No. **C-9199**

NAME

	MORN.	NOON	NOON	NIGHT	EXTRA	
	IN	OUT	IN	OUT	IN	OUT

TOTAL TIME................HOURS

RATE................

TOTAL WAGES FOR WEEK $................

INSTRUCTIONS

This PAY-CHECK must be cashed by the owner.

If lost, the Time-Keeper should be notified immediately, and if it has not been cashed prior to the notification, payment will be stopped and a new check issued to the loser.

The COMPANY will not be responsible for the loss of pay due to the cashing of this PAY-CHECK when presented by the wrong party.

Ford Motor Company

THIS SIDE FRONT

No. **C-9199**

NAME

THE TIME CARD PRESS, SYRACUSE N. Y.

Ford Clock Card, Face and Back

The number and date are inserted by rubber stamps.   Ruled side printed in black—reverse in red

main entrance, through basement doors, passing the time clocks and making their time-card records.

International Time Clock and Time-Card Racks, at Manchester Avenue Entrance
to the Machine Shop

Returning to the Ford employment-department routine, the applicant, having obtained medical-department approval, returns to the
employment department and gives the replies needful for filling the
employment record form, printed in black on white paper, 5 inches
wide by 7⅝ inches high, reproduced on page 47 on a smaller scale.

The employment record is filled by the employment department, and
receives the applicant's signature in the indicated space. Next, the
employment department selects a badge and clock-card number not then
in use in the department to which the applicant is assigned, fills the
name space and also fills out an identification ticket, separates the iden-
tification-ticket coupon, and files it by date. This coupon seems to be a
negligible item, said to be "seldom referred to." The clock card and
identification ticket are then given to a messenger, who first takes the
applicant to the particular time clock belonging to his shop location,
where the messenger instructs the applicant in the art of making clock
records on the clock card and leaves the clock card in its rack. From the

time clock the messenger then guides the applicant to his department foreman, who receives and files the applicant's identification ticket, which act places the applicant in work.

TIME CLOCKS

All clocks are electrically synchronized with one master clock, which is kept to Western Union time, and all time clocks are supplied by the the International Time Recording Company, of Endicott, New York, price $250 each. One hundred and twenty-nine clocks are in constant use, and there are six spare clocks, all under charge of one individual, who visits each clock daily, examines it to see that it is in working order, and, if not, replaces it with one of the spare clocks, and as soon as may be repairs the faulty clock.

THE CLOCK CARD

This is a regular International clock card, printed in black on one side as here reproduced, and in red on the other side, save the serial letter and number, which appear in black on both sides. The card body is stiff manila $3\frac{3}{8}$ inches long by 9 inches high, with workman's pay check coupon at top, $2\frac{1}{16}$ inches high, and duplicate timekeeper's pay record below.

RECORD OF EMPLOYEE

No.

Name

Dept. Occupation

Hired		At			Advanced		To		
Advanced		To			"		"		
"		"			"		"		
"		"			"		"		
"		"			"		"		
"		"			"		"		
"		"			"		"		
"		"			"		"		

Left

"Record of Employee" Envelope

This clock card is used as follows:

The first time the workman makes a clock record on his card he removes the coupon pay-check, and retains it until paid; the regular pay-day is five days after written date on card. If the workman loses this coupon he notifies the time office at once, where payment is stopped on the lost coupon, and upon convincing evidence the time office issues a duplicate pay-check coupon to the workman, who is penalized for carelessness by an added three days of delay in pay-receiving. All clock tickets are removed daily by the time-office manager, who takes them to the time office where the time is extended into the right-hand column of day spaces, and the time office returns the clock card to the clock rack in time for the next record by workmen. All clock-card racks are covered by a

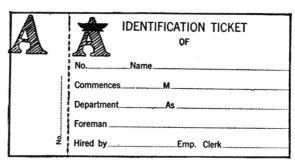

IDENTIFICATION TICKET
OF

No.............Name............

Commences............ ....M............

Department............ ....As............

Foreman............

Hired by............ ....Emp. Clerk............

Identification Ticket
The letter is stamped in red

door which is kept locked by its department time keeper, who opens it 30 minutes in advance of bell-time, and stands guard over it until the ringing of the time-bell, when the department time keeper closes and locks the clock-card rack door. This routine has been forced upon the time office to prevent fraudulent practices of workmen in making clock records. One clock card remains in the rack for 14 days, and is then removed to the time office, which fills a new clock card, same badge number, and places it in the clock rack, ready for the next 14 days' time-clock record.

RECORD-OF-EMPLOYEE ENVELOPE

Substantial manila stock, open at right-hand end, with flap, not gummed; size, 6 inches wide by 4 inches high, printed in black, on one side only, as here shown.

So long as any pay is due workman, this record-of-employee envelope is kept on file in the time office. When the workman is paid in full, and leaves the Ford service, the time office encloses a "Discharged" form in the record envelope, crossing out the "discharged" and filling in the "reason" space with appropriate record if the man quits of his own notion, and then sends the record envelope to the employment department, where it is filed under an alphabetical record of the first three letters of workman's surname.

IDENTIFICATION TICKET

Size, 5 inches long by $2\frac{1}{2}$ inches wide, with coupon at left end 1 inch wide, large letter in red, same on coupon and on body. Filled by employment department. Coupon filed in employment department, body sent with applicant to department foreman, who places man in work by act of filing body of identification ticket in foreman's cabinet file. Material, stiff white cardboard.

The red letters on the identification ticket are the serial letter of the workman's badge number. The identification ticket is filed and permanently retained by the workman's foreman save in case of workman's transfer to another department, when it goes with the man to his new department, where the identification ticket is filed by the foreman as before.

REPORT OF PERSONS TRANSFERRED

TO THE MANAGER: DATE_____191__

I HAVE TRANSFERRED

NAME_____ NO.__

FROM THE_____PLANT AS A__

TO THE_____PLANT AS A__

TO TAKE EFFECT____M._____191____NEW NO.__

REASON __

SIGNED O. K.

FOREMAN SUPT.

MANAGER

APPROVED

D FORM 23

Transfer Report

RECOMMENDATION FOR ADVANCE

Printed in black on one side only of pale pink form, $5\frac{1}{4}$ inches long by $3\frac{1}{2}$ inches high. Filled by applicant's foreman, sent by foreman to superintendent's office for approval, and then sent to time office, where it is enclosed in workman's record envelope and held so long as the man remains in the Ford service.

TRANSFER REPORT

Printed in black on one side only of yellow paper, size, $4\frac{3}{4}$ inches wide by 3 inches high. Filled by workman's foreman, accepted by department superintendent, transmitted to time keeper, filed in workman's record envelope in time office, so long as man remains in the Ford service.

RECOMMENDATION FOR ADVANCE

No._____   Date_____19____

NAME_____   Approved:

Dept. _____   _____

Date Hired_____at_____Skill Rate_____

Last Advance_____to_____ "   "_____

Date _____New Rate_____ "   "_____

Sub-Foreman_____Mach._____

Class of Work_____

Part No._____No. Pieces_____Max. No. Pcs._____

Foreman's Remarks_____

Signed   O. K.

_____   _____
Foreman   Supt.

Recommendation for Advance

DISCHARGE

Printed in black on salmon-colored sheet, 5½ inches wide by 3½ inches high. Filled by foreman, and given by foreman to discharged workman, as warrant to paymaster for instant payment; taken up by paymaster on payment, filed and held by paymaster. This "discharged" form does not go into the workman's record envelope.

REPORT OF DEPARTMENTAL DISCHARGE

This form became necessary when the workman's right to appeal from discharge by foreman was inaugurated. The foreman can discharge a man from his department only. The man may protest his discharge and seek employment in some other Ford department if investigation proves him worthy.

Upon discharge by departmental foreman, the foreman fills out Form 868, addressed to the employment office and by him transmitted thereto, accompanied by the man's

DISCHARGED

NAME_____   NO._____

To Take Effect_____M_____1913.

TAKE THIS NOTICE WITH CLEARANCE
CARD AND PAY CHECK TO PAYMASTER
AT ONCE.

_____
FOREMAN.

Discharge

identification ticket and clock card and the workman himself. The man may then protest his discharge to the head of the employment department, who passes on the case and may either make the discharge final, or decide that the man may be a worthy servant. In the latter case, he files the man's name as an applicant for Ford service, and if possible places the man at once in another department, using the "Report of Persons Transferred" form to place the man in work in his new department.

DEPARTMENTAL DISCHARGE FORM

The word "Over," lower right corner, merely gives room on the back for added discharge-causes specification space, should more space be needed.

Size 5 inches wide by 7⅝ inches high. Printed in black, on white paper.

This foreman's discharge notice is held and filed alphabetically in the employment department for future consideration, in case the man should be again discharged by another departmental foreman, and should again protest his discharge.

TO EMPLOYMENT DEPARTMENT

No._____

NAME _____

OCCUPATION _____

DATE HIRED _____

HIRED AS _____

MEMO.
SEND LATEST IDENTIFICATION TICKET WITH MEMO.
STATE FULL AND ACCURATE REASONS WHY YOU CANNOT USE MAN

SIGNED BY FOREMAN _____

DEPT. _____   DATE _____

TIME   A. M.
            P. M.   - OVER -

Departmental Discharge Form

TIME TICKETS

For convenience in accounting, the Ford Company uses two "nonproductive" time tickets, and one "productive" time-ticket form.

The "non-productive" time-ticket form having the more extended use is shown in Form 759. Form 764, "Time Ticket, Tools and Patterns," is used as specified, while Form 915, "Productive Time Ticket," is used for all persons directly engaged in Ford car production.

Form 759

Acct. Nos.	CHARGE MANUFG. EXPENSES	HOURS	Acct. Nos.	CHARGE MANUFG. EXPENSES	HOURS
182	Crating and Shipping		118	Sweeping and Cleaning	
103	Experimental Miscellaneous		115	Misc. Handling and Trucking	
103½	" —Model		144	Watchmen	
135	Foremen		131	Drawing-Machine Model	
101	Insurance Workingmans Compensation				
110	Heat, Light and Power				
111	Inspection			Plant R. & C. Order No.	
112	Messenger Service			" " " " " "	
113	Misc. Non-Productive		8	" " " " " "	
138	Store Room				

EMPL. NAME *John Smith*   NON-PRODUCTIVE No. *9999* DATE *2/7/03*

O. K. *John Doe* FOREMAN   TOTAL *8*

Form 759 for All Unproductive Time Except Tool and Fixture Draftsmen, Tool Makers and Pattern Makers

ORDER NUMBER	CLASS OF WORK	ACCT. No.	HOURS

TIME TICKET TOOLS AND PATTERNS
DEPT. W. 8-1
EMPL. No. 191
EMPL. NAME
DATE
FORM 764
O. K.   FOREMAN   TOTAL

Form 764, Time Ticket, Tools and Patterns

Form 764, "Time Ticket, Tools and Patterns," is used for tool and fixture designers and draftsmen, wood-pattern makers and metal-pattern makers, and tool-makers. It is a stiff manila card, printed in black, one side only, size 3¾ inches wide by 6⅜ inches high, shown here reduced. Form 915, productive time ticket, is used by all workmen or workwomen directly employed in production of the Ford car. It is a stiff manila card, printed in black on one side only, size 3¾ inches wide by 6⅜ inches high.

Form 759. This form of non-productive time ticket, is used by all Ford employees save tool and fixture draftsmen, tool-makers, and pattern-makers, who all use Form 764 time ticket. Form 759 is a stiff manila card, 6½ inches wide by 3¾ inches high, printed in black, on one side only.

CHANGE OF ADDRESS

The Ford Company prints in black, on white paper, one side only, size 5 inches wide by 2¾ inches high, a notice in these languages: English, Italian, German, Polish, Greek, Turkish, Russian and Roumanian, and places it in the hands of every employee whose name is on the pay roll. Great inconvenience was at one time experienced from failure of hands to give notice of habitation change. This notice, in the eight languages mentioned, is reproduced on page 59.

Productive Time Ticket

BETTER ADVANTAGE NOTICE

This is a request to workers to advance their own and the company's interests by advising foremen of the workman's own opinion of his most useful sphere of activity. Mr. Ford wanted a Swiss watchmaker for work of his own, outside of the shops. One was found, running a drill press. The heat-treat department wanted a skilled firebrick layer, for furnace work. He was found, also running a drill press, proved master of fire-brick handling and construction, and now holds the position of general inspector of furnace condition and furnace repairer, very much to his own gain and that of the company.

The man who is down and out is, as a rule, little inclined to talk when he has faced starvation and has obtained work which puts food in his mouth. This form of the Ford Company goes to every worker, and, while it simply offers to use the man for the Ford Company's best purposes, it also gives the man the hope that his own best estimate of himself will be gladly listened to by his employer. This is a wise and kind

---

Form 946

FORD MOTOR COMPANY EMPLOYEES.

We realize that quite a number of our men are qualified to do different work, other than that at which they are at present engaged; in other words are working out of their trades, or regular lines, of employment, as followed previous to coming to work for this company.

Kindly notify your foreman just what you are best qualified to do, as we may be able to use you to better advantage elsewhere.

Ford Motor Company

EMPLOYMENT DEPARTMENT

Better Advantage Notice

FORM 947 **OCCUPATION RECORD**

EMPLOYEE NO._____ NAME_____

ADDRESS_____ AGE_____

EMPLOYED IN DEP'T._____ PRESENT OCCUPATION_____

KIND OF WORK BEST ADAPTED FOR_____

EXTENT OF EXPERIENCE_____

Occupation Record

encouragement to the worker, which is probably always of value in case of immigrant employment.

To meet the requirements of this request, Form No. 947, "Occupation Record," is provided and given out to employees, to be filled and signed by any employee and given by him to his foreman, who may transfer the applicant to a more suitable department, or send the filled and signed occupation record form to the employment office for suitable attention. The "Occupation Record" is a stiff white card, 5 inches wide by 3 inches high, printed in black on one side only.

FORD EMPLOYEES WHO DO NOT COME IN THROUGH THE EMPLOYMENT DEPARTMENT

Administration building department heads select their own departmental assistants and office help.

FORD FACTORY WOMEN WORKERS

About 250 names of women are on the factory pay roll; their time is kept at the factory time-keeper's office. Applicants are invariably friends of employees, and make personal application to forewoman of department they wish to enter. In case the forewoman views the applicant favorably, she fills a regular application for employment form and sends it to the employment department, and the routine is then the same as for male applicants. The women workers have an exclusive entrance at the northwest corner of the factory, from Woodward Avenue.

FORD PLANT WORK HOURS

March 9, 1914, work hours and labor recompense at the Ford Motor Company's Highland Park plant were as follows:

Eight hours constitute a day's work. This rule is rigidly enforced, save in maintenance or alterations, where the workmen are forced to work such hours as factory conditions demand or permit, making avoidance of overtime impracticable; in case of maintenance and alterations overtime the pay is one and one-half day rates.

For sufficient reasons the working hours of day-wage earners are fixed as follows, at the present time.

OFFICE-FORCE HOURS

Begin at 8:15 a. m., work to 12:00, noon, take one hour for lunch, begin at 1:00 p. m. and work to 5:15 p. m., making an 8-hour day. Males over 22 years of age contributing to the support of others and of "approved" personal conduct, receive $5 for 8-hours work. No overtime.

ΕΙΔΟΠΟΙΗΣΙΣ ΠΡΟΣ ΟΛΟΥΣ ΤΟΥΣ ΥΠΑΛΛΗΛΟΥΣ

"Οταν ἀλλάσσετε διεύθυνσιν, νὰ εἰδοποιῆτε ἀμέσως τὸν ὑπάλληλον εἰς τὸ Τμῆμα ἐπου ἐργάζεσθε ἤ, νὰ τὸ ἀναφέρετε εἰς τὸ Γραφεῖον τοῦ Γουάτσμαν διὰ νὰ συμπληρώσῃ τὸ δελτίον ἀλλαγῆς διευθύνσεως. Παράλειψις τοῦ νὰ μᾶς εἰδοποιήσετε περὶ τῆς ἀλλαγῆς τῆς διευθύνσεως, εἰμπορεῖ νὰ συνεπιφέρῃ ἀπώλειαν τῆς θέσεώς σας.

ΜΑΘΕΤΕ ΝΑ ΔΙΑΒΑΖΕΤΕ ΚΑΙ ΝΑ ΓΡΑΦΕΤΕ ΑΓΓΛΙΚΑ
Ford Motor Company.

اعلان لجميع العمال

اذا غيرت عنوانك حالاً بلغ كاتب الادارة التي تشتغل بها أو صرّح

في مكتب الحارس وذلك بان تملأ ورقة العنوان بعنوانك الجديد ان سهوك عن

ابلاغك ايانا تغيير عنوانك ربما ادى الى خسارتك شغلك

تعلم ان تقرأ وتكتب الانكليزية

Ford Motor Company

Объявленіе Для Всѣхъ Служащихъ

Въ случаѣ перемѣны вашего адреса, извѣстите конторщика того Цеха, въ которомъ вы работаете, или объявите въ контору еторожа и проеите выполнить для ваеъ бланкъ для перемѣны адреса. Вамъ могутъ отказать отъ мѣста, еели вы не извѣстите наеъ о перемѣнѣ адреса.

Научитесь читать и писать по-англійски.
Ford Motor Company

AVVISO AGL'IMPIEGATI

Quando si cambia di casa bisogna avvisare immediatamente lo scrivano del Dipartimento in cui si lavora, o farne rapporto all 'Ufficio del Custode, e far riempire il modulo del cambio d'indirizzo. La mancanza di questa notificazione di cambiamento di domicilio può cagionare la perdita dell'impiego.

Imparatevi a leggere e scrivere Inglese
Ford Motor Company

ZAWIADOMIENIE
do wszystkich pracowników

Jeżeli zmienicie swój adres, zawiadomcie natychmiast pisarza w Departamencie, w którym pracujecie, albo donieście o tem do Biura Szwajcara i odnotujcie zmianę adresu na właściwym druku. Zaniedbanie zawiadomienia o zmianie adresu, może spowodować utratę posady.

Uczcie się czytać i pisać po angielsku.
Ford Motor Company

AVIS PENTRU LUCRĂTORĬ

Dacă vě mutațĭ șı vě schımbațĭ adresa, ınștiințațĭ ındată biroul Secțieĭ în care lucrațĭ saŭ biroul păzitoruluĭ, dându-ĭ noua voastră adresă scrisă pe una din formularele din biroŭ pentru acest scop. Cine nu se va conforma acestuĭ avıs póte să-șı pearză locul.

Invățațı să cetıțĭ şı sě scrieţĭ
ın Englezește.
Ford Motor Company

NOTICE TO ALL EMPLOYEES

If you change your address, immediately notify the Clerk in the Department you work or report to the Watchman's Office and have change of address blank made out. Failure to notify us of change of address may mean a loss of position.

LEARN TO READ AND WRITE ENGLISH
Ford Motor Company

ZUR BEACHTUNG
AN UNSERE SÄMTLICHEN ANGESTELLTEN

Bei Wohnungsänderungen haben die betreffenden Angestellten unverzüglich dem Bureaubeamten der Abteilung, in der sie beschäftigt sind, Anzeige zu erstatten, oder sich im Bureau des Fabrikwachters (Watchman's Office) zu melden zwecks Ausfüllung eines Wohnungswechsel-Formulars, widrigenfalls Entlassung aus ihrer Stellung erfolgen kann.

Lernet englisch lesen und schreiben
Ford Motor Company

Change of Address Notice. The Eight Slips Are Shown Here in One Group

Girls and women, of whom there are many employed in the administration building, draw a minimum rate of $65 per month. This rate was $40 per month previous to the bonus declaration of January 5, 1914.

Department heads are recompensed by salary and bonus both, in varying sums not made public. Previous to the bonus declaration officials had a three weeks' vacation with full pay in each summer. This vacation gift is now withdrawn, all vacations being had at the vacator's own cost.

Factory Workers' Hours

Factory workers may work in one, two or three shifts.

Three-Shift Hours

Shift I.   Begin at 12:00 midnight. Stop at 8:00 a. m.; 10 minutes gift for eating, from 4:00 a. m. to 4:10 a. m. The workers do not leave their places during the eating time, as a rule.

Shift II. Begin at 8:00 a. m. Stop at 4:00 p. m., with 10 minutes gift for eating, from 12:00 noon, to 12:10 p. m.

Shift III. Begin at 4:00 p. m., work to 12:00 midnight, with a gift of 10 minutes eating time, from 8:00 p. m. to 8:10 p. m.

At the time of this writing, March 9, 1914, the core-makers, the heat-treating men, the watchmen, 45 in each shift, and the watchmen's record keepers in their room in the administration building, are working three shifts, the full 24 hours.

Machinists, Car Assemblers, Testers, Shipping and Stores— Receiving Force, Laborers, and Truckers, Working Two Shifts

Shift I.   Start at 6:30 a. m., stop at 10:30 a. m.; take 30 minutes of their own time for lunch, start at 11:00 a. m., and stop for day at 3:00 p. m.

Shift II. Start at 3:30 p. m., stop at 7:30 to eat, taking 10 minutes of their own time; start work at 7:40 p. m., stop 11:40 p. m.; 29 cents per hour is the low wage rate; over 22 years of age and aiding in support of others and "acceptable," $5 for 8-hours work.

Girls and Women in Factory

One shift only, 32 cents per hour minimum wage.

Start at 7:30 a. m., stop at 12:00 noon, taking 45 minutes, own time, for lunch; start at 12:45, stop at 4:45.

Saturdays, start at 7:30 a. m., stop at 11:30 a. m. Work 44 hours per week, full time.

Draftsmen

One shift, from 8:00 a. m. to 12:00 m. Take one hour of own time, start at 1:00 p. m., stop at 5:00 p. m.

OTHERS WORKING ONE SHIFT ONLY

From 8:00 a. m. to 12:00 m., 30 minutes of own time for lunch; start at 12:30 p. m., work to 4:30 p. m.

If over 22 years of age and contributing to support of others, and also "acceptable," $5 per day of 8 hours.

What is here detailed as to the relations of employer and employed in the Ford shops does not in any way or at any point cover the subject, but will enable the factory manager who follows these articles to form a general conception of the Ford animus toward workmen. At the date of this writing, March 28, 1914, 57½ per cent of Ford workers have been pronounced "acceptable," and have been placed on the pay roll at "bonus" rates, which in many instances bring the workman's pay close to that of his foreman's. Naturally, the foremen are looking forward to some "readjustment" which will recognize their own superior value to the Ford Company. Prophecy is out of place here. It is the eventuation, the grand average of final eventuation, which interests the world at large.

The Ford Company has no socialistic leanings, and is not making any claim to placing a shining example before the world's employers of labor. It simply has the cash on hand, and believes it will continue to have the cash on hand, to try to help its own hour-wage earners in its own way. That is the whole story up to date.

CHAPTER III

HOW THE WORK IS DONE

A DETROIT daily newspaper not long ago printed a story anent a new farm tractor, said soon to be placed on the market by the Ford Company, and added, in the fulness of reportorial wisdom, that while the Ford factory was at present equipped for building Ford cars only, yet all of the machine-tools had been designed with such cunning foresight that "by merely changing the dies" they would produce farm tractors just as well as they had before produced Ford cars.

Probably the average Ford factory visitor has the same general broad conception of the "How" of making 1,000 automobiles (it is now more than 1,100 automobiles) per day.

The man who really knows anything of the entrails of a machine shop, who knows that nothing, of advantage, at least, ever "happens" in a machine shop, has plenty to think about as he stands at the "start-to-run" end of the Ford chassis assembling lines. This man of experience asks himself how the component production is evened up to assembling requirements. Here are, say, from 1,000 to 4,000 separate pieces of each chassis component to be supplied daily, infallibly, and constantly. How is this done?

In brief, first, by unremitting record-keeping of every finished component produced. Hour by hour, with endless toil and pains, an absolutely correct record is kept of the Ford component production and of the Ford factory out-put.

The factor of safety of component supply is placed by the official production head at a sufficiency for 25,000 cars, a month's assembling supply at the production rate of 1,000 cars per day. This is official, but, as will be seen from the "shortage-chaser" story, the factory practice does not follow the production-head schedule, but quite to the contrary, places a maximum component supply at a sufficiency for 5,000 cars, three-days' assembling, with a danger line at components enough for 3,000 cars.

Is it easy to hold these figures by accurate factory superintendence and accurate production accounting?

Easy or difficult, the accurate factory accounting records are made, but are not used for emergency decision in directing component production.

Seeing is believing. When a Ford car assembled-component assembler suddenly discovers that his requisition on finished stores for components wanted at once is not filled because there are no such components in finished stores, no grand conclave of factory accountants is summoned.

Quite to the contrary, a brisk and intelligent young man, styled the "Shortage Chaser," whose face already begins to show fine lines etched by the stress of concentrated attention, boards the department drifting within sound of breakers, seizes the helm of component production, and pilots the department into smooth water again—sometimes but barely escaping the surf-line, it is true, but yet always managing to escape disaster.

The Shortage Chasers

In point of fact there are two shortage chasers—the day shortage chaser, and the night shortage chaser who combines shortage chasing with other duties from the time he goes on duty at 3:30 p. m.; he stops at 7:30 p. m. to eat 10 minutes on his own time, begins again at 7:40, and works to 11:40 p. m.

At 3:30 p. m. when he goes on duty, the night shortage chaser first inspects the day shortage-chaser's final report, made at 2:30 p. m., and is thereby informed as to the condition of all assembling departments which are working through his shift, the day shortage chaser specifying in his 2:30 p. m. report what component production is most needed and specifically calling the night shortage-chaser's attention thereto. Guided by the day shortage-chaser's report, the night shortage chaser urges the most needed component production, has checkers and counters under him, and fills tags authorizing the removal of finished components from their production department to the assembling department which needs them. Before leaving at 11:40 p. m. the night shortage chaser makes a record of components which he has moved from a production department to an assembling department, for information of the day shortage chaser, who comes on duty at 6:30 a. m.

The usual number of reports made by the night shortage chaser to the day shortage chaser is about six.

The Shortage-Chaser's Desk. Shortage Chaser at the Left and Clearing-House Chief Clerk at the Right

THE DAY SHORTAGE CHASER

The story of the shortage chaser must be told as briefly as is consistent with intelligibility. His desk is about 50 feet north of the machine-shop superintendent's office; he has a desk and one assistant.

At 6:30 the day shortage chaser, henceforth specified as "the shortage chaser" only, first inspects the night reports, making notes of impending shortage; next he notifies the "checkers" who direct the movements of components reported at or below the 3,000 danger limit; this is done at 7:00 a. m., the shortage chaser making a personal delivery of his own pencil memoranda to the proper "checkers." Next the busy shortage chaser goes in person to each assembling station reporting shortages and informs himself by personal observation of shortages—this because the final reports were made to component-production officials at 2:30 p. m. of the previous day. Being then advised of actual conditions by personal observation, the shortage chaser goes to the foreman of the machine department producing the most needed component, informs

Office at the Clearing House with Shortage-Chaser's Blackboards

The same office is used by the general stock superintendent (standing at the right of the picture) and the clearing-house head (seated at the large desk in the center).

him of conditions, and from this department foreman to such other department foreman as he may deem needful to see in person, say from three to ten individuals. Next the shortage chaser makes his 8:30 a. m. report at the checker's office by writing the same on his checker's office blackboard, 40 inches wide by 40 inches high, with 59 lines for writing in chalk. On this blackboard the chaser makes his reports by first inscribing each symbol and following the symbol with numbers of this individual component finished since 6:30 a. m. of the current day.

This blackboard record is then typed in manifold in the clearing house; one copy is sent to each department foreman interested, and one copy is sent to the shortage-chaser's desk, these typed report copies being distributed at about 8:40 a. m.

The next succeeding morning the shortage chaser compares his shortage reports for that day with the typed record of his shortage reports made on the blackboard at 8:30 of the previous day. He adds, in pencil, to the typed report of the day before such shortages as may be revealed by the reports of the current day, and delivers this added-to-in-pencil typed list of yesterday's shortages to the clearing house tag-blank filler, who is a clearing house official, but is placed at the shortage-chaser's desk for speedy communication. His duties are explained below.

The day shortage chaser makes three reports daily to the clearing house, at 8:30 and 11:30 a. m. and 2:30 p. m.

From 6:30 a. m. to 11:30 the shortage chaser covers all factory production departments and all assembling departments, and at 11:40 a. m. he chalks all production results from 6:30 a. m. to 11:30 a. m. on the clearing house blackboard. The shortage-chaser's clearing-house blackboard reports are thus made the guide for the activities of the checkers and counters and the checker's truckmen in moving components first to such departments as are most in need of replenishments.

Having made his 11:30 a. m. reports on the clearing-house blackboards in the stock superintendent's office, the day shortage chaser then again turns his attention to such assembling departments as most need his presence, and at 2:30 p. m. makes his final blackboard records in the stock-superintendent's office, which is also the "clearing-house" head's office.

THE CLEARING HOUSE

The function of the "Clearing House" is to initiate and control the movements of foundry finished product, in the form of snagged and tumbled, patched and sand-blasted castings (forming the entire finished product of the foundry), the completed machine-shop departments product, and the products of the snagging department, pressed-steel department, bushings department, magneto department, fender department, gasoline-tank department, coil-box department, brake-band department, muffler department, and painting department, which finishes certain components checked into and out of the painting department by the clearing-house checkers.

CLEARING-HOUSE OFFICIALS

The Clearing House has one head, one chief clerk, stationed at the shortage-chaser's desk, and above referred to as the tag blank filler, thirteen "checkers," and fifty "counters," under the checker's orders.

THE CHECKERS

When any component production department has completed a production order the department foreman reports to a clearing-house checker orally, and the checker then takes one or more counters, as may be needed, with him to the production department and there proceeds to count the product into suitable receptacles, to enter the quantity on a proper tag, and to wire the body of the tag, or all of the tag, to the component receptacle, to serve as a direction for delivering the components to the proper department by crane, mono rail or otherwise, and he also takes such other steps as are needful to give the clearing house a record of the components transfer, all as fully detailed in the description of the use and functions of the clearing-house tags, presently following.

Form 708. Machine-Shop
Components

Clearing-House Original Records

These are all made on wired tags and the coupons of these tags, presently to be described as to forms, colors, and functions.

The Clearing-House Chief Clerk

The chief clerk is the responsible official of the clearing house, who collects, compiles, and separates into appropriate groups and divisions all the tag records which comprise the entire original records of the clearing-house transactions.

The clearing-house chief clerk is stationed at the shortage-chaser's desk and has three clerks and one messenger. The clerks are located close by the chief clerk, and are employed solely in transferring production records, taken from tags filled by checkers, to certain "record boards" and books.

Each day's component-production records for the entire factory are completed at the end of each day, but the chief clerk consults the shortage-chaser's clearing-house blackboard reports, and also the shortage chaser himself, to aid in producing completed records of components which are short, first, before completing the records of components which are in good supply, so that early attention will be given to shortage production.

CLEARING-HOUSE TAGS

The only form blanks used by the clearing house are wired tags, suitable for attaching to component receptacles. Their size, color, and use are as follows:

FORM 708, BLUE, WITH COUPON

Filled by checker in a production department from counter's report to checker, body and coupon both; checker separates coupon and sends it

Form 820. Rush Tag

Partial Quantity Tag

Form 705 is similar to Form 820, but is red in color and is used for machine-shop components

to the clearing-house chief clerk, and then wires blue tag body to the component receptacle, which then passes into control of the shop transportation system. Used for components produced in the machine shop, only.

Form 708, wired blue tag, $3\frac{1}{8}$ inches wide by $6\frac{3}{8}$ inches high, coupon $2\frac{9}{16}$ inches high; stiff card, printed in black on one side only, with duplicate serial numbers in red on body and coupon. Used for components produced in the machine shop only, which may be delivered either to the finished-stock department or to an assembling department, "Stock Advance" Tag.

Form 709, Pressed-Steel Components

Form 709 is same as 708 in all particulars save color, which is bright green, serial numbers in red. Its use is the same as that of Form 708, save that the component originates in the pressed-steel department.

Form 705, Deep Red, Rush from Machine Shop

Used for components produced in the machine shop to be delivered directly to an assembling department.

Two coupons are filled by the checker from the counter's report. The checker removes the end coupon and sends it to the clearing-house chief clerk, who transfers the record to his production records. The checker also removes the second coupon and sends that to the finished-stock department. He then wires the body to the component receptacle which is transported to the specified assembling department. The finished-stock department then fills an assembling-department requisition and sends same with the second coupon to the assembling department, where the department foreman compares the amount, and if alike, signs the requisition and returns it to the finished-stock office.

All the clearing-house tags are the same over-all dimensions—a stiff tag deep red, with two coupons; the first is $1^7/_{16}$ inches high, the second 2 inches high, printed in black, on one side only, body and both coupons bearing same serial number.

Form 820, Rush for Pressed-Steel Components

Form 820 is the same in all particulars as 705, for the same use, but is yellow in color, and is the rush tag for pressed-steel department production, printed in black on a deep yellow tag, serial numbers printed in red.

Partial-Quantity Delivery Tag

Form (no number) "Stock Advance Tag," "Series C" "Partial-Quantity" delivery tag is filled by the checker, both body and the one coupon. The coupon is detached by the checker and held by him until the quantity for the day is known, when he makes out a department requisition for the total coupons quantity, and sends same with the coupons to the department which verifies the quantity, signs the requisition, and returns the requisition with the verifying coupons to the checker, who retains the coupons and delivers the requisition to the clearing-house chief clerk. This form is used for one or more partial deliveries from the same department, all on one day, in all departments save and except the machine-shop departments and the pressed-steel department. Color, vivid salmon; coupon 1¾ inches high, printed all in black, on one side only.

This story has told how workmen are taken into the Ford shops, and enough of the finished-components handling is given to show how the men are kept busy, and to show the duties of the shortage chaser, who is a result of the closely limited maximum production working of the Ford factory, which has never yet been able to produce cars enough to enable the acceptance of immediate delivery orders during the spring and summer.

If the shops at Highland Park were not worked to maximum capacity continuously, the shortage chaser would be superfluous. With the factory production capacity in excess of the demand for cars, the finished stock (that is to say, the finished components in the finished-stock department), would always be kept sufficiently in advance of the requisitions of the assembling departments to meet all requisitions promptly and certainly—a condition of affairs which would at once eliminate the shortage chaser, because there would then be no shortage possibility. This story shows how the Ford shops manage to face a constant shortage probability—perhaps it might be said that the real condition is that of actual shortage of components constantly—and yet escape serious delays.

If the factory production capacity were in excess of the Ford car demand, and the component production were in excess of assembling demand, there would then be an overhead interest and storage charge against the factor-of-safety excess of finished components held in the finished-stock department, which does not now exist.

On the other hand, the shortage chaser now avoids disastrous shortages only by the use of extraordinary care and exertions, together with sudden changes, which are always costly factory expedients and conditions. The entire situation at the Ford shops is novel, and is met by novel methods, and is of much interest to factory managers in general. The ideal factory condition is undoubtedly that of perpetual tranquillity, all operations balanced and co-ordinated, so that there is no "hurry up" pressure required in any direction whatever. Yet this condition of perpetual tranquillity necessitates the carrying of large values of finished components, with an inevitable increase of fixed charges, greater or less as the margin of safe component-excess supply is fixed at a higher or lower level. There is a point, of course, where abundant component supply carried in the finished-stock department becomes an extravagance, and is hence reprehensible; so that it is not easy to say with certainty that the hand-to-mouth component production, even when coupled with the anxieties and make-shifts of the shortage chaser, really costs more than it would cost to carry an ample supply of finished components of all kinds. Leaving these ultimate considerations out of view, this story simply shows the practice of a factory which is so fortunately situated that its market is ready-made, so that the selling of the factory product is of negligible importance, while the constant maintenance of the factory production-capacity at maximum becomes the one objective of vital importance and all absorbing interest to the management.

Six Views of the Ford *en bloc* Cylinder Casting

CYLINDER MACHINING, CRANK-BOX CONSTRUCTION, AND BRAZING

It is to be regretted that space does not permit each of the subjects specified in the above title to be treated in a chapter by itself, so that each story might be written in full detail, because each one, as practiced by the Ford Company, is of interest at every point and well worth complete illustration and description.

On the other hand, the factory manager has no time to spare for reading which is merely of general interest, but wishes concentrated and suggestive mention of causes and methods, rather than facts and details merely, so that the necessity of condensing the three specified divisions of Ford practice into the space of a single chapter may best suit the desires and purposes of production managers at large.

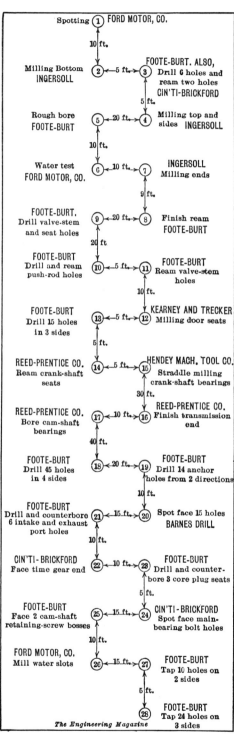

Spotting (1) FORD MOTOR, CO.

10 ft.

Milling Bottom (2) ←5 ft.→ (3) FOOTE-BURT. ALSO,
INGERSOLL   Drill 6 holes and
         ream two holes
         CIN'TI-BRICKFORD

       5 ft.

Rough bore (5) ←20 ft.→ (4) Milling top and
FOOTE-BURT   sides INGERSOLL

10 ft.

Water test (6) ←10 ft.→ (7) INGERSOLL
FORD MOTOR, CO.   Milling ends

       9 ft.

FOOTE-BURT. (9) ←20 ft.→ (8) Finish ream
Drill valve-stem   FOOTE-BURT
and seat holes

    20 ft

FOOTE-BURT (10) ←5 ft.→ (11) FOOTE-BURT
Drill and ream   Ream valve-stem
push-rod holes   holes

       10 ft.

FOOTE-BURT (13) ←5 ft.→ (12) KEARNEY AND TRECKER
Drill 15 holes   Milling door seats
in 3 sides

   5 ft.

REED-PRENTICE CO. (14) ←5 ft.→ (15) HENDEY MACH. TOOL CO.
Ream crank-shaft   Straddle milling
seats   crank-shaft bearings

    30 ft.

REED-PRENTICE CO. (17) ←10 ft.→ (16) REED-PRENTICE CO.
Bore cam-shaft   Finish transmission
bearings   end

    40 ft.

FOOTE-BURT (18) ←20 ft.→ (19) FOOTE-BURT
Drill 45 holes   Drill 14 anchor
in 4 sides   holes from 2 directions

    10 ft.

FOOTE-BURT (21) ←15 ft.→ (20) Spot face 15 holes
Drill and counterbore   BARNES DRILL
6 intake and exhaust
port holes

    10 ft.

CIN'TI-BRICKFORD (22) ←10 ft.→ (23) FOOTE-BURT
Face time gear end   Drill and counter-
        bore 3 core plug seats

       5 ft.

FOOTE-BURT (25) ←15 ft.→ (24) CIN'TI-BRICKFORD
Face 2 cam-shaft   Spot face main-
retaining-screw bosses   bearing bolt holes

    10 ft.

FORD MOTOR, CO. (26) ←15 ft.→ (27) FOOTE-BURT
Mill water slots   Tap 10 holes on
        2 sides

       5 ft.

       (28) FOOTE-BURT
The Engineering Magazine   Tap 24 holes on
        3 sides

**Diagram of Processes and Average
Travel, Ford Cylinder Casting**

Machining the Ford *En Bloc* Cylinder

The Ford *en bloc* four-cylinder casting form (see the illustration, which shows six different views of this component) is very far from being a simple affair, either in the foundry or in the machine shop. It is a piece designed to meet a great number of conditions of importance, quite regardless of moulding and finishing costs, yet it is actually machined in 45 minutes of working time, including the time of placing and removal from machines, but not including the time of transportation from one machine to that making the next cuts. There is no hand work on this cylinder, there are but few operations made on one cylinder only at a time, and these single-cylinder operations are rapid. The long-time operations are performed on milling machines having long tables, and the table feed is started as soon as the first cylinder is clamped in place on the table, while removal from the table begins as soon as the cylinder is fully exposed after passing the milling cutters. A sufficient number of spare milling cutters are provided for each operation to ensure having a newly ground set of cutters on hand before change is needful. Each set of cutters is worked through one 8-hour day, and the setting of the cutters is

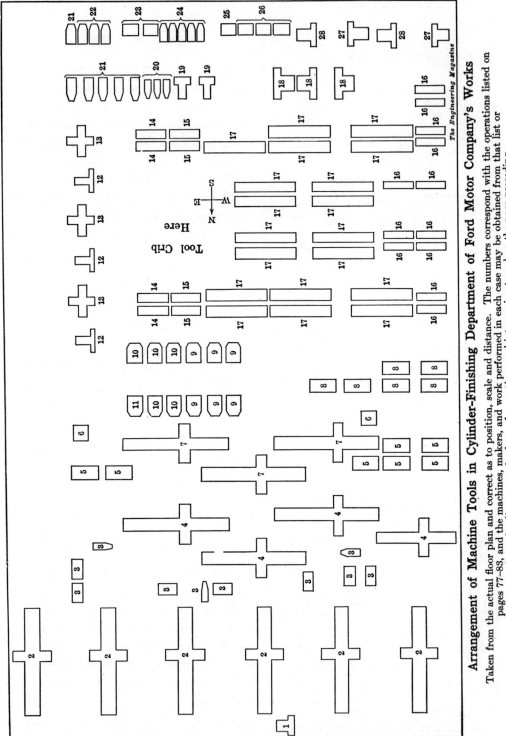

Arrangement of Machine Tools in Cylinder-Finishing Department of Ford Motor Company's Works

Taken from the actual floor plan and correct as to position, scale and distance. The numbers correspond with the operations listed on pages 77–83, and the machines, makers, and work performed in each case may be obtained from that list or from the diagrammatic chart of operations and intervening travel on the page preceding

The Engineering Magazine

facilitated by table marks and suitable straight edges so as to consume the least possible time, and to ensure the utmost attainable accuracy in cutter placing.

GAUGING AND INSPECTION

The cylinders receive twenty-one inspections and gaugings in the course of finishing; all inspection results are fully recorded, and the machining is so carefully conducted that less than one-half of 1 per cent of the cylinders are spoiled in machining. Somewhere about 8 per cent of the cylinders moulded are lost in the foundry, and of 1,000 apparently perfect cylinder castings sent from the foundry to the machine shop about 100 are thrown out as wasters because of spongy or "stodgy" spots. Where the leaks shown in the hydraulic test (which is made following operation 5, in the series of machining operations described below) are susceptible of plugging they are plugged and saved. This 1,000 good cylinders from

Operation 1 of Cylinder-Finishing Series

General view of cylinder casting located on fixture and held in place by turning the two top hand wheels. The fixture is shown on larger scale on page 76

1,100 rough cylinders sent from the foundry to the machine shop is favorable practice, and the wasters percentage may rise very considerably from unanticipated causes.

But this matter of cylinder-wasters percentage belongs more especially to the Ford foundry chapter, which shows what is believed to be the most advanced foundry equipment so far placed in any foundry anywhere. All fuels burned and irons melted in this foundry are subjected to chemical analysis and everything is done under strictly scientific regulations, yet the percentage of cylinders lost varies greatly. The cylinder is difficult because the water jacket is only $\frac{1}{8}$ inch thick, to begin with; but as before said, this whole matter belongs to the Ford foundry story, where the cylinder-founding practice is detailed at length and day-by-day cylinder-castings production-results are given.

The first cylinder-machining inspection follows operation 2, and inspection also follows operations 3, 4, 5, 7, 8, 11, 13, 15, and 17. From operation 18 to operation 28, inclusive, the cylinder is gauged after each operation, making a total of 21 gaugings altogether, the last 11 being made by one single inspector. A full and complete inspection record is kept so that the faulty cut in each waster is known and the machine fault, if such exists, is remedied at once. Should the fault be due to any workman's act, he is, of course, duly informed and his faulty practice changed.

The finishing routine is shown in the chart, "Cylinders-Finishing Routine Diagram," given on page 73, the legends specifying the nature of the operation, while the floor travel of the cylinder from one operation machine to the next in sequence is given in feet between the operation numbered circles, and the name of the supplier of each machine-tool is also given in juxtaposition with each operation circle, while half-tone illustrations of many of the machines are shown, with appropriate captions.

Besides this operation diagram, a scale drawing of the actual placing of the various machine tools on the shop floor is reproduced on page 74, each tool ground-plan having the operation number shown, so that the actual relative positions of all the machine-tools used in machining Ford cylinders are placed before the reader.

As to the mill cuts made, they are all end cuts, no mill cut being made with the circumferential surface of the milling cutter, and almost

Operation 1 of Cylinder-Finishing Series, Showing the "Floating" Core-Spotting Fixture

The rigid bar, F, has vertical cross pieces at the ends, of length to fit crank-box coring inside. The top end of cylinder is laid on two widely-separated hard plugs. The crank-box coring may be a little high at one end and low at the other end, as regards the top surface spots. Therefore F is jointed to the upright integral with foot-frame B, which rests on the wedge-block W. The height of the cylinder crank-box end is varied by the hand-screw-moved wedge-block, W, until index I, fixed to F, registers with the index mark on the upright integral with B. This brings the middle of the crank-box coring right with the cylinder top-end spotting plugs, and divides whatever twist there may be in the crank-box coring evenly, one end down as much as the other end of the crank-box coring is up, which is best that can be done in spotting the cylinder for the first spotting cut

Operation 4 on Cylinder Casting.   Surface Tops of Cylinders, and Mill Top-End Sides
Ingersoll milling machine

without exception the mills have inserted teeth.   None of the mill cuts are made by driving the milling-machine table both ways, though some of them might be so made.

The cylinders are pickled perfectly clean before reaching the machine shop.

Ford Cylinder-Machining Operations

Here follows a brief detail of the twenty-eight machine operations required to machine completely the Ford four-cylinder *en-bloc* casting, which is shown in six positions on page 72.

Operation 1.   Spot the cylinder by two rough-casting-surface points near the top end of the cylinder, directly under the two hand wheels on top of the cylinder fixture and by four points of the crank-box coring, these cored surfaces being located by an "evener" internal spotting gauge, placed inside the crank-box coring.   The cylinder crank-box end rests on a screw-adjusted wedge at the middle point of the cylinder length; this wedge, in connection with the two fixed supports, widely separated, near the top end of the cylinder, gives the cylinder casting a three-point support.   By adjusting the wedge position the crank-box end of the cylinder is raised or lowered to bring the two index marks on the "evener" (placed inside the crank-box coring) into registry with

Operation 6. Hydraulic Test for Possible Leaks in Water Jacket
Ford machine, design and construction

each other. See enlarged view of the "evener" in position in the crank-box cored opening. This fixture spots the rough cylinder at four points—two exterior, near the top end of the cylinder, and two interior, near the bottom end of the cylinder, while the first cut, surfacing the four "spots" on the top end of the cylinder, is made. The illustrations on pages 75, 76, with their captions, will make this cylinder holding for the spotting cut clear to the reader. Machine designed and built by the Ford Motor Company.

Operation 2. The cylinders are next placed in fixtures on an Ingersoll milling machine, where each cylinder stands top-end down on its milled spots, and is clamped against two hardened plugs which bear on the outside cylinder-surface spotting points made in operation 1. This second operation cut then cleans the flat bottom-surface edges of the crank-box end and also, with a half-round mill, cleans the babbitt seats of the three crank-shaft boxes.

Operation 3. Drill the six crank-box-cap holding-screw seats, ream one end hole, letting the reamer follow the drilled hole, and then, with jig having a pin in the reamed hole, jig-ream one of the cap-screw holes in the other end of the cylinder.

Operation 8 on Cylinder Casting. Finish-Ream Four Cylinder Bores at Once
Foote-Burt machine

Operation 7 on Cylinder Casting. Milling Both Ends of Cylinders at Same Time

Ingersoll two-spindle milling machine

These two reamed holes then become the spot-holes by which the cylinder is located for all succeeding cuts.

Operation 4. The cylinders stand on their bottom ends, position fixed by fixture pins which enter the two reamed spot-holes, and the mill cuts surface the top ends and sides of the cylinders. Ingersoll machine.

Operation 5. Rough bore the four cylinders at the same time. Machine supplied by Foote-Burt Company.

Operation 6. Hydraulic test of water-jacket, sixty-pounds pressure; machine designed and built by Ford Motor Company. If leaks are shown they are marked by red paint circles around them and the cylinders go to the pluggers, if leaks can be plugged; if impossible to plug them, the cylinders go back to cupola. If no leaks are shown the tester makes his "O. K." mark on the cylinder and passes it for succeeding operations.

Operation 7. Ingersoll machine, milling both ends.

Operation 8. Finish reaming cylinder bores; Foote-Burt machine.

Operation 9. Drill valve-stem holes and finish valve ports; Foote-Burt machine.

Operation 10.   Drill and ream push-rod holes; Foote-Burt machine.

Operation 11.   Ream valve-stem holes; Foote-Burt machine.

Operation 12.   Mill door-seats, Kearney and Trecker knee milling machine, with end-mill in vertical spindle.

Operation 13.   Drill fifteen holes at once, from three directions; Foote-Burt driller.

Operation 14.   With reaming arbor, carrying three reamers, arbor

Operation 18 on Cylinder Casting. Drill 45 Holes at Once from Four Directions

Foote-Burt machine.   Note steel-pipe ways for sliding cylinders, lower left corner

Drill and Counter-Bore Intake and Exhaust Port-Holes
Operation 21 on cylinder casting. Foote-Burt machine

on lathe centers, cylinder standing on bottom end, spotted by two reamed holes, ream the crank-box babbitt seats, previously rough-finished by half-round mill, operation 2. (Refer back to the description of this second operation, page 78.) This brings the babbitt seats in to exact position with relation to the two reamed spot-holes; Reed-Prentice lathe.

Operation 15. Cross cuts over ends of the three crank-box bearings, six cuts; Hendey Machine Tool Company.

Operation 16. With two cylinders, crank-box ends together, on arbor on lathe centers, finish transmission seats; Reed-Prentice lathe.

Operation 28 of Cylinder-Finishing Series.   Tap 24 Holes from Three Directions

Last machining operation. All subsequent operations go in the motor-assembling series, fully described
in Chapter IV.   Note steel-pipe work-supporting ways, lower left corner.   Foote-Burt machine

Operation 17.   Ream crank-shaft babbitt seats; Reed-Prentice lathe.

Operation 18.   Drill forty-five holes at once from four directions; Foote-Burt drilling machine.

Operation 19.   Drill fourteen babbitt anchor holes from two directions, on Foote-Burt driller.

Operation 20.   Spot-face fifteen holes; Barnes drilling machine.

Operation 21.   Drill and counter-bore intake and exhaust port holes; Foote-Burt machine.

Operation 22. Face time-gear; Cincinnati Drilling Machine Company's driller.

Operation 23. Drill and counterbore three core-plug seats; Foote-Burt driller.

Operation 24. Spot-face main-bearing bolt holes; Cincinnati Bickford Company's driller.

Operation 25. Face two camshaft retaining-screw bosses; Foote-Burt machine.

Operation 26. End-mill cleaning of the arc-shaped water jacket openings to the cylinder-head water-jacket space; Ford Motor Company, designer and builder of machine.

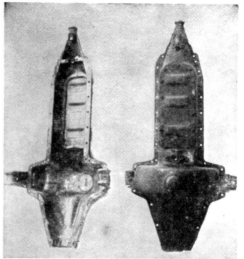

Complete Crank Box

Operation 27. Tap ten holes from two directions; Foote-Burt machine.

Operation 28. Tap 24 holes from three directions; Foote-Burt machine.

This completes the machining of the cylinder, ready to go to the assemblers, who grind the valve seats, babbitt and bore the crank-boxes, and fit the crank shaft to its boxes.

The entire time occupied in placing on machine, making cuts, and removing from machine, is 45 minutes for each cylinder. The total floor-travel of each cylinder, between operations, is 334 feet. The floor-travel time is not included in the 45 minutes of cylinder-finishing time.

The highest work-

Annealing Crank Boxes after the First Draw
Operation 5, second anneal

Line of Bliss Drawing Presses for Drawing the Pressed-Steel Crank Boxes

man's pay on the cylinder-machining job is $5 for 8 hours, 62½ cents per hour, say a fraction over 1 cent per minute. Add another cent for cutting-edge up-keep and one more for overhead charges, we have 3 cents per minute for the workman's time, all charges included, which is probably somewhere near total per-minute shop cost, and the machining cost of Ford cylinder, 45 minutes time, is $45 \times 3 =$ $1.35, only, certainly much below what seems possible in the way of low cost for this job involving 28 operations.

This is an instructive example, as showing the very great labor-cost reductions made possible by an unchanging model of the salable product.

The Ford Motor Pressed-Steel Crank Box

The illustration on page 83 shows a number of the finished pressed-steel crank-boxes so placed as to show the form of the box completed. This crank-box begins with large sheet-steel plate, No. 13 gauge or 0.093 inch thickness.

The principal drawing and shaping operations on the crank-box are worked on the row of E. W. Bliss presses, shown in the illustration on page 84, but the drawn shape produced by the press dies has a considerable number of added members of various forms, pinned and riveted and brazed or soft-soldered in unit assembly with the drawn sheet-steel shell, and many drilling, riveting, grinding and lathe operations are required to complete the pressed-steel crank-box and give it its finished form.

Crank-Box Press Work and Annealing Operations

The sheet-steel stock, 0.093 inch thick, comes to the press line in sheared sheets large enough for one blank, and the blank is punched out of this sheet on the first press at the west end of the line, this act of blanking out being crank-box operation 1. Blank over-all dimensions, 46 inches long by 24 inches extreme width.

Operation 2. The blank is stiff from the finishing rolls of the plate-

Supplementary Operation 11 on Crank Box. First Braze
Braze rear-end annular drop-forging reinforce into rear end of crank-box shell

steel mill, and is placed at once on a steel-roller gravity-incline and carried to the annealing ovens, 1500 degrees F., where the blanks are piled, one hundred and fifty on each one of six oven cars, which fill the oven with nine hundred blanks. As at present worked the six cars go into the annealing oven at 8:00 p. m., remain until 12:00 midnight, are then withdrawn and left in piles on the cars until 6:30 a. m., when they are cool enough to be worked in the drawing press.

This first annealing practice will soon be obsolete. A furnace now under construction is served by an endless chain moving up and down,

Supplementary Operation 12 on Crank Box. Braze Globe Seat to Crank-Box Shell
Stationary flames below, with swinging flames above. Four brazing fires, independent but close together, are used by one man

which is fitted with pendulum blank-carriers to take the blanks individually as they come through the press die, carry them upward about 60 feet in the furnace uptake, giving ample heating time, and then carry the blanks downward 60 feet in the open air, giving plenty of cooling time before the blanks reach the oiling table, where two oiler men with oil brushes cover both sides of the blank with lubricant before it is given draw No. 1, on the large drawing press next east of the oiling table.

Operation 22 on Crank Box
Drill 31 holes. Bausch driller

The first anneal is operation 2, and the oiling is operation 3.

Operation 4. First draw, Bliss press, $5\frac{1}{2}$ inches deep. The maximum depth of draw is $8\frac{1}{2}$ inches (operation 7) and the finished depth of draw is $8^3/_{16}$ (operation 10).

Operation 5. Second anneal. The crank-boxes are placed individually on a gravity roller-incline and go down hill to the annealing furnaces, where they enter the oven on a single car in piles of fifty, nested, remain one hour, and are then cooled for an hour, when they are cool enough for the second draw.

Operation 6. Second draw, brings up and shapes the drain-cock seat.

Operation 7. Third draw, carries stock down to maximum depth of $8\frac{1}{2}$ inches, with several other changes of form.

Operation 8. Fourth draw, finishes corners and fillets and brings job to shape generally.

Operation 9. Anneal: carried down roller-slide by gravity to annealing oven. Nested 120 on one truck into oven, oven one hour, and one hour to cool. All these blank ovens are kept at about 1500 degrees F.

Operation 10. Final draw; puts in U-shaped brace, gives general finish to corners, fillets and flats, and reduces maximum depth from $8\frac{1}{2}$ inches to $8^3/_{16}$ inches.

Operation 11. Trim, pierce, and cut out the transmission door in bottom.

Operation 12. Stiffen. Again down a roller-slide to large furnaces, where the crank-boxes are heated individually on large-area furnace floors and are then individually quenched in tank of soapy water.

Operation 13. Straighten up in operation 10 die.

From operation 13, the crank-box goes to the component appliers and brazers and grinders and turners and soft solderers, all listed as follows:

Supplementary Operation 37 on Crank Box

Straighten trunnion to place by hand, and gauge for position with forked and sliding gauge. Workman is bending over to see how trunnion stands up and down in gauge fork

Operation 1. Apply drop-forging half-ring to rear end, drill three pin holes, put in pins.

Operation 2. Rivet pins both ends; John F. Allen, N. Y., pneumatic riveter.

Operation 3. Seat and drill front vertical wall for four rivets.

Operation 4. Burr up rivet ends to retain rivets.

Operation 5. Head front-wall rivets, by hand.

Operation 6. On anvil with hand-hammer and "staking" tool, stake front wall to fill.

Operation 7. On surface plate, gauge and with hand hammer bring job to over-all length.

Operation 8. Apply globe seat for front-axle globe-end radius-fork.

Operation 9. Drill for two rivets, to fix globe-bracket position.

Operation 10. In press, rivet ends of globe-bracket.

Operation 11. First braze; rear-end reinforce, made in a four-fire, hand-revolved brazing-furnace. See illustration on page 85. Ford Company design and construction.

Operation 12. Braze globe-seat bracket. Vertical flames both

With Angle Plate on Lathe Face-Plate and Back-Rest Fixture, Turn Trunnion
Supplementary operation 39 on crank box. Five Reed & Prentice lathes and one Warner lathe on this job

upward and downward. Ford construction, shown in the illustration on page 86.

Operation 13. On emery wheel, polish arm-seats.

Operation 14. Face end of rear annular collar flush with crank-box shell end.

Operation 15. Back to big press line, and in final die straighten up the job, far as completed.

Operation 16. Re-rivet front-wall rivets, stretched by preceding operation.

Operation 17. Bring walls to length with press surface-jig.

Operation 18.   Grind flat over walls at ends.

Operation 19.   Pierce two holes for drain-cock flange; also, same operation, seat and close in the drain-cock seat ready for tapping.

Operation 20.   Rivet splash-plate.

Operation 21.   On driller, half-globe ream front-axle radius-ball seat.

Operation 22.   Drill thirty-one holes, Bausch Machine Company's driller.   See illustration, page 87.

Supplementary Operation 40 on Crank Box
With crank box clamped to lathe-saddle fixture, bore and face rear-end annular collar

Operation 23.   Burr thirty-one drilled holes; Bausch Machine Company's driller.

Operation 24.   Punch three rivet holes in each arm-seat.   Ferracute Machine Co. press.

Operation 25.   Drill fourteen transmission cover holes, Bausch Machine Company's driller.

Operation 26.   Burr fourteen drilled holes, Bausch Machine Company's driller.

Operation 27.   Punch three holes in front and bottom; Ferracute Company, Bridgeton, N. J., press.

Operation 28. Ream front wall for starting-crank sleeve seat. Motch and Merryweather Machine Company.

Operation 29. Punch overflow screw-seat-bush holes.

Operation 30. Fix front-end malleable-iron casting trunnion in place with two rivets.

Operation 31. Drill six more trunnion rivet holes. Wormer Machine Co. driller.

Operation 32. Hand-rivet six rivets in trunnion.

Operation 33. Close in the two overflow-plug bushes, to be tapped

Brazing Hangers to Crank-Box Shell

Supplementary operation 43. Four fires in a bank—stationary flames below, with two swinging flames above

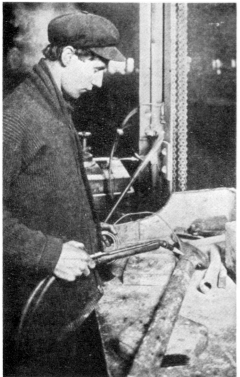

Spot-Brazing with Oxygen Torch

Correcting any defects in the brazing of the steering-post flange

to take the overflow screws. These screws are at different levels, to show maximum and minimum oil plash-pool depths in crank-box fly-wheel-housing depression. E. W. Bliss press.

Operation 34. Press-rivet six rivets in end trunnion shell, Toledo Machine Tool and Press Company.

Operation 35. Turn crank-box shell projections down over trunnion shell, with hand-hammer.

Operation 36. Braze trunnion shell to crank-box shell, in four-hole, hand-revolved brazing furnace. Same style of furnace as is used for operation 11.

Operation 37. On a large cast-iron jig, with legs and clamp and

Continuous Brazing with Turret Work-Carrier and Arc-Shaped Heating Chamber on Top

spotting pins, gauge and straighten the trunnion. See illustration on page 88.

Operation 38. Drill trunnion hole. Foote-Burt driller.

Operation 39. With angle plate on face-plate and lathe and back-rest fixture, turn trunnion; five Reed-Prentice lathes and one Warner lathe on this job. See illustration on page 89.

Operation 40. With crank-box clamped to lathe-saddle spotting-fixture, bore and face rear-end brazed-in drop-forging annular collar. See the illustration on page 90.

Operation 41.   Drill and tap screw holes in rear-end collar.

Operation 42.   Place the two pressed-steel hangers by which crank-box is held to chassis frame, drill for and insert three pins, and rivet pin ends, to hold hangers to crank-box shell.

Operation 43.   Braze crank-box hangers to crank-box shell, four fires in a bank, with swinging flames on top, stationary flames below. See upper illustration on page 91.

Operation 44.   By hand, with big file end, scrape and clean inside of crank-box shell.

Operation 45.   By hand, finish-tap rear-collar screw holes.

Operation 46.   Place transmission covers, with gaskets applied to covers; place horse-shoe reinforces inside of crank-box, and put in fourteen transmission-cover screws, through covers, through gaskets, through crank-box shell, and turn screws down hard; screws threaded into the two horse-shoe reinforces.

Operation 47. In large fixture, with gauge and hand-hammer, bring the crank-box hangers to place.

Operation 48. Lay crank-box, flat side down, on large surface plate, and with hand-hammer make the crank-box top flange lie down on the surface plate, all the way around.

Operation 49. In a large fixture, with clamps, with hand-hammer, bring the hanger holes to slide on fixture pins.

Operation 50. Tap globe-seat cap holes for cap retention.

Operation 51. Tap drain screw seat.

Operation 52. Tap the two overflow screw seats.

Operation 53. Fill overflow screw seats with temporary brass screws, screw-driver cuts, to close holes for gasoline leak tests.

Operation 54. Tap two holes in rear-end annular collar, and two holes in front vertical wall.

Operation 55. Heat front side of front wall, and clean wall and box wall seat with muriatic acid, to clean the surfaces for soft-soldering.

Operation 56. With tinning fluid and hand soldering-copper, soft-solder front wall in place to the crank-box shell inside.

Operation 57. With hand copper, fill joint with soft solder and also fill top joint between box wall and the front wall, if joint is open on top side.

Operation 58. With hand-file end clean off surplus solder.

Operation 59. Place drain screw and turn it down hard.

Operation 60. Press the hand starting-crank bushing into place in center of trunnion.

Operation 61. Place crank-box, open side up, in gasoline vat and see if any gasoline leaks into the box at any point. If leak shows it is made tight.

Operation 62. Final. Dip in air-drying japan vat, to japan outside of crank-box.

The over-all dimensions of the completed crank-box are $42\frac{7}{8}$ inches long, $22\frac{3}{4}$ inches extreme width, over the hangers, $18\frac{1}{8}$ inches extreme width of shell, and $8\frac{3}{16}$ inches depth inside. The weight of the finished crank-box assembly is 29 pounds. The factory cost, including all materials and overhead charges, was, through the month of February, 1914, $2.26274, or about 2.26\frac{1}{4}$. Of this total, according to the Ford costing department, labor and overhead charges make up $1.63749 and material is $0.625. This is, of course, far below what the cost would be in smaller numbers. The production averages about 900 per day, giving opportunity for elaborating the plant to the economical limit of special-tool installation.

The finished crank-box of pressed-steel is extremely strong, not liable to fracture from blows, and gives a very stiff and substantial support for the entire power plant of the Ford car, and, beyond doubt, the reliability of the Ford car is vastly enhanced by using wrought steel instead of cast metal as a crank-box construction material. So far as I am aware, no other small gas-engine has been fitted with a pressed-steel crank-box, and in my own opinion, the Ford crank-box is far and away the best ever used in a motor car.

The brazing fires are specialized and differentiated to such an extent as to afford a highly valuable study to those who make continued use of brazing, especially in view of the assertion made by Ford officials that no Ford car ever came to grief through brazing failure.

An illustration of a Ford revolving-work-carrier continuous-process brazing machine is given, showing the latest Ford practice in that direction.

In all Ford brazing operations where the conditions permit, the flame is directed downward on the brazing and a pit of melted borax is maintained directly under the braze. The brazing material is in all cases brass wire. For most of the brazing operations the wire comes to the brazer in coils about as big as a man's fist; the wire is soft, and the brazer straightens out what length he desires, and bends the end to suit his work. The brass which runs off the braze falls into the melted-borax pit, which is cleaned out with a ladle every day, these cleanings being treated to recover the brass they contain.

Most of the Ford brazing is done with the brazing wire in hand-coils, as shown in the illustrations. In no case is granulated spelter used. Where the long wire cannot be conveniently used, the same brazing wire is cut into lengths about ½ inch long and laid upon the surface before the work is put in the fire.

Ford Spot Brazing, with Oxygen Flame

The one fault with brazing as a method of uniting metal pieces is the impossibility of full inspection without cutting the job to pieces. A braze may be good all round the visible junction of the pieces and yet may not cover the broad meeting surfaces of the two components.

To make a certainty of full brazing the Ford Company introduces the secondary operation of "spot" brazing, done by an experienced workman, who handles an oxygen and gas torch (which gives a fine-pointed pencil of extremely hot flame) in his right hand, and a coil of brazing wire in his left hand and carefully inspects the braze made and patches it up with "spot" brazing wherever his experienced eye detects a possible fault. The oxygen flame is very hot and melts the brass rapidly, and as the pencil of flame is small the spot brazer can place his work exactly, and make the braze good with certainty.

Page 92, the final illustration of this chapter, shows a Ford "continuous" brazing machine, a hand-revolved vertical turret work-carrier, with over-head, arc-shaped, heating chamber, worked with two men, one to place the work and move turret, while the other does the brazing and removes the work. This picture is given here because this is the brazing story of the Ford series.

The Ford assembling practice, both of motor and of the chassis, is of the highest importance, and demands a separate chapter of its own to give even so much as a general showing of the unique "moving assembly" Ford practice, in which the assembly itself slides on ways, slowly chain-driven, from one group or pair of assemblers to the next assemblers, instead of the component under assembling standing still while successive groups of assemblers perform their operations on the stationary component. At first the work was pushed along by hand; but it has very lately been discovered by the Ford engineers that a slow chain-drive much reduces assembling labor costs, and now most of the Ford assembling slides are being fitted with endless-chain drives.

The moving of the assembly to successive groups of workmen of itself made a very great reduction in Ford assembling costs, the work being pushed along by hand at first; but now it is fully decided that the slow chain-drive is vastly superior to hand moving, as it brings all the groups of assemblers to a uniform speed rate, hurries the slow men and restrains the too swift men, and as before said lowers the assembling labor-cost while improving the quality of the product. This practice will be shown in detail in the fourth chapter.

CHAPTER IV

INSPECTION AND ASSEMBLING

FORD shop inspection is, of course, thorough, and begins before the unloading of incoming rail shipments, by analysis of samples of bar steel and forgings, and pig-iron.

The inspection of material and components in process of finishing in the various shop departments, is in charge of one chief inspector, who began as machinist with the first Ford car model built in the shop at 81 Park Place, 1901-2. It is worthy of note that when Henry Ford began at 81 Park Place, 1901, he worked as a machinist on the first Ford car with his own hands and had with him one young machinist, one draughtsman, and one boy. The draughtsman is now Ford factory superintendent, the young machinist is now chief inspector, and the former boy is now the metallurgist-in-chief of the Ford Highland Park plant, which may be taken as evidence that Henry Ford was unusually fortunate in the selection of his first three men, or, again, as evidence that he is willing to aid in advancing individuals who once begin to work for him.

The head inspector has three assistants, two for day work and one for night work, and about six hundred others under him, variously employed but all classed under the general title of "inspectors."

All inspectors take orders from the head inspector only, but of course respect the convenience of the foreman of the department in which they are stationed.

The inspectors are divided into classes having special duties and designations.

The "incoming-material inspectors," one hundred and twenty in number, deal with all material received partly finished from outside suppliers, inspecting to Ford Company's specifications and drawings.

The fifty foundry inspectors inspect every piece of casting made by the foundry, first in the rough, then as to tumbling, snagging, and visi-

97

Inspector-in-Chief in His Office.   Office Assistant Seated at Typewriter

ble defects, and see that all work sent from the foundry to the machine shop is to all appearance satisfactory.

The incoming-material inspectors and the foundry inspectors pass upon materials entering the factory departments where they are to be finished and completed.

The factory departmental inspectors are divided into three classes, as follows:

(1) "Machine inspectors," who are inspectors of machine work in progress.

(2) "Operation inspectors," who inspect work after the completion of individual operations.

(3) "Floor" or "final" inspectors, who inspect completed components only.   These are day inspectors.

In addition there are about one hundred night inspectors, mostly acting as machine inspectors, some six or eight "rejected-components" inspectors, and finally, about twenty "scrap" inspectors, whose duties will be presently specified.

The machine inspectors, one or more in each machine-shop component-production department, move from one machine to another and note work in progress.   There are about one hundred and twenty day machine inspectors and about one hundred night machine inspectors. The machine inspector notes any fault in any operation in progress, and may either correct faulty tool-setting himself, or may call the department-foreman's attention to the fault, or may order a change of tools or may call a tool-setter to remedy a fault. Machine inspectors enough are placed in each department to cover all operations in that department at frequent intervals, so that no faulty operation shall proceed for any great length of time. The office of the machine inspector is highly important and his powers are large and are exercised at discretion.

The operation inspectors inspect the work at certain periods in progress of finishing.

The floor or final inspectors deal with components in completed form.

Each department is cleared daily of wasters or components rejected by the final inspectors, and all wasters from all machine-shop departments are taken at once to the same room, close to the machine-shop superintendent's office, where each waster is carefully examined by one of the six or eight wasters inspectors to see if the rejected component can be made good.

All wasters finally condemned by these wasters inspectors then go to the "scrap" inspection department, and

Form 706. Shop Inspection Tag

there undergo individual examination by the twenty scrap inspectors who place the blame of the scrap-making where it belongs.

The wasters inspectors may call on the head inspector, and the head inspector may summon the foreman of the production department where the waster was originated, and the machine-shop superintendent may be notified, so that the waster makes plenty of trouble for those whose faults assisted in its production. The same procedure may be followed in the scrap-inspection quarters, so that all in fault are very likely to be made fully aware of vigorous disapproval of scrap production even as a rare performance.

Every effort is made to save everything which can be profitably saved, and to place blame where it belongs, with a view to curing faulty practice of every description.

THE TRAVELING INSPECTOR

It often happens that matters under discussion with an outside

Form 933.   Inspection Report on Defective Material

supplier can be soonest brought to a mutual agreement by a face-to-face talk and in such instance a traveling inspector is sent to the outside supplying factory.

In cases of sufficient importance the head inspector may go to an outside factory, though this official has plenty to do at home, and leaves the Ford shops in cases of emergency only.

INSPECTION FORM BLANKS

Form 706, "Shop Inspection Tag," size $2\frac{1}{16}$ wide by $4\frac{3}{8}$ inches long, is wired to the receptacle containing finished components by a floor, or final inspector, only.   No other inspection official is authorized to

Inspector's Report

use Tag 706. It is printed in black on stiff white paper, filled by the final inspector, who makes the inspection and wires the tag to the components receptacle, where it remains until the components are used in an assembling department. The inspector dates the tag, fills in the component symbol space, directs the finished components to destination, signs his initials, and certifies accuracy of dimensions and finish.

Form 933, Inspection Report on Defective Material. Printed in black on one side only of substantial white-paper form, $8\frac{1}{4}$ wide by $5\frac{1}{4}$

inches high. Filled by the department inspector with carbon duplicate, sent to the head inspector, who signs his name to both original and carbon, sends the carbon to the purchase agent, and files the original; when final adjustment is made it is recorded by the head inspector on his filed original, completing the entire record.

INSPECTOR'S REPORT

Triplicate form, green, pink and yellow colors, printed in black, serial letter black and same serial number in red, on one side of thin paper, only, 8 inches long by $5\frac{1}{4}$ inches high. Green original and pink and yellow carbons. This is the report on incoming material, filled by

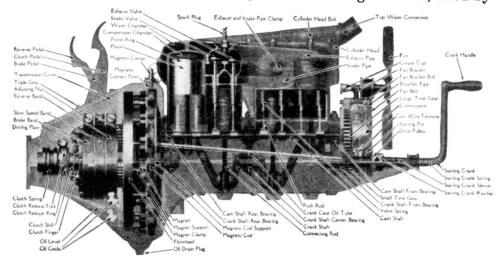

"Ghost" View and Partial Section of Ford Motor
Giving a good idea of the problems and the work involved in its assembly.

incoming-materials inspector, signed by his shop number; the three forms are sent to the head inspector, who appends his signature to all three forms, sends the green original to the purchase department, the pink carbon to the stock department, and files the yellow carbon in his own department.

FORD SHOPS ASSEMBLING

Ordinary machine-shop assembling practice stations the principal component in a convenient place on the shop floor, sometimes over a pit, or on a suitable platform having more or less elevation above the shop floor, on horses or on the bench, as may seem best, and proceeds with the assembling by bringing the other components to the principal component and applying and fixing them to the principal component which remains in the one place until the assembly is completed.

It is also ordinary practice to place all the components of a given assembly, as of a lock, or a dozen locks, in a box, or in a box with twelve compartments, and to pass this box to an assembler, who may wholly assemble each lock, or perhaps may partly assemble each lock and pass the box on to one or more assemblers who complete the assembling; or to place the components of (say) a watch movement in each of a series of boxes and pass these boxes to the first one of a line of assemblers, who does his part of the watch assembling and passes the box on to the next man, and so on, until the watch is completely assembled. All of this well-known practice may divide the assembling operations needful to produce the completed unit assembly more or less minutely, and, up to a certain limit the greater the number of the assemblers in the line, the less the total assembling time will be and the better the work of assembling will be done.

These methods are used for small unit assemblies only, and the Ford motor and chassis assembling methods are believed to show the very first example of minutely dividing the assembling operations of so large and heavy a unit assembly as an automobile. These Ford motor and chassis assembling lines are believed also to show the very first examples of chain-driving an assembly in progress of assembling, and hence are worthy of the closest study by all builders of comparatively small assemblies of any description.

The Ford shops assembling practice is to place the most suitable component on elevated ways or rails, and to carry it past successive stationary sources of component supply, and past successive groups of workmen who fix the various components to the principal component, until the assembly is completed and ready to leave the assembling line.

In some cases, where the shape of the component is unsuited to travel on rails, the principal component is pushed along on a finished iron table from one man or group of men to another man or group of men, past sources of component supply, each workman or group of workmen completing the placing, or the placing and fixing, of one component before moving the assembly in progress to its next station.

In case the assembly in progress moves on elevated rails or ways, it is common Ford practice to drive the assembly in progress by means of a slow-moving chain, and if the components are perfectly to gauge, so that all operations can be performed in predetermined times, it is better to drive the assembly in progress at a fixed suitable speed by chain, at a uniform rate, than to move it on the ways by pushing.

This Ford method of moving the assembly in progress has effected remarkable labor-saving gains over stationary assembling with all components brought to the one point for each assembly, the labor-saving gains being in all cases accompanied by great reductions in floor space required for the assembling operations.

Thus, up to September, 1913, the Ford car chassis assembling occupied 600 feet length of floor space, and required 14 hours of one man's time to assemble one chassis, standing still in one place while being assembled.

April 29, 1914, with the chassis chain-driven while assembling, 1,212 Ford chassis were assembled on three parallel elevated-rail assembling lines, by 2,080 hours of labor, giving one chassis assembled for each 93 minutes of labor, as compared with 840 minutes of labor in September, 1913.

The stationary chassis assembling in 1913 took 600 feet in length of floor space, while on April 29, 1914, the assembling lines were only 300 feet long.

As for Ford motor assembling, in October, 1913, 9,900 labor hours were required to assemble 1,000 motors in one day, which gives 9 hours 54 minutes = 594 minutes for each motor assembled; May 4, 1914, 1,003 motors, chain-driven on rails, were assembled with 3,976 labor hours, or 238,560 minutes = 237 minutes and 52 seconds time for each motor-assembly completed, a saving of 356 minutes 8 seconds = 5 hours and 56 minutes, per motor. In other words, more than 2½ motors were assembled on May 4, 1914, in the time it took to assemble 1 motor in the month of October, 1913, when the motor assembly was made by first-class American mechanics, working in what was believed by the Ford engineers in the month of October, 1913, to be the very best manner possible.

Besides these almost unbelievable reductions in assembling time, the Ford shops are now making equally surprising gains by the installation of component-carrying slides, or ways, on which components in process of finishing slide by gravity from the hand of one operation-performing workman to the hand of the next operator, this use of work slides being in some instances combined with operation divisions.

All of this Ford practice is of great importance to manufacturers at large, because the Ford engineers assert that these improved methods of handling work by slides, of moving assemblies in progress, and of minutely dividing assembling operations, can be applied to any and all small-machine manufacturing, with very large reductions of labor-cost.

The writer of these Ford stories has had sixty years of machine-shop

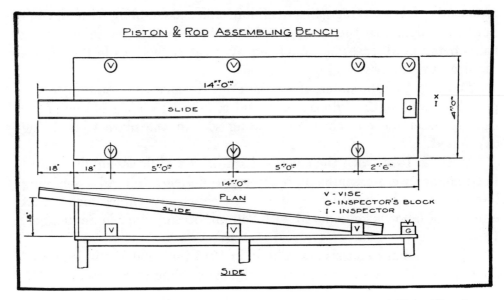

Plan and Elevation of Piston-and-Rod-Assembling Bench and Slide, Showing Dimensions

experience, ranging from cleaning castings and helping in the blacksmith shop to holding the position of chief draftsman and superintendent, and he believes that these assertions of the Ford engineers as to the extended scope and applicability of these new methods of work-in-progress handling and assembly moving, are broadly true.

I should say, in addition, that it was only at the end of three weeks of study and photograph-taking in preparation of this chapter that I became aware of the underlying principles by the application of which these incredible labor-savings of the Ford shops have but very recently been obtained.

What is more, if the reader experiences but a very small part of the surprise and admiration the writer experienced upon being made aware of this new Ford practice, he will certainly approve of the space devoted to full illustrations and descriptions of the Ford new practice in the directions specified. The Ford engineers are now moving over 500 machine tools in the Highland Park shops, and are having a large number of new machine tools constructed, many of them showing striking novelties of design, in order to take full advantage of the new things they themselves have learned in the last ten or twelve months.

The new Ford method of finishing the cylinder bores of small gas-engines by a rolling process, illustrated on page 126, gives an excellent interior cylinder surface, and is here first illustrated and described. This method of cylinder-bore finishing costs but very little, and is believed to produce results far superior to those obtained by the very best cylinder grinding practice, at a small fraction of cylinder-bore grinding costs, and this first disclosure of the Ford cylinder-bore rolled finish is highly important gas-engine construction news.

THE FORD PISTON AND CONNECTING-ROD ASSEMBLING

To show what may be done by simply dividing an operation seemingly already reduced to its lowest terms, and placing a short work-slide lengthwise of the assembling bench; the first example of the improved Ford practice here illustrated and described is the piston and connecting-rod assembling, changed within the last two months, so that now 14 men assemble 4,000 pistons and connecting-rods in one 8-hour day, instead of the 28 men employed to do exactly the same work less than two months ago, and with no change whatever in the tools used, nor in the ultimate operations performed.

In addition to the labor-time saving, the present practice of piston and rod assembling includes an inspector, who gauges and inspects each piston and rod assembly, with the result of no rejections from the motor-assembling line. With the former practice, where one man did the

Piston-and-Rod-Assembling Bench with Men at Work
South bench, looking east; inspector at left front.

whole job of piston and rod assembling, numerous returns were made from the motor-assembling line, causing costly delays in the motor assembling, to say nothing of the costs of pulling down and reassembling the faulty piston and rod assemblies.

FORD PISTONS AND PINS

The finished weights of Ford pistons vary, maximum, about six ounces. Each piston is weighed and marked on the head by a heavy center-punch used without a hammer, with one, two, three, or four center marks, dividing the pistons into four weight classes, maximum weight variations in each class three-quarters of an ounce. After inspection, the inspector places the assemblies on one or another of four shelves, according to center marks on the piston head, and the pistons are paired for weight on opposed crank-throws by the motor assembler.

The pistons and pins come to the piston-and-rod-assembling bench with the pins in the pistons. The rods come to the bench by themselves.

PISTON-AND-ROD-ASSEMBLING BENCH

The work bench is covered with sheet metal on top. In the old style, where each man did the entire job (average time about 3 minutes), each bench had 7 piston-holding special vises on each side, with no inspector, and no inclined work-slide over the bench—14 men to each bench, 2 benches, 28 men in all, who assembled 175 pistons and rods, average, in 9 hours of each man's time, or about 3 minutes 5 seconds time, each. Operations, tools, and benches were the same as now used in working the new methods, save that 7 of the 14 vises are now removed from each bench. No inspection, and many returns of faulty piston-and-rod-assembling from the motor-assembling line attended the older practice. The flat-top sheet-metal covered benches are 14 feet long and 4 feet wide.

Here was a 3-minute operation, very simple: push pin out of piston, oil pin, slip rod in place, slip pin through rod and piston and tighten the pin-pinching screw in the rod top-end, and place and open the pinching-screw split pins; and, although the time was not very small and the work not faultless, no one had studied the job carefully, or held a stop-watch on the operations to find how the 3 minutes were actually expended. Finally the motor-assembling foreman analyzed the time with the stop-watch and found that 4 hours out of the 9-hour day were spent in walking—that is to say, in body movements of each assembler made by moving his feet.

In a day or two the foreman had split the single man into 3 men, and reported to the machine-shop superintendent that he had no use for 14 of

North Bench for Piston and Rod Assembling
Looking from the southwest corner; inspector at the left front

Another View of the North Bench for Piston and Rod Assembling
Showing four assembling shelves at the left; the inspector, also at the left, is trying the stiffness of the rod movement

the 28 men on the piston-and-rod-assembling job, and the superintendent laughed at him.

Seeing convinced the superintendent that the laugh was misplaced, and he then said that it was surprising that the job had not been changed before.

It is of no use whatever to tell this story without detailing it as minutely as a split second-hand details operation-motion time-losses; therefore, one diagram and three photographs are shown, together with a fairly complete operation-time analysis so that the reader can see for himself much more than he could learn as a mere uninstructed spectator in the Ford shops, watching this piston-and-rod-assembling job in actual work.

OLD-STYLE, ONE MAN PERFORMING SIX OPERATIONS

Operation 1.   Drive out pin, with special hand-hammer.

Operation 2.   Oil pin, by dipping end in box of oil.   Hand.

Operation 3.   Slip pin in rod-eye.   Hand.

Operation 4.   Turn pin to take screw.   Screw-driver.

Operation 5.   Turn in pinch-screw.   Hand brace.

Operation 6.   Tighten screw, with open-end wrench, and put in cotter-pin; spread pin-end with special tool.

Time 3 minutes and 5 seconds; no inspection; 14 men on one bench. Average production per man, 175 pistons and rods assembled in 9 hours working time.

NEW-STYLE, OPERATION SPLIT INTO THREE DIVISIONS

Bench provided with slide, 3 men on each side of bench and inspector at one end of bench.

Operation 1.   Drive out pin, oil pin, enter pin-end in piston, average time, 10 seconds.

Operation 2.   Place rod in piston, pass pin through rod and piston, with screw-driver turn pin to position to take screw, turn screw in with brace.   Time 10 seconds.

Operation 3.   Tighten screw with open wrench, place cotter-pin, by hand, spread cotter-pin ends with special tool.   Time 10 seconds.

Operation 4.   Inspection.   Inspector gauges piston with flat steel gauge, places piston in pin-holding jig, tries rod to see if rod is pinched tight on pin, then holds piston horizontal in both hands and vibrates it slowly in vertical plane to see that the weight of rod free-end will barely rock pin in piston-pin bushes, and that pin has friction enough in bushes to keep rod from moving freely, a delicate test for pin-fit in piston-bushes. If rod works either too stiffly or too freely the assembly is rejected, goes back to assemblers, and has a larger or smaller diameter pin put in, as case may demand.

Actual inspecting time about 8 seconds, leaving inspector 2 seconds time to place the assembly on its proper shelf, according to the weight as shown by the center-punch mark or the marks on the piston head.

The best time record for 7 men, 6 assemblers and 1 inspector, is 2,600 piston and rod assemblies turned out in 8 hours, equal to one assembly in $77^1/_{13}$ seconds of one man's time. Average time, 2,400 assemblies in 8 hours, with 7 men, gives one assembly in 84 seconds of one man's time, or better than double the work of one man doing the entire job with no inspector, and with a saving of 101 seconds of time of assembling.

With inspection, under new style, as said before, there are no returns of pistons from the motor-assembling line.

This piston-assembling job teaches two lessons of first importance. The first is that there are great savings in labor to be made by splitting operations to such an extent that the workman

West End of Flywheel-Magneto Assembling Line

This is the first of the Ford sliding assembly lines, and at this end the old pipe construction yet remains in place.

does not need to change the position of his feet, and the second lesson is that a work-slide so located that the workman can drop his completed operation out of his hand in a certain place, without any search for a place of deposit, and also can reach to a certain place and there find his next job under his hand, is also a very important time-saver.

The vises are 60 inches apart, so that there is only 30 inches reach required for the pistons and pins, which are placed on the bench after operation 1, ready to hand to the man who performs operation 2, who in turn places the pistons where they are readily reached for operation 3. The slide is used for the completed assembly only, and delivers the com-

Middle of Flywheel-Magneto Assembling Line
Showing the gray-iron and angle-bar construction now adopted in the Ford assembling lines, and the bottom line of the driving chain.

pleted assemblies close in front of the inspector so that not a movement need be wasted anywhere.

In commenting on the late change from the old routine of piston and rod assembling to the new method by which 14 men are made to do more and better work than 28 men did before, the foreman of assemblers said, "We were asleep over that job, asleep and dreaming. I don't see how we came to overlook the possibilities the way we did."

Eastern End of Flywheel-Magneto Assembling Line, Showing Part of Chain Drive
The chain is belt-driven to a worm shaft with worm gear on the outside (rear) end of sprocket shaft.

Height of Moving Assembly Lines

It was in this same assembling department that the first moving assembly line, that for assembling the Ford fly-wheel magneto, was installed. Of course, every one had everything to learn, and this first Ford assembling rail-line was built 8 inches lower than it should have been. The correct height for the magneto assembling, three illustrations given herewith, is 35 inches above the floor for this job. There were the same uncertainties as to the best height in the case of the chassis-assembling ways. In all instances it is of first importance that the

Assembling Transmission Casings
Two gray-iron finished flat-top benches are used, that at the right rear being higher than the one at the left front.

workman should stand upright. A stooping posture very soon tires the workman, and greatly reduces his efficiency. When the chassis ran on its own wheels on the floor it brought things about "work-high"; some of the operations were too high for convenience, and platforms were placed on the floor where needful. When the first high line was placed for chassis assembling, with the chassis sliding on its axles on top of the rails, it was made $26\frac{3}{4}$ inches high; two other chassis lines were installed each $24\frac{1}{2}$ inches high, one on each side of the middle $26\frac{3}{4}$-inch rail-line. These two heights, $26\frac{3}{4}$ and $24\frac{1}{2}$ inches, are retained with much satisfaction, the tall men being worked on the high line and the shorter men placed on the two low lines. The Ford engineers attach so much importance to this "work-high" condition that they are now placing a great number of gray-iron raising bases under various machine tools, particularly under presses, to bring the work at such a height that the workman can either stand or sit erect, any stoop being now well known to cause a marked reduction in the worker's output.

The first fly-wheel magneto moving assembling line was installed, ready for work, about May 1, 1913, but the desirability of general application of the moving assembly line to the Ford motor assembling and the chassis assembling was not at once fully conceded by all the Ford engineers.

Fly-Wheel Magneto Moving Assembly

This moving-assembly line is of historical importance as being the first moving assembly placed in work anywhere, so far as revealed by information to date. It is, of course, possible, or perhaps probable is the better word, that the moving-assembly line has been used somewhere in the world, but it is new to the Ford engineers and entirely novel to me. If the moving-assembly line has been used elsewhere, probably this publication will bring the previous use to public knowledge.

The fly-wheel-magneto-assembling story will not be told in full at this time. The Ford motor is the only one used for automobile driving which fires the charge by current generated by a magneto built directly on the fly-wheel, and hence sure to run as long as the fly-wheel revolves —which, of course, gives a more direct and certain magneto drive than can be had with a separate magneto, gear-driven from the motor crank-shaft, after the usual practice. Besides this, the Ford fly-wheel magneto is a novel construction, and it is hoped that it may be fully described at a future date, but at this time such description is outside of the line of thought.

Previous to the installation of this moving magneto-assembling line, the Ford fly-wheel magneto had been a one-man assembly, each workman on this job doing all the assembling of one fly-wheel magneto and turning out from 35 to 40 completed assemblies per 9-hour day. The work was done by experienced men, but was not so uniformly satisfactory as was desired, and was costly as a matter of course, as all one-man assembling must of necessity be forever.

Forty assemblies per 9-hour day, best time for one-man work, gives nearly 20 minutes time to each one.

When the moving-assembly line was placed in work with 29 men, splitting the one-man operations into 29 operations, the 29 men began turning out 132 magneto assemblies per hour, or 1,188 per 9-hour day, one man's time producing one fly-wheel magneto assembly in 13 minutes 10 seconds, a saving of nearly 7 minutes time on each assembly, or more than one-third of the best one-man time.

First Operations in Motor Assembling

Pouring crank-shaft boxes with two babbitt ladles, one in each hand; babbitt-melting furnace at the right.
Cylinders slide over hot plate before babbitting and are heated so that thin babbitt will pour well. The
man in the middle puts on and takes off the babbitting jig; the man at the left
chops off the babbitt risers.

Operation 10—Cleansing the Cylinders

The cylinder castings (which weigh 101 pounds rough as sent from the foundry) are placed on pendulum
carriers pivoted to a slowly revolving gray-iron wheel, turning top to left, which carries the cylinders
down through a hot cleansing bath. The operation requires two men, one to place the cylinders on the
shelves and the other, standing at the right, to take them off and place them on the assembling line.

A new high line with chain-drive was installed for magneto assembling about March 1, 1914, when the Ford work day had been shortened to 8 hours.   At that time the magneto-assembling force had been improved by substitutions and experience, and 18 men were assembling 1,175 magnetos in 8 hours, or a little more than 7 minutes of one man's time to assembling one magneto.

The chain-drive speed was a matter of trial; it was first made 5 feet per minute, which was much too fast; then 18 inches per minute

Operation 14—Finish Valve Seats on Foote-Burt 8-Spindle Drilling Machine

was tried, and found much too slow; the third trial was 44 inches per minute (3 feet 8 inches), and is yet in use, though the foreman believes it could now be increased

Operation 15—Grinding in the Valves
The work of two men was saved by moving this Foote-Burt machine from its original place on the floor into the assembling line.

to advantage. The chain drive proved to be a very great improvement, hurrying the slow men, holding the fast men back from pushing work on to those in advance, and acting as an all-round adjuster and equalizer.

As soon as the men became accustomed to the automatically moving assembly 4 men were taken out of the line and the production was 160 in excess of previous performance; 14 men working 8 hours assembled 1,335 magnetos, making 5 minutes of one man's time assemble a magneto, as against 20 minutes when one man assembled the entire job.

The next attempt at moving the assembly in progress was made with the job of placing the crank-shafts in the *en-bloc* cylinders. An accident occurred which resulted in personal injury and put a stop to new installations of the moving assembly for a time, but in June, 1913, the foreman of the assembling room took courage and split the transmission-cover assembling into 23 operations, not on rails but on flat-top metal tables, the shape of the transmission cover making rail-sliding impracticable.

One man assembling the entire transmission cover produced from 20 to 30 assemblies per 9-hour day, 18 minutes for each one.

At the present time 23 men, each working one of the 23 operations for 8 hours, complete 1,200 transmission assemblies, which gives 9 minutes 12 seconds for each assembly, or a little more than one-half the best time with one man doing the whole job.

These great labor savings led to the first trial of full-length assem-

Operation 17—Cleaning Cylinders by Live Steam
They are lifted into a steam box, which is closed tight by toggle levers, and cleaned by 72 live-steam jets. The washing-wheel hot bath (Operation 10) stands at the left. The machine is of Ford design and construction.

Operation 19½—Hydraulic Testing of Cylinders for Leaks

It was impossible to place this machine in the line. At the left is the long inclined gravity cylinder-carrier, down which the cylinders run upon rollers. The machine is of Ford design and construction.

bling ways for motor assembling, in November, 1913. Motor assembling on separate benches gave, in October, 1913, 1,100 men working 9 hours to assemble 1,000 motors.

By installing full-length motor-assembling lines and building some new tools to go into the motor-assembling line, along which the motors in process of assembling are moved by hand, now, May 8, 1914, 472 men working 8 hours assemble 1,000 motors.

In November, 1913, it took nearly 594 minutes of one man's time to assemble one motor.

Now, one motor is assembled in 226 minutes of one man's time, as against that 594 minutes in November, 1913.

This very great saving is due to the continuous line assembling, to the installation of work-carrying chutes, and to holding the motor as nearly as may be at one level during the entire course of motor assembling.

Some of the savings effected by placing the machines in the line-level are noted in the illustration captions.

A complete list of the motor-assembling operations is given on pages 118-127, each followed by the time of performing the operation.

A number of the most typical operations are illustrated; and inspection of the machines and methods thus shown, together with the descriptive legends and the data of the number of men employed on each job, will give a much more comprehensive idea of Ford practice in this department than could be obtained from any mere verbal description.

Operation 36—Ream Crank-Shaft Bearings; Performed on Reed-Prentice Lathes, of Which the Ford Shops Use Many

The lower view shows a slide installation by which the cylinders are carried by gravity to Operation 28.

FIRST ASSEMBLING LINE

	Number of Men	Time, Sec.
1. Put cylinder on hot plate and plug holes with asbestos...	2	6
2. Put cylinder on babbitting fixture.....................	1	4
3. Put on babbitting bar and plates.....................	1	7
4. Pour babbitt.......................................	1	4
5. Take off babbitt bar and plates......................	2	6
6. Take off cylinder..................................	1	3
7. Chop gates..	1	12
8. Peen babbitt......................................	1	11
9. File gates...	1	15
10. Wash cylinders....................................	2	18
11. Clean out chips and knock out babbitt chips...........	1	5
12. Put in broaching tools in 8 push-rod guide holes........	1	30
13. Take cylinder from rack and broach 8 holes in punch press	1	13
14. Seat 8 valve seats in 8-spindle press.................	1	101
15. Put in valves in motor while other one grinds valves.....	1	71
16. Wash and inspect valves............................	2	32
17. Steam cylinder. Blow out with 72 steam jets...........	2	33
18. Put valves back in cylinder.........................	1	8
19. Assemble springs and spring seats to motor............	4	21
19½. Water-test cylinder. Made outside of the line........	1	1
20. Assemble valve-spring seat pins.....................	1	45
21. File burrs from cylinder case and gauge holes with bolts..	1	14

Operations 29 to 34, Inclusive—Beginning of Second Assembly Line; Placing the Crank Shafts

Operation 35—Running the Crank-Shaft. Ford Machine

Bearings must come off this machine smoking hot. If they are not hot, it shows they do not touch the crank-shaft.

	Number of Men	Time, Sec.
22. Assemble front and center bearing with liners and bolts...	1	20
23. Assemble rear cap and bolts and put on 2 nuts..........	1	25
24. Tighten nuts on front bearing and put 2 nuts on center bearing..	1	25
25. Tighten center-bearing bolt nuts.....................	1	24
26. Tighten main bearing and take case from bench.........	1	21
27. Take cylinder from lime. In lathe, ream. Put on slide...	1	160
or	2	98
28. Round corners of bearings, special Ford machine........	1	35
SECOND ASSEMBLING LINE		
29. Take off caps, punch oil holes, countersink and mark caps	1	124
30. File angle on bearing, wipe out dirt and chip gear cover and lay crank in place..................................	1	100
31. Oil-stone crank-shaft and fit liners below bearing caps....	1	100
32. Put in 6 bearing bolts, tighten nuts on main bearing bolt and tighten nut on one center bearing bolt...........	1	115
33. Tighten front bearing nuts and one center bearing nut....	1	105
34. Put in cotter pins and clean out front-cover end with wire brush...	1	100

Operations 44-47—Placing the Cam-Shaft and Gear Assembly
This operation is performed on a Ford gray-iron flat-top bench of the same height as the assembly line.

Operations 48 to 57—Ford Motor-Assembling Line

	Number of Men	Time, Sec.
35. Run in crank-shaft..............................	2	105

Operations 36 to 43, inclusive, serve to place the cam-shaft and gear assembly and are worked on a bench level with the assembling lines.

36. Ream bearing.....................................	1	7
37. Break bearing....................................	1	10
38. File bearing	1	14

Operation 58—Running in the Pistons, Cam-Shaft, Cams and Valves
Performed on a Ford machine, a duplicate of that shown on page 119.

39. File off burrs on cam-shaft flange....................	1	9
40. Assemble front bearing to cam-shaft..................	1	10
41. Assemble spring to bearing and assemble center bearing..	1	14
42. Assemble gear to cam-shaft..........................	1	44
43. Test out size of cam-shaft gear......................	1	10
44. Drive brass bushing in case and line-ream same........	1	70
45. Assemble push rods in push-rod guides................	1	52
46. Drive cam-shaft in cylinder and blow out motor........	1	53

Operation 59—Ford Motor Assembly

On a separate iron-top bench of the same height as the assembly lines, the gap between lifter and valve stem is fixed to gauge. If the gap is too great the valves are ground down in the seat. If it is too small the valve-stem ends are ground off. The workman reaching upward on the right is grinding off the stem end on a high-up emery-wheel. All men at this bench are Americans and all-around machinists; they see that the valves are correctly timed and the motor assembly so far as completed is correct.

Operation 72—Tighten Bolts with Electric Drill and Turn Motor Half Around on the Ways, Placing its Front End toward the End of the Assembling Line

	Number of Men	Time, Sec.
47. Put in cam-bearing set screws and inspect and take push rods from below the valves..........................	2	60
Piston and rods assembling is a separate job, on piston-and-rod-assembling bench.		
48. Gauge pin bearing on crank-shaft and scrape off burrs on cylinder bores....................................	1	57

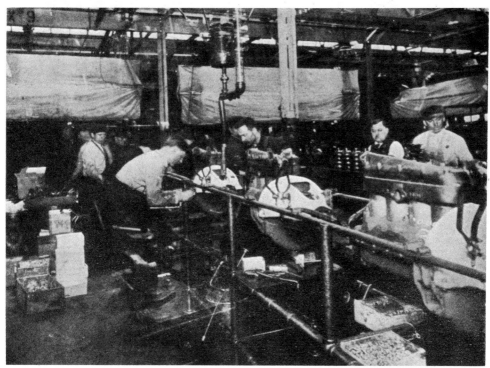

Operation 78—Tighten Transmission Cover Bolts and Put Lubricating Oil into the Crank Box through an Overhead Oil-Measuring Rig

When the two-way cock is opened to admit oil to the overhead measuring cylinder, a float-carrying valve rises until it closes the top air vent. When the cock is opened to deliver oil to the motor-crank box, the float descends, admitting air to the measuring cylinder. Placing this oil-measuring device overhead saved the work of five men. The crank-box oil filling now takes only the time required to move the valve.

	Number of Men	Time, Sec.
49. Fit pistons..	3	70
50. Fit rings to pistons..................................	1	24
51. Stone burrs on crank-shaft pins and turn over motor.....	1	85
52. Mark caps on rods and retry pistons and pull wire from water jacket....................................	1	28
53. Take off caps and file same..........................	2	106
54. Put on two top rings and push pistons in cylinder........	1	50
55. Pull No. 1 and No. 4 rods to crank pin and put on nuts and cotter pins....................................	1	60

Operation 84—Paint the Motor and Remove it from the End of the Assembly Line to a Small Wooden Stand on Rollers

	Number of Men	Time, Sec.
56. Turn over crank and assemble No. 2 and No. 3 rods and caps to crank....................................	1	63
57. Assemble nuts and cotter pins to No. 2 and No. 3 rods and take motor off bench...............................	1	75
58. Belt piston in belting-out stand. Run in pistons in cylinders...	2	55
59. Time motor. Separate bench operation................	1	355
60. Drive studs by machine—6 studs.....................	1	45
61. Clean cylinder and put on head and gasket and drive 15 bolts...	2	48
62. Tighten 15 cylinder-head bolts and put in 4 bogus plugs..	1	45
63. Put on magneto coil................................	1	51
64. Wire coil and put in oil tube and clamp and gauge coil...	1	38
65. Assemble cylinder front cover........................	1	50
66. Hand transmission.................................	..	235
67. Assemble fan pulley................................	1	60
68. Assemble commutator...............................	1	80
69. Inspect motor and blow out valve doors................	1	53
70. Blow out motor. One man will take care of two lines....	..	25
71. Put on bands, universal ball cap, pan on motor and put in pan bolts..	2	61

Turn in the Globe-Joint Cap Screws

The Man at the Left is Numbering the Motor. The Man at the Right is Trying the
Standard Starting Crank for Its Engagement with the Crank Shaft

These operations are performed as the motor stands on the small truck.

New Method of Finishing Inside of Cylinder Bore After Reaming

A cage of hard-steel rollers running at 450 r. p. m. with $\frac{1}{16}$-inch feed is passed down through the bore and up again. Now worked on drill presses, one bore being rolled at a time: a four-spindle machine now under construction will roll all four cylinder bores at once. The hard-steel rollers are ground in a curve, making then 0.001 inch larger in diameter at the middle, and the cage of rollers is oiled freely while passing through the cylinder bore. This makes an excellent cylinder-bore surface. The Ford model T cylinders, which are $3\frac{3}{4}$ inches in diameter, were not finished in any way after reaming up to about April, 1914, when this rolling process (believed to be original with the Ford Company and a new operation in gas-engine finishing) was introduced.

	Number of Men	Time, Sec.
72. Tighten bolts with electric drill and turn motor on ways..	2	65
73. Put two front-cover bolts in pan and put transmission-cover gasket on cylinder.	1	78
74. Assemble transmission cover to motor and put in two rear bolts.	1	70
75. Tighten engine-pan bolts and put in cotter pins.	2	75
76. Adjust bands.	1	60
77. Put in transmission cover-to-pan bolts and put on nuts...	2	70
78. Tighten transmission cover-to-pan bolts and put in cotter pins and oil.	2	72
79. Assemble slow-speed connection and adjust same.	1	67
80. Assemble exhaust and intake pipe clamps and 6 screws in transmission-cover door.	1	55

	Number of Men	Time, Sec.
81. Assemble magneto contact and tighten transmission-cover-door screws...	1	71
82. Assemble exhaust and intake pipes with carburetor......	1	50
83. Put on side and top water connections..................	1	55
84. Paint motor—remove from line........................	1	68

The next chapter of this book on the Ford plant will show the chassis assembling, the body placing on the chassis, and the loading of the Ford cars into railway cars. Succeeding chapters will show the results which the Ford engineers gain by the moving of over 500 machine tools, now in transit. The Ford shops, now having reached a production capacity of 1,200 cars per day, if urged, for the first time are giving the Ford engineers opportunity to draw breath and look about, and do some things that they have never before had time to do. The results of this general overhauling will be fully told in following chapters.

CHAPTER V

MOTOR-TEST BLOCKS AND CHASSIS-ASSEMBLING LINES

A GRAY-IRON foundry is not an automobile-body upholstering shop, and an automobile-upholstering shop is not a gas-engine assembling nor a chassis-assembling department. These assertions will be accepted by all without argument or demonstration.

How, then, can the Ford engineers be expected to reduce labor-costs enormously in the gray-iron foundry, in the motor-assembling department, in the chassis-assembling department, and in the body-upholstering department, by use of one and the same mechanical element, a slowly-moving, endless chain?

The Ford engineers certainly do make great labor reductions in the foundry, the machine shop, and in body-upholstering by simple endless-chain installations, because in all assembling operations it costs much less in labor-time expenditure to move an assembly in progress past fixed points of component supply than it costs to hold the assembly in progress stationary and bring the components to the one assembling location, and because the moving assembly gives more floor space for assemblers and hence permits the more minute subdividing of assembling operations.

In the foundry, in ordinary practice, a poured mould is neither more nor less than an assembled unit, all assembling operations being performed in the one fixed location where the flask is first placed on the foundry floor. The sand is brought to the flask by hand and shovel, the pattern, gaggers, parting-sand, and cores are brought to the mould by hand and assembled, and, as the last operation, the melted metal, final component of this foundry assembled unit, is brought to the finished mould and poured into it.

The Ford four-cylinder *en-bloc* casting, the rough casting weighing 101 pounds, is made in this way at this time. The Westinghouse air-brake-cylinder mould is made and poured and shaken out on an inter-mittingly-moved endless train of cars (240 in number, if memory serves

129

correctly), drags and copes on separate cars moving to stations under the overhead sand-chute, past the groups of moulders and core-setters and flask-closers, to the cupolas where the moulds are poured; then over shake-out grates where the sand falls into low troughs, provided with spiral conveyors, wherein the sand is moistened, cut-over, and led to an elevator which lifts it to supply the sand chutes filling the flasks. Undoubtedly the Ford *en-bloc* cylinders might be moulded and poured on a Westinghouse endless chain of cars running on two parallel tracks, connected by semi-circles of track at the ends; but the Ford cylinders are not so moulded and poured; they are moulded on the floor and poured from ladles hung from overhead rails.

All the Ford-foundry small work is machine-moulded, copes and drags separately in most instances; then the moulds are placed on endless-chain-driven mould-carriers which take them past the pouring

Single Motor-Testing Block, with Motor in Place for Running in

From the Test Block the Motors Are Taken to within Reach of the Chassis-Assembling Line in Truck Loads of 5 Motors Each, 200 Truck Loads per Day of 8 Hours for 1,000 Autos Assembled

zone and over the shake-out gratings, as in the Westinghouse method. The Ford moulding machines stand under sand chutes which are served by an endless chain of sand-distributing blades or pushers, slowly moving in troughs placed above the heads of the machine moulders.

The Ford gray-iron foundry is now installing a new core oven, served by two endless-chain lines, all as will be fully described in the chapter on the foundry, later in this book. The main themes of this chapter are the motor testing and chassis assembling; but the spectacle of the body-and-top chain-driven assembling led to a general survey of the Ford endless-chain assembling lines, which naturally recalled the Westinghouse endless-train air-brake-cylinder moulding and pouring, and so suggested the close analogy between machine-shop assembling and foundry moulding operations, notwithstanding the fact that foundry operations and machine-shop operations are so universally regarded as widely dissimilar.

Before following the chassis assembling in detail, however, further attention must be given to the motor block-test and the details of motor "running-in" on the block. These important operations conclude the motor assembly (which was described in the preceding chapter) and precede the delivery of the motor, with its motor-assembler's record, to the automobile-assembly line.

THE MOTOR-TEST BLOCKS

The motor blocks are nineteen in number at the date of this writing (June 1, 1914) and the day's motor production, whatever it may be, must be handled on the nineteen blocks. This number will soon be increased.

Each test-block consists of a Westinghouse direct-current shunt-wound motor, constant speed, showing 20 horse power at 230 volts, 73 amperes and 750 revolutions per minute, equipped with Weston instruments and supported on a stand adapted to take the motor and hold the transmission shaft in line with the motor-armature shaft. The motor under test is placed on the block and driven at 750 revolutions per minute until the needle drops to a 20-ampere reading, this operation taking, say, from 3 to 5 minutes; each motor is given as much time on the block as may be, but the floor must be kept clear of untested motors. No motor is ever passed until it makes 750 revolutions per minute with 20 amperes of 230-volt current.

The head block-tester has one assistant, one tester to every test-block, and enough helpers to handle the motors on and off the test-blocks. Each block-tester has an alphabetical steel stamp with his own individual letter, and marks a certain screw-head with hammer and letter stamp at the end of each test, and also paints one other certain screw-head red when a motor is passed from the test-block for use in the chassis-assembling line.

The block-tester examines the motor while on the block for all the possible imperfections enumerated in the list on the following page.

Imperfections discovered are noted in pencil, on small, white, stiff cards, using list terms, and a straight vertical pencil mark is made in the corresponding blank space at the left of the specified fault. One card is filled for each fault found, and all cards are fixed by one particular screw to the faulty motor, which is then sent to the motor-repairs department, working four men only, who are all-round machinists, and who take care of all the motor repairs when as many as 1,100 motors per day are being turned out.

This list of motor repairs is long because it includes every fault which has been so far discovered in any Ford "Model T" motor.

Each day's report of motor repairs is sent by the head motor assembler to the machine-shop superintendent. After repairing, the motor goes back to the tester, with its fault-cards, is placed on the block and given another trial, and so on until the motor shows no faults. By applying test certification marks to two specified bolt heads, finishing record-spots on motor castings is avoided; also, if the two specified screws should be removed, no one could be sure the motor had been tested, as it would then be without test certification marks.

MOTOR-ASSEMBLY RECORD

Triplicate sheet, Form No. 386, printed in black, on one side only, as shown on the next page, thin paper, three colors, size $9\frac{3}{4}$ inches wide by $8\frac{1}{4}$ inches high. Filled by head of motor assembling, one original and two carbon copies. The green original is placed by the head assembler in a heavy envelope, wired to the pedal, and goes

LIST OF POSSIBLE IMPERFECTIONS FOR WHICH EVERY FORD MOTOR IS TESTED

Oil leaks in transmission covers.
Oil leaks around pedals.
Oil leaks between transmission cover and pan.
Oil leaks at door of transmission cover.
Oil leaks between transmission cover and crank case.
Oil leaks at magneto contact.
Oil leaks between crank case and pan.
Oil leaks at end of cam shaft.
Oil leaks at end of crank shaft.
Bottom door bolts leaking.
Loose rods of gasket knocks.
Rods striking pan.
Manifolds, cracked, reset, etc.
Defective cylinder heads and cylinder-head gaskets.
Tight piston rings.
Bent cam shaft.
Valve trouble, push rods, bent valve stems.
Change water connection.
Metal in transmission.
Hole in cylinder.
Change cam shaft, bearing frozen.
Put on water connection.
Intake pipe leaks.
Noisy transmission.

Cylinder head bolts won't go down; dirt in hole, etc.
Clutch won't release.
Adjust transmission bands.
Hole in crank case.
Crank case arms out of line.
Put in pet-cocks.
Change small gear.
Repair carburetor.
Clutch shift grinds on shaft.
Broken gear cover.
Hole in leather pipe too small.
Tight ball-cap bearing.
Loose front-cam bearing.
Threads stripped in drain-plug hole.
Tight cam-shaft bearing.
Cam-shaft brass bushing too tight.
Magnets striking spool.
Change fan pulley—wabbles.
Cracked and leaky pans.
Noisy gears.
End play in clutch-lever shaft.
Clutch adjusting-screw too tight.
Motor out of time.
Hole in cylinder base.
Hole in water jacket.
Motor pumps oil.

with the motor to the chassis-assembling line. The yellow carbon is filled by the head assembler and also placed in the envelope wired to pedal, going with the motor to the chassis-assembling line. The white carbon is filled and filed by the head motor assembler as his own record of production.

All of these motor-assembly triplicate record forms are numbered in red, in numerical sequence, as are also the automobile-assembly records described near the end of this chapter, and to be more fully explained by an examination of the Ford sales and shipping practice.

Motor-Assembly Record.   Filled in Triplicate.   One Copy Wired to Motor, the Others Filed as Explained on the Preceding Page

FORD SPECIAL NUT-BRACE

The Ford shops have brought out no end of original small tools and fixtures, and a considerable number of highly original machine-tools, but this is the only hand-tool involving notable invention that has so far been brought to my attention in the Ford assembling.

In case of placing a free-body-fit bolt, the head of the bolt must be held while the nut is turned on and forced to place. With ordinary wrenches, the assembler holds the head from turning with one wrench, held in one hand, and turns the nut home with another wrench, worked by his other hand—a slow operation at best, and, in many cases, very difficult because of obstructions which prevent ready access to the bolt-head while turning the nut to place.

With the special brace (page 135), which has a solid nose fitted to the nut at N, a block, $S\,B$, fitted to slide on the brace-body, $B\,B$, with an off-set extension, fixed to $S\,B$, reaching outward beyond N and then bent inward and ending in the head-holder, $H H$, concentric with $B B$ and N, the bolt-seating operation becomes easy and rapid.

The bolt-head and nut are shown as holding the plates P, Pl, together, the plates being cut away to show the bolt. An open coil-spring, S, is placed be-tween $S B$ and N. With the bolt in the holes in P, Pl, and the nut carried in N, $S B$ is pushed towards N until HH can be slipped over the bolt-head; then $S B$ is released, S pulls H H onto the bolt-head,

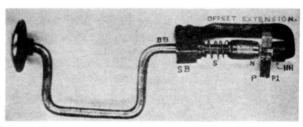

Special Brace, Evolved by Ford Chassis Assemblers
See pages 134, 135

and the assembler then has both hands free to run the nut home by operating the brace in the usual manner.

Three of these bolt-head-holding nut-braces are used on each auto-mobile assembling line, nine braces in all, saving three men on each line, $15 per 8-hour day, or $45 per day on the three assembling lines, which is a large interest on the brace cost.

Ford Chassis Assembling

The Ford chassis assembling in moving lines affords a highly impres-sive spectacle to beholders of every class, technical or non-technical. Long lines of slowly moving assemblies in progress, busy groups of suc-cessive operators, the rapid growth of the chassis as component after component is added from the overhead sources of supply, and, finally the instant start into self-moving power—these excite the liveliest inter-est and admiration in all who witness for the first time this operation of bringing together the varied elements of the new and seemingly vivi-fied creation, on the three Ford chassis assembling lines where over 1,200 have been put together and driven out of doors into John R Street in one single 8-hour day.

Chassis Assembling in Chain-Driven Lines

Up to August, 1913, the Ford chassis was assembled in one location. First the front and rear axles were laid on the floor, then the chassis frame with springs in place was assembled with the axles, next the wheels were placed on the axles, and the remaining components were suc-cessively added to complete the chassis. All components needed to make up one chassis had to be brought by hand to each chassis-assembling location. This routine of stationary chassis assembling was, in September, 1913, worked with two lines of assembling-floor space, 600 feet long, 12 feet chassis-to-chassis centers, 50 assembling locations in each 600-foot line, 100 cars in process of assembling in the two lines. Working in this routine 600 men were employed, 500 being assemblers who were supplied with components by 100 men acting as component carriers.

About April 1, 1913, the first sliding assembling line, used for assembling the Ford fly-wheel magneto, was placed in work and immediately showed a large reduction in assembling labor-cost. Consequently, the possibility of lowering chassis-assembling costs by introducing the moving assembling line for chassis assembling became a matter of discussion among the Ford engineers.

In the month of August, 1913 (the dull season) 250 assemblers, with a stationary assembling location for each chassis, the assemblers being served by 80 component carriers, worked 9 hours per day for 26 days to turn out 6,182 chassis assemblies. Total labor hours $330 \times 9 \times 26 = 77,220$ hours, giving 12 hours and 28 minutes for labor time on each chassis, about as good as was ever done with stationary chassis assembling.

The assembling line was long—600 feet—but even at that did not give room enough, and $12\frac{1}{2}$ hours of labor time seemed altogether too much for one chassis. It was in the dull season, and an experiment was made with rope and windlass traction on a moving assembly line 250 feet long. Six assemblers traveled with the chassis as it was slowly pulled along the floor by the rope and windlass past stationary means of component supply, and the chassis-assembling time was reduced to 5 hours and 50 minutes of one man's time, over 50 per cent saving.

October 7, 1913, on a moving-assembly line 150 feet long, with no helpers, components being piled at suitable locations, 140 assemblers in the line completed 435 chassis assemblies in one 9-hour day, 2 hours and 57 minutes of one man's time for each chassis assembling.

The assembling line was lengthened by degrees to 300 feet, giving the men more room, and on December 1, 1913, 177 assemblers working 9 hours turned out 606 completed chassis assemblies, about 2 hours 38 minutes of one man's time to each chassis.

December 30, 1913, working two assembling lines, 191 men completed 642 chassis assemblies in one 9-hour day, a little less than 2 hours 40 minutes of one man's time for each chassis, the cars being pushed along by hand.

January 14, 1914, one assembling line was endless-chain driven, with favorable results.

Construction of Chassis-Assembling Line of Elevated Rails

Showing the endless-chain idler at south end of chain. The crosswise-placed gasoline-tank platform is shown filled two-high, with tanks standing on end

January 19, four chassis-assembling lines were worked, only one line being chain-driven. The wheels were put on as soon as the axles and the chassis frames were assembled, and the assemblies in progress ran with their front wheels on the floor and their hind wheels carried in 3-wheeled cradles, used to give easy

Another View of the Chassis-Assembling Lines, from a View Point North of the Tank-Platform

The chain is in place, but not stretched. Pile of mufflers at left hand

placing of the rear wheels on the motor-starting drive at the end of the line.

February 27, 1914, the first high line of rails with chain drive was used. The chassis slid on its axles as pulled by the chain, and the wheels were applied only a short distance before the motor-starting was reached. This first high line was made with rails 26¾ inches above the shop floor, and at once showed great advantages, the best time for one chassis assembling being only 84 minutes, while the worst time was 2 hours. Two other high lines were soon installed, 24½ inches high, with chain drives; tall men worked on the line 26¾ inches high, and short men on the other two lines, 24½ inches high.

The Ford engineers make a point of "man-high" work placing, having learned that any stooping position greatly reduces the workman's efficiency. The differing heights of the chassis-assembling high lines are believed to be decidedly advantageous.

On these three high lines, on April 30, 1914, 1,212 chassis assemblies were completed in one 8-hour day, each chassis being assembled in 1 hour 33 minutes of one man's time, as against 12 hours 28 minutes, the best time with stationary chassis assembling, September, 1913—93 minutes as against 728 minutes—and it must be borne in mind that the September, 1913, Ford practice in chassis assembling was fully abreast of the best known in the trade. Very naturally this unbelievable reduction in chassis-assembling labor costs gave pause to the Ford engineering staff, and led to serious search for other labor-reduction opportunities in the Ford shops, regardless of precedents and traditions of the trade at large.

The chassis was not completed when it ran out into John R Street, and the first practice was to let the driver run the chassis up and down until he thought best to abandon it to the motor inspector and the rear-axle inspector, and to return to the end of the assembling lines for another chassis to drive out into John R Street. The bodies were allowed to slide down an incline from the second floor, and were then dragged along the pavement by one man and stood on end in a bunch south of the chute.

When the assembly was completed on the John R pavement, and had been inspected by the motor inspector and the rear-axle inspector, it was again boarded by a driver and taken to the bunch of bodies, where four men lifted a body into place on the chassis, and the completed automobile assembly was then driven to the shipping-clerk's office, between the railway tracks, ready for shipment.

This procedure afforded plenty of gaps and vacancies for discretionary proceedings on the part of all the men working outside under the head assembler. The next radical improvement was made by laying down the angle-iron John R street track, running southward from the exit door, under the body-chute and something more than a chassis

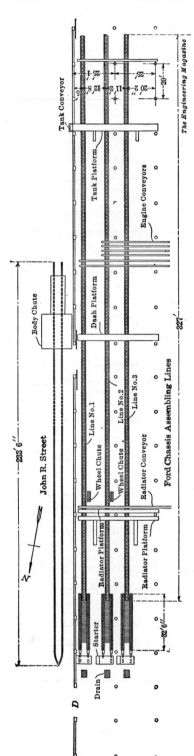

Plan of Chassis-Assembling Lines

The chassis assemblies begin at the south (right-hand) end, and move to the north (left-hand) end, under the overhead gasoline-tank platform, the motor-carrying chain-hoist tracks, the dash assembly platform and the radiator platform. They then take the wheels, run on the wheels on roller frames over the pit where a workman caps the front-axle bracing globe, and then down a short incline onto the motor-starting drive for the rear wheels. Then the chassis is driven under its own power, through the door, D, and on the John R street track to the southward

The Engineering Magazine

length to the south of the chute; and the chute itself was presently equipped with a car-body handling rig, not regarded as the final thing, but serving to place a body on the chassis with one handling only. The ground plan of the three chassis-assembling lines inside the shop, and of the John R street track, is given to scale on this page and the numerous illustrations in half-tone will give the reader a fair idea of the chassis-assembling procedure.

CHASSIS-ASSEMBLING OPERATIONS

It must be clearly understood that the moving-assembly speed is varied to suit exactly each individual assembling job. As each operation is performed while the work passes slowly across the station occupied by each assembler or assembling gang, the time of transit past this station must be sufficient for good work and no more.

The first assembling line established in the Ford shops (for the magneto) was originally speeded at 60 inches per minute, which proved much too fast. The next speed tried, 18 inches per minute, was found to be as much too slow. The third guess, 44 inches per minute, answered so well that it is yet retained.

The dash-assembly line travels 72 inches per minute; the front-

Mounting Chassis Frames on Springs
View looking southeast, toward the gasoline-tank platform

Press Operator Fixing Fender and Run-Board Brackets to Chassis Frames
This view is at the north end of the chain-driven chassis-and-springs assembling line, on which the chassis
frames are carried to the south for various operations after the frames are mounted on the springs

141

axle assembling line 189 inches per minute, and the body-and-top assembling line 144 inches per minute. The speed of the chassis-assembling line is 72 inches (6 feet) per minute.

The work is so divided among the assemblers that each operation is performed in 7 minutes and 36 seconds, turning out 300 complete chassis assemblies on each chassis-assembling line in 8 hours of working time, save in case of operations 1 and 2.

Placing Axles under the Chassis Frames and Springs

OPERATIONS

1. Three men; one press man and two chassis-frame handlers. Fix 4 mud-guard brackets, 2 on each side, to the chassis frame, 600 in 8 hours.

2. Six men. On moving line, fix rear spring to chassis frame, 600 in 8 hours. Operations 1 and 2 are on a side line, work moving from north to south, and this side line turns out 600 chassis frames with 4 mud-guard brackets and rear springs in place in 8 hours, enough to supply two lines of automobile assemblers, work moving from south to north, each line turning out 300 automobile assemblies in 8 hours. The Ford Highland Park shops on June 11, 1914, were turning out 600 automobiles per day, and about 400 more per day were assembled at the various Ford branches, making about 1,000 new Ford automobiles assembled per day.

To assemble more than 600 automobiles per day, two presses and 18

Chassis Lines after Passing to North of Tank Platform, Looking to Northwest, Approaching Motor-Hoist Rails

143

men are worked in operations 1 and 2, and three automobile-assembling lines are worked. The high production and the record at that date were 1,212 automobiles assembled in one 8-hour day at the Highland Park plant.

From operation 2, all operations are performed on two automobile-assembling lines simultaneously, same number of men and same operations on each line, assemblies moving from south to north. Operations performed and men used on one automobile assembling line only, here follow.

Lowering Motor to Place on Chassis
Looking to southwest; shows overhead chain-hoist rails

3. Three men. Two men place and fix the rear axle, connecting the rear spring to the rear-axle spring shackles; one man working simultaneously with the other two places and fixes the front-axle assembly under the chassis frame.

4. Two men. One completes the fixing of front axle, places the two combined lamp-brackets and front mud-guards, and catches nuts on, while the other man places and fixes the mud-guard bracket truss-rods.

5. Two men. Place nuts on truss-rods. Place and fix control-lever rock-shaft.

6. One man. Fixes front spring, tightens nuts, and puts in 4 split pins.

7. Two men. Complete fixing of combined front fender-irons and lamp brackets.

7½. Place one gallon of gasoline in the gasoline tank, on gasoline-tank bridge.

8. Two men. Place gasoline tank and fix same, also place gasoline

feed-pipe. The tank receives one gallon of gasoline before leaving the gasoline tank bridge.

9. One man. With hard-grease syringe ("dope gun") injects 4 pounds of heavy grease into the bevel gear and differential hous-

After Taking the Dash Assembly
Looking southward from radiator platform

ing. Also places 1 pound heavy grease in universal-joint globe housing.

10. Two men. Place motor and connect the universal joint of propeller shaft to the change-gear shaft.

11. Two men. Line up mud-guard brackets. Tighten rear-spring perch nuts and place the cotter pins in same.

Applying Radiator to Chassis
Looking southward, showing radiator platform

Applying Wheels to Chassis
Looking northward from radiator platform

12. One man. Places spark plugs. Fixes same.

13. One man. Seats and caps motor front-support and wires 2 cap screws.

14. Two men. Fix globe housing to end of transmission case, place 2 bolts and 2 cap screws.

15. One man. Put cotter pins in the nuts placed in operation 14 and wire the cap-screw heads placed in the same operation.

16. Two men. Place and fix the 2 rear crank-case bracket bolts and 2 bolts with split pins.

17. One man. Places 4 grease cups, 2 in universal-joint casings and 2 in rear-axle gear housings.

18. Two men. Place dash assembly. Place 4 bolts.

19. One man. Places muffler and fixes exhaust pipe, also replaces rear-axle bevel-gear housing grease-plug, after first making certain that grease has been properly supplied.

20. One man. Nails name plate on dash board.

21. One man. Adjusts pedals travel.

22. One man. Fixes steering-column end to chassis frame.

Workman in Pit under Chassis, Capping Front-Axle-Brace Globe

The last operation in chassis assembling. The figure at the right is handling the exhaust hose

23. One man. Places and fixes commutator.

24. One man. Places acetylene-gas pipe and its supporting bracket inside chassis frame.

25. Two men. Place split pins in fender and lamp-bracket bolt nuts; also put split pins in 4 dash-board bottom holding-bolt nuts.

26. Two men. Place and fix motor-hood clips and hood "blocks" (wood-strips) and connect the spark-plug wires.

27. One man. Places radiator support and spring studs and nuts, and places split pins in nuts.

28. One man. Tightens and pins muffler-fixing bolt nuts.

Chassis Leaving Rails on Which the Axles Slide, to Run on Its Own Wheels

The sheet-steel casings enclosing the chain-driving belt are shown at upper left. All bolts which could touch workmen in these assembling lines are fully encased

Filling Radiator and Starting the Motor

The driver is sitting on the gasoline tank. The lever man stands on a lever hooked over the rear axle, to give adhesion of the rear wheels to a friction drive (seen in the floor) to start the motor

29. One man.   Secures gasoline feed-pipe to carburetor; also connects brake-rod.

30. Two men.   Place motor pans, one on each side, under chassis frame, and pan-holding bolts and nuts.

31. Four men.   Tighten motor-pan-bolt nuts and place split pins in same.

Chassis Standing with Rear Wheels on Ball-Bearing-Supported Idlers, So That Motor Can Drive Wheels at Any Speed during the Rear-Axle and Transmission Running Test

32. One man.   Pins steering-gear bracket nut, and adjusts spark-time.

33. Two men.   Put on wheels, place wheel nuts.

34. One man.   Connects carburetor "pull rod" (gives more or less gasoline) and adjusts the carburetor, and turns on the gasoline.

35. Three men; one head checker and 2 checkers, one on each side, also act as inspectors.   Record chassis numbers and car numbers, fill

blank records in record sheets, Form 14. The third man is record inspector, and filler of his own number record book; superior to the two checkers.

36. One man. Caps steering connecting-rod globe end, places 2 cap bolts, places nuts and pins them.

John R Street Rail Line Filled with Cars

37. One man. Connects magneto wire, and paints bolts and nuts on right side of chassis.

38. One man. Places radiator and its water connection and top stay-rod, and places carburetor priming rod.

39. One man. Tightens radiator water connection.

40. One man. Places nuts and split pins, radiator-support studs.

41. One man. In pit, caps front-axle radius-rod globe, and puts on two stud nuts and wires same.

42. One man. Paints bolts and nuts on left side of chassis and radiator.

43. One man. Final inspector, tags defects.

44. Two men. Fill radiator with water, handle starting weight lever on rear axle, and lift rear wheels off starting friction-wheels and attach exhaust hose.

45. One man. Driver, drives car on to John R street line.

THE JOHN R STREET TRACK

In regular course of events the chassis is driven from the motor-starting drive at the north end of the assembling line, through the door to John R street, directly on to the John R street track, and is there left by its driver, who walks back into the shop and takes out the next chassis which has had its motor started. The John R street track was not placed until after the need for it was plainly apparent. The early practice included a run up and down John R street at discretion of the driver, who did not leave the car until he saw fit to do so. The consequence was, that with new cars coming out of the shop door at 40-second intervals, the street was filled with cars running up and down in no regular sequence and with a considerable waste of the time of the drivers, as was shown by the fact

Body Chute, John R Street, Looking Northwest

Body at top right, on chute platform, ready to go down the chute, endless-belt control by man at lever at extreme right of platform. Two handlers on top of platform to left of the lever man are ready to start the next body down the chute. Near the foot of the chute, under the rocking gallows frame, two men, one on each side of body, are making slings, hung from the gallows cross-bar, fast to the body. The chassis stands at the left, ready to take the body. The man on the box, at right gallows upright, controls the movement of the gallows frame. The man at left gallows upright stands ready to direct the body when launched.

that six drivers were taken off as soon as the John R street track began to be used. The John R track also cleaned up the traffic congestion at that point, and the placing of idlers on ball bearings at one point in the John R street track made the rear-axle running inspection possible without taking the cars off the track and placing the rear-axle housings on small wooden horses so that the rear axle could be motor-driven without moving the chassis. These idlers in the John R street track at once showed their value by almost entirely clearing that thoroughfare of all new cars save those on the track itself.

Placing the Body on the Chassis

A very considerable list of chassis-assembling operations, performed formerly between the shop door whence the cars came out and the body chute, are now performed on the John R street track, with that notable time-saving which always followed keeping work in progress in one well-

Looking East from Body Chute, to Railway Shipping Platforms. The Middle Building is the "Hospital," where any Chassis Showing Fault in Tests on John R Street Rails Goes for Such Repairs or Replacements as May Be Needed

The shipping clerk's office, or, in the Ford nomenclature, "The Finishing Department," is seen in the distance, east of the hospital. Before placing the John R _ _ _ _ _. This picture was taken during a 1,000-cars-shipped day; note

Applying Tops to Bodies

There are two lines, one driven to deliver some 8 or 10 bodies per hour more than the other. The fast line is used when haste is important, the slow line when there is plenty of time

defined line and thus leaving as little as possible to the whim or choice of the individual workman.

As soon as a chassis is driven onto the John R track the clutch is

South End of Body-and-Top Assembling Line, 340 Feet Long, Endless-Chain Driven

This page and pages 154, 157 show the variety of assembling operations to which chain-driving on siding ways is applicable.   Until very lately this body-and-top-assembling was performed by placing each body on a four-wheeled truck and moving the trucks by hand; the line was long, and all the trucks were moved at once in obedience to the blast of a horn.   Now, with the chain-driving, everything proceeds in perfect order, and with a large reduction of labor costs.   The bodies are received at the south end of the line and delivered with tops applied at the north end

North End of Body-and-Top-Assembling Lines, Showing Drive of the Chains

There is yet much difference in the mechanisms of the Ford chain drives, which will probably soon find
a standard form

adjusted so that, with the motor running, the chassis will "creep" at
something less than walking pace along the unobstructed track, southward toward the body chute. The man who tightens the clutch also
throttles the motor to low speed.

Automobile Assembly Record, Triplicate Form. See Pages 157, 158

Form 842. Chassis Assembler's Daily Report to Machine-Shop Superintendent
8 by 5 inches, very thin white paper. See pages 157, 158

Next the water connection to the radiator is made tight, if it shows any leak.

Then the top nut of the steering shaft, which holds the hand-wheel, is put on, after inspection to make sure that the hand-wheel key is in place.

This is followed by careful carburetor adjusting. The Ford cars are equipped about half and half with Holly and Kingston carburetors.

Endless-Chain Lowering Tanks from Top Floor, Outside, to the Tank-Platform Inside

John R street side of the shop, looking northwest

Next the motor inspector, who must be an expert and must hear well, puts the motor through its paces, and if he detects any fault the chassis is taken out of the line and goes to the "Hospital," across the street, where the motor is made to run right or is exchanged for one that does run right. The Ford *en-bloc* cylinders castings are piled in the open air for 30 days to "season" before machining, but may develop leaks when placed in actual work in spite of the shop hydraulic test, and the highly specialized motor inspectors can rightly interpret every sound made by a running motor, and so are able to locate accurately the point where any abnormal sound originates.

Finally, the hind wheels of the chassis are brought to stand on four flanged-sleeve ball-bearing idlers and the rear axle is run at various speeds and its noises are carefully noted. Here, again, experience and quick hearing are indispensable. The rear axle makes but little noise and the inspector must be able to locate certainly the cause of any unusual sound.

The rear-axle inspection takes place under the body chute, and when everything is right the chassis runs to the south end of the chute and has a body placed on it, and is then ready to be driven out to the shipping platform.

The illustration on page 152 gives an excellent idea of the orderly conditions secured by the present methods. Anyone who saw John R street in the strenuous days preceding the installation of the track will appreciate thoroughly the improvement in methods represented by this item alone.

Every motor has an individual number, as each chassis and body have, but these two numbers are not the same in any one car, and it is

Fitting Top on Body, on Chain-Driven Line

Note the ease of attitude of the workmen, and the orderly appearance of this scene of active employment
under favorable conditions

needful the factory should have a record of the number of the motor and of the chassis and the body which are assembled together to form one complete automobile.

AUTOMOBILE-ASSEMBLY RECORD

Triplicate Form No. 14, printed on thin paper in three colors, is filled by the head of the chassis assembling, one original and two carbon copies being made. It carries the entire specifications of an automobile on a sheet $9\frac{3}{4}$ inches wide by $8\frac{1}{4}$ inches high.

Use of the green original; after the dash assembly is fixed to the chassis, the motor-assembly record envelope (Form 386) is removed from the pedal and fixed to the steering wheel. The green original automobile record is placed in the same envelope. The yellow carbon also is placed in this envelope with the green original. The white carbon is filed by the head automobile assembler as his own record of production.

Daily "Car" Report

"Car" here signifies either a chassis without a body, or a chassis with a body making the assembly a complete automobile. The word "Decked," in this form, signifies "Body on Chassis."

"L.H.R." means left-hand control, regular.

"L.H.M." means left-hand control, metric (for foreign trade).

"R.H.R." means right-hand control, regular.

"R.H.M." means right-hand control, metric.

"L.H. 60 ins." means left-hand control, 60-inches gauge, for southern trade.

This Form 842, a single sheet of thin white paper, printed in black, 8⅛ inches wide by 5¼ inches high, constituting the chassis-assembler's daily report to the machine-shop superintendent, is filled daily by the head of the chassis-assembling department and by him sent to the machine-shop superintendent, who files it in his office, as his own record of production.

CHAPTER VI

MACHINING AND ASSEMBLING THE FRONT AXLE

THIS description of Ford practice in finishing front-axle components and carrying them to final assembly supplies a concrete example of actual machine-shop results obtained by carrying out certain definite principles. These underlying principles are:

(1) A broad survey of the field of effort with a wholly free and unfettered mind.

(2) The careful examination of existing conditions.

(3) The elimination of every needless muscular movement and expenditure of energy in the shop-production routine.

What is more, these demonstrations of Ford practice show the ultimate results of ideal factory conditions—conditions in which there is absolute freedom both from any restraint of individual effort toward labor-cost reduction, and from that still more often imposed limit, the inability to incur necessary money cost. It happens that the Ford shops have several capable engineers working together in perfect harmony, and that these men of ideas are so fortunately placed that the cost of changes and improvements need have no determining influence whatever on the carrying out of new methods and means by them devised.

At the date of this writing, June 9, 1914, the Highland Park shops are working altogether fifty-nine men in the tool and fixture drawing room, forty pattern makers and four hundred and seventy-two tool makers, and there are besides these, three hundred men in outside machine-tool shops—say a total of eight hundred and seventy-one men employed in reducing to practice two broadly new methods of lowering Ford shop-production labor-cost, viz., by the placing of work slides of greater or less length, and by the use of the moving assembly.

In addition to this work on installations which are supposedly new, the Ford shops are simultaneously completing the moving and replacing of more than five hundred machine tools to carry out what is termed in the Ford shops "progressive production"; that is to say, the scheme of

159

placing both machine and hand work in straight-line sequence of operations, so that the component in progress shall travel the shortest road from start to finish, with no avoidable handling whatever.

In other words, the Ford shops at this time present a large-scale laboratory demonstration showing results which conform absolutely to the theorems formulated by Professor Jones and Mr. Knoeppel.* It certainly is not often that theory and practice, abstract reasoning and the results of such reasoning in actual working form, can appear in one publication in such prompt succession and in such convincing coincidence.

The finishing of Ford front-axle components with work-slide installations, and the front-axle preliminary and final assembling lines, are of course purely technical examples of advanced machine-shop practice; but it is this very fact which makes this actual shop-practice story available as a demonstration of the correctness of the labor-cost reduction theorems formulated by Professor Jones and Mr. Knoeppel.

Again, while it is undeniably true that thought must precede action, and right thinking alone can show the road to right doing, it is also undeniable that the sight of the actual right machine working in the right manner is far more impressive to the rank and file of "industrial economists," the practical shop-men working to reduce shop labor-costs, than any printed words can ever be; and because of this a fully illustrated story of ultimate shop practice, like this description of Ford front-axle production, has a highly efficient educational value of its own, because an actual presence is more impressive than a mental conception.

The study of the finishing and assembling of front-axle components shows how labor-costs may be very greatly reduced by three expedients:

(1) By placing tools and men in operation sequence, so that each component shall travel the least possible distance while in process of finishing.

(2) By the use of work slides, placed so that upon the completion of one operation the workman can drop the component in one unvarying place, convenient to his hand, and so that gravity shall carry the component to within the easy reach of the workman who is to perform the next operation on the component.

(3) By the use of sliding assembly lines, chain-driven for the final assembling, but having the partial assemblies moved by hand.

---

*The Business Administrator; Edw. C. Jones.   The Engineering Magazine Co., N. Y.   Installing Efficiency Methods; C. E. Knoeppel, *Ibid.*

The Complete Front-Axle Assembly

This front-axle assembling job also shows one original machine tool by which two hand operations and one machine operation are ingeniously combined, and the moving assembly line is the latest Ford installation of that class, and shows some labor-saving peculiarities of much importance.

The illustrations given herewith show the complete front-axle assembly, a sectional view of the stub-axle and spoke flanges and the ball bearings, a floor-plan of the machine-tool placing for finishing of components, a sheet of rough and finished drop-forged components with their symbols, and many pictures of component finishing, together with views of the various novel aids in assembling.

Ford's Globe-Jointing of Axles

The Ford Model T car places a half-elliptic spring, convex side up, on each axle, and perches the chassis frame on the tops of these half-elliptic springs, which are shackled to the front axle and to the rear-axle housing. The rear-axle housing is prolonged to a forward globe-end, which is taken by a globe bearing, fixed to the chassis frame.

The front axle is fitted with two horizontal diagonal braces, reaching to rearward, ending in a globe, and this globe is seated in a globe bearing, also fixed to the chassis frame.

The ends of the springs can safely endure a very considerable torsional flexure; hence the spring-hangers, or shackles, which secure the spring ends to the axles, are brass-bushed, with closely fitted pins and oil cups, all with the highly desirable result of making the car of this model extremely well adapted for the roughest of rough-road work; in point of fact the Model T car can stand a twist of 24 inches in its wheel base, 12 inches for each wheel above or below level, on contrary sides front and rear.

Ford's conception* of the low-cost car for the average man included the necessity of good performance on bad roads, or no roads at all, and this requirement was met by globe-jointing the axles to the chassis frame, thus giving the car the power to run over any surface, no matter how rough, whereon the motor could be made to turn the wheels without injury. This unique conception for satisfying the engineering requirements of the problem will be yet more fully understood from an inspection of the illustration on page 161.

The front-axle body, T-202, is milled on a large and very peculiar Ingersoll milling machine having a hand-revolved and machine-fed work-carrying fixture, of which two views are given.

The feature of prime novelty and interest shown in this front-axle-components finishing job is the work slides, placed wherever they can be of obvious advantage and in many places where they seem at first sight to be needless, yet in every instance making large labor-cost reductions, some of which are specified later in this story.

Of course, speaking broadly, there is nothing new in the use of troughs by which material or components under construction are moved by gravity from one location to another location. But the placing and using of such metal troughs, or "work slides" as they are here named, in the manner in which they are now (since 1913) placed in the Ford shops, is new to me, and the labor-savings effected by these work slides are incredibly large—vastly greater than at first expected by the Ford engineers themselves, who believed that the general use of these work slides would be advantageous, but had no expectation of such unbelievable labor-cost reductions as followed work-slide installation in every instance. The true cause of these labor-cost reductions is now known to be the saving of thought and of muscular movements gained by furnishing a fixed point where the workman may drop a component when his operation thereon is completed, and a second fixed point where the workman who is to perform the next succeeding operation can certainly pick up the piece when he wants it. This is the whole story, and the

*This conception is patented the world over. The American patent applications and issue dates are as follows:

Subject	Application Date	U. S. Pat. Date	U. S. P.
Rear-axle globe joint	Feb. 24, 1903	Dec. 22, 1903	747,909
Front and rear globes	July 21, 1909	Oct. 14, 1913	1,075,557
Front and rear globes	Oct. 13, 1911	Nov. 12, 1912	1,044,038

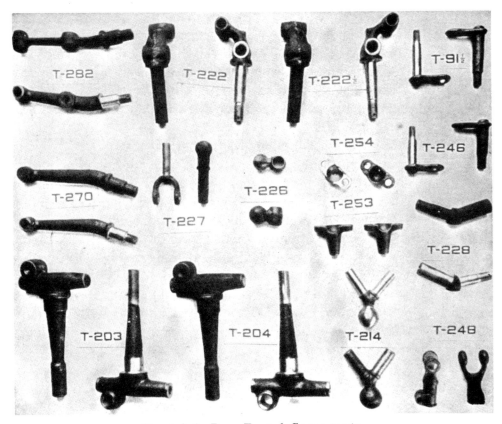

Front-Axle Drop-Forged Components

Ford engineers are now placing these work slides everywhere, always with marked reductions of labor costs.

The second astonishing feature shown by this front-axle job plant is the inverted drillers, shown working, front elevation, on page 168, and commented upon at length elsewhere.

The third notable machine-tool novelty shown on the front-axle component-finishing floor is the large front-axle body T-202, milling machine, shown in three views, page 165 front, and page 166 right end and rear. Of course, there is nothing broadly new in fitting a multi-spindle milling machine with a revolving work-holder; but the large size, peculiar construction, and excellent performance of this front-axle-body fork-and-spring-perch milling machine, supplied by Ingersoll to Ford engineers' specifications, give this tool novelty and interest.

There are four mill-carrying spindles overhead, each of the outside spindles carrying four pairs of straddle mills adapted to mill the fork bosses of two axle bodies at once, while each of the inside spindles carries two pairs of straddle mills to mill the four spring-perch seats of two axle bodies at the same time.

The axle bodies are clamped to a revolving work-carrier which has four faces at right angles to each other, these faces being long and wide enough each to take two axle bodies laid flat, side by side, and leave room between the axle bodies for the straddle mills on the four mill spindles to work.

This large and heavy hand-revolved axle-body fixture has journals at each end, carried in slides which are moved up by action of an underneath cam-shaft, driven by worm-gear and tangent-screw, and has also a large capstan wheel at the right end by which the fixture may be hand-revolved; the fixture can be latched in four positions, 90 degrees apart. The four flat faces of this revolving and lifting horizontal work-carrier are provided with studs, clamps, and nuts at each end to hold two axle bodies on each flat face of the carrier, the pair of axle bodies being located on the carrier faces by two swinging spotting fixtures, one at each end, which are jointed to the end frames to swing in a horizontal plane.

This work-carrier is counterbalanced by two 1,200-pound weights, suspended from chains which pass over two idlers for each one and then take hold of the slides in which the revolving fixture is journaled.

Two workmen, one at each end, fix two axle bodies to one fixture-flat standing vertical before the men, locating the position by the swinging spotting fixtures and fixing the two axle bodies to the work-carrier by means of the clamps, studs, and nuts. Then the spotting fixtures at each end are turned out of the way, and the man at the right unlatches the revolving fixture and gives it a quarter turn by means of the capstan at the right, and then latches the fixture in position, the four mill-carrying spindles running continuously. The man at the left then starts the cam-shaft running, and the cams lift the fixture, carrying two axle bodies clamped to its top horizontal flat face, up to the straddle mills, soap and water lubricated, and feed the cut up to top position, when the cams permit a quick gravity drop of the fixture, the cam-shaft drive being automatically knocked off when the fixture reaches low position. Meantime the two men have fixed two more axle bodies to the next vertical face of the work-carrier in front of them, as before, and when the work carrier rests in low position the man at the right again indexes the work-carrier a quarter turn, front side moving upward, and then the man at the left again starts the cam-shaft, all as before. At the fourth indexing of the work-carrier the men have to take off two milled axle bodies before they can place two more on the vertical flat of the carrier in front of them, and so on.

At first all the journals were oiled by individual oil-cups, time wasters and uncertain in action, which were soon changed for automatic, 25-lead mechanical oilers at each end of the machine, best shown in the right-hand end view.

The four mill spindles are worm-gear- and worm-driven, as shown in the rear view, which also shows the worm and worm-gear drive of the cam-shaft, the belt drive of the soap-and-water return pump, and the belt drives to the automatic oilers. There is no return of the lubricating oil, which runs down into the machine base. The work-carrier balance-weight chains are shown at each end in the rear view, taken with the machine in work. The front view was taken with the machine idle, because the flood of soap and water applied to the mills in work runs over the fixture and obscures details.

One grinding of the gangs of mills of this milling-machine will mill from 150 to 175 axle bodies, T-202, to within gauge limits. The gangs of mills are on individual arbors, so as to be removed from the machine and replaced as unit assemblies. Five tool-grinders are constantly em-

Front View of Ingersoll Special Milling Machine for Milling the Front-Axle Body
This machine is provided with a horizontal four-sided, cam-lifted and hand revolved work-holding fixture
as described on pages 163–165.

Right End of Axle-Body Milling Machine

ployed in keeping up these gang-mill assemblies, several complete sets of which are used, so that there is no delay in changing.

The regular practice is to change these gang-mill assemblies once in four hours, removing them from the milling machine before the work shows any sign of not being within gauge limits.

Speaking from the tool-maker's side of this axle-body milling job, there is no uniformity of mill-life for "once grinding." The best record is four-days work for once grinding: poorest, part of one axle only, a hard axle taking the edges off six pairs of the straddle mills before completing the first cut. The grand average is about four-hours life, changing the gangs of mills twice in each eight-hour day.

This machine finishes the twelve surfaces on each of two axle bodies, twenty-four cuts in all, at the same time, and turns out about 450 milled axle bodies in eight hours, with two men, and uses about one pint of lubricating oil per hour. Three other milling machines of different forms are now used to bring the milling up to 900 axle bodies in eight hours, but these will soon be displaced by a second machine of the same general design as this with many changes and improvements, the two Ingersoll machines together being expected to mill about 1,000 axle bodies in eight hours.

Rear View of Axle-Body Milling Machine

Page 169 shows the front-axle-body-drilling Foote-Burt special four-spindle driller. The holes are first jig-drilled to rough diameters, then the jig-bushes are changed to finish diameter, and the drills are changed for reamers to ream the holes to finish diameter. One man on this four-spindle driller drills and reams six holes in each one of about 130 front-axle bodies per eight-hour day.

It is a proverb among special-tool designers that a man will walk round and round the best method for any job and not see it for a long time, if ever. The more common event is that some other man, a stranger to the job, finally discovers the one best scheme.

Stub-Axle and Steering Arm, with Ball Cone and Nut

The spring-perch seats in this axle-body drilling job are about 2½ inches through, and the chip-clearing spiral of the drills clears the hole of lubricant just as surely as it carries the chips upward, thus forcing the drills to work dry in heat-treated stock and making a very hard job indeed, almost as bad as the stub-axle hub-drilling.

Suppose the same general form of a horizontal work-carrier as that on the axle-body milling machine were used, stationary axis, no rise and

fall action, with, say, the lower third of the horizontal-axis-fixture diameter submerged in lubricant, and suppose the lubricant reservoir to be fitted with four horizontal driller-quill receiving sleeves, in which eight driller quills were spiral-gear-driven, drills at right angles to the fixture axis, and the correct distance below it, the four spindles on one side to carry drills and the four

Stub-Axle and Axle-Body Assembly, with Spoke-Flanges in Section

on the other side to carry reamers. Then all the drill and reamer work could be submerged and perfectly lubricated, the reamers following the drills back, and the workman having nothing to do save to index the fixture round and put on and take off the finish-reamed axle bodies.

Then this drilling and reaming job would be performed under the most advantageous conditions, with a large reduction in first cost of the drilling machine, a saving of drill wear, and considerable saving in labor cost.

One word here as to the practical designing of special labor-cost-reduction machine tools.

It is a common saying among shop men that "everybody takes the hardest way first," and every machine-tool designer can recall many an instance in his own work where a later idea was much better than the first one, although the first idea was so good that it was eagerly reduced to practice in a greater or less extent before the unsought, later, and better scheme forced itself upon the designer's attention with the result of throwing away the previous work.

To avoid such unpleasant events it is surely time well spent, before beginnings drawings, to consider fully and impartially every plan and method which might possibly serve the occasion, no matter how strange or absurd the plan appears at first sight; and such consideration of seemingly unavailable methods should not be superficial, but most careful and painstaking. It is excellent practice, when undertaking a new construction, to write, in full detail, every thought and scheme that can be mentally evolved before going to the drawing board at all, and the

Front View of Four-Spindle Inverted Drillers with Celfor Drills

In this job of drilling ⅝-in. holes in T-203 and T-204 the work is above the drills. The cutting edges cannot be lubricated, but must work dry in heat-treated steel, which is externally cooled by soap and water flooding

Drilling the Fork-Ends and Spring-Perch Hole in the Front-Axle Body T-202
The fork-ends are drilled with ordinary twist drills and the spring-perch holes with Celfor drills, soap and water lubrication

designer who follows this practice will very seldom find that he has wasted any time by delay in using the T-square and scale.

The "inverted drillers" used for drilling the stub-axle hub-holes (time $3\frac{1}{2}$ minutes, drill lubrication, drill spindle and drill feed underneath, with work-cooling overhead and drilling from one way only) might have been amplified and changed as follows, and probably would have been so changed had the conception occurred to the designer:

The $3\frac{1}{2}$-minutes drilling time is more than twice the time of any other machining operation on the "steering spindle," or stub-axle. The stub-axle hub is strong and gives plenty of hold for chucking; hub axis and spindle axis might both be horizontal, the stub-axle to stand still and be completely finished, except the split-pin hole, at one chucking only, the hub to be drilled from both ways at once, reducing drilling time to, say, 100 seconds, the axle being finished while the axle hub is being drilled and reamed, and all cuts made submerged in lubricant.

This method of chucking and finishing avoids placing the stub-axles

Finishing Components T-270 and T-282 on Reed-Prentice Special Integral Lathe Head-Stock Spindle and Two-Jawed Clutch Disk

A self-opening threading die is fixed to the free end of an arm jointed to the tail spindle, to swing in an approximately horizontal plane through the live-spindle and tail-spindle axis. The tail-spindle is moved by a hand lever. When T-270 or T-282 is turned ready to thread, the workman moves the threading die to concentricity with the blank to be threaded and then starts the die on the work by pulling the tail-spindle hand lever. When the tail-spindle reaches its stop, the dies open, permitting the tail-spindle to be drawn back and the die is then pushed out of the way. This rig threads T-270, T-282 without reversing the lathe spindle

on lathe centers, hence avoids centering, and could be made to finish the stub-axle with a considerable saving of time, all cuts submerged in lubricant.

The "inverted drillers," shown in the illustrations, direct an upward jet of lubricant to the bottom end of the hub, but cannot possibly give effective drilling lubrication through the entire length of the stub-axle hub-hole. Where a piece is submerged in lubricant atmospheric pressure ensures the presence of lubricant at the tool cutting edge, constantly, all as is well known and commonly practiced.

In these "inverted drillers" all the lubricant jet from below can do is to lubricate the drill jig-brushing and the point of the drill when starting.

Drilling ⅝-Inch Holes in Hubs and Stub Axles T-203 and T-204

Foote-Burt special four-spindle driller with Celfor drills, soap-and-water lubricated and placed above work

Drilling ⅝-Inch Diameter Holes in Components T-203 and T-204

The work is done on a four-spindle inverted drill with Celfor drills. Note the work slides conveying the drilled parts by gravity to the anvil. Here a workman straightens such as need straightening to enable the stub-axle to be turned at the proper angle to the stub-axle hub holes.

171

Finishing the Rear-Axle Spring Perch

This component is not shown among the components illustrated on page 163. The illustration is introduced to show the inexpensive work slides. Before these were placed six Reed-Prentice lathes and two helpers were needed to produce the 6,400 spring perches in eight hours. With the work-slides four lathes do the same work in the same time, requiring no helpers to move the stock, and saving two lathes, two lathe-hands, and two helpers

Reaming Stub-Axle Hubs for Bushing on a Special Three-Deck Six-Spindle Machine

The work is held stationary in a fixture and reamed from both ends at once, with soap and water lubrication. The operator is constantly employed putting in and taking out work

To keep the hub cool as may be while being drilled, a large jet of soap and water lubricant is directed on the exterior of the hub from above.

This exterior cooling of the stub-axle hub while drilling the ⅝-inch diameter pin hole makes it barely possible to drill this ⅝-inch hole through 4½ inches of heat-treated steel with ordinary twist drills, and to drill these same ⅝-inch holes with "Celfor" twist drills with some degree of comfort, though Celfor drills work much better on this job with drillers of the ordinary form, spindle and lubrication both above the work, than with the "inverted" drillers.

This comment and suggestion is an unavoidable result of inspection of the unique and most surprising "inverted" drillers used for the larger part of the stub-axle pin-hole drilling. It is not uncommon to place drill spindles underneath the pieces to be drilled, for convenience in submerging the work in lubricant and so forcing the lubricant by atmospheric pressure to fill the hole and follow the drill cutting edges as they enter the metal; but in these "in-

Ford Special Centering Machines with Two Live Spindles

The work is held stationary; each spindle carries a centering drill and reamer combined, to center both ends of components T-203 and T-204, which are spotted in the fixture by the hub holes. Two machines with two men center 1,800 stub-axles per eight-hour day. The axles are inclined 3 degrees to the hub holes, right and left

Rough- and Finish-Turn T-203 and T-204 on Reed-Prentice Lathes

The axle is three degrees out of square with the hub-pin holes. Note again the work-slides save two lathes, two lathe-men and one helper on this job

verted drillers" the work is not submerged, and the drills are not lubricated, but are forced to drill $4\frac{1}{2}$ inches through the heat-treated steel absolutely dry, with no lubrication whatever, and depend upon exterior cooling of the work to make the drilling possible. Such a job could not be passed without special mention, because it shows drilling practice not to be seen, probably, anywhere else in the world.

FORD FRONT-AXLE COMPONENT FINISHING

Neither brass bushes, connecting-rod bodies, nuts, nor stub-axle pins are shown in the plate of components on page 163, and all stock has the following list of operations, as may be needed, performed upon it before being brought by monorail to the front-axle components finishing job, viz.: heat-treat, anneal, rough-straighten, finish-straighten, snag and tumble.

The front-axle body is first of all inspected for straightness, and such bodies as are not satisfactory in this particular are returned to the heat-treating department for correction before beginning machine work on this component.

Here follows the long list of finishing operations on components shown on the components and symbols sheet, page 163. The name of each operation is followed by the name of the machine used for performing that operation, the number of working spindles of the machine, the number of men employed upon the operation, and the operation time. This list is given in full on the following pages.

STUB-AXLE ARM, RIGHT—T-282

Op. No. Name of Operation	Name of Machine	No. of Spindles	No. of Men	Time of Operation
1. Turn and thread.....	Seven Reed-Prentice lathes..	$3\frac{1}{2}$	$3\frac{1}{2}$	1 min. 9 sec.
2. Drill one 43/64-in.....	Two 4-spindle Foote - Burt drill presses............	8	2	850 in 8 hr.
3. Burr...............	Barnes drill press..........	1	$\frac{1}{3}$	850 in 8 hr.
4. Press in bushing T-225	Ferracute press............		$\frac{1}{2}$	850 in 8 hr.
5. Ream bushing T-225 to 9/16-in.............	Barnes drill press..........	1	$\frac{1}{2}$	850 in 8 hr.
6. Face bushing to 1-in...	Cincinnati drill press........	1	$\frac{1}{2}$	850 in 8 hr.
7. Drill 5/32-in. cotter-pin hole............	Allen 2-spindle drill press....	1	1	850 in 8 hr.
8. Drill 25/64-in. hole...	Cincinnati drill press........	1	1	850 in 8 hr.
9. Bore 1/2-in. by 3/8-in. deep and ream taper hole 4-in. per foot....	Cincinnati drill press........	1	$\frac{2}{3}$	850 in 8 hr.
10. Spot face...........	Cincinnati drill press........	1	$\frac{1}{3}$	850 in 8 hr.
11. Burr 5/32-in. cotter-hole................	Barnes drill press..........	1	$\frac{1}{2}$	850 in 8 hr.

STUB-AXLE ARM, LEFT—T-270

Op. No. Name of Operation	Name of Machine	No. of Spindles	No. of Men	Time of Operation
1. Turn and thread......	Seven Reed-Prentice lathes..	3½	3½	1 min. 9 sec.
2. Drill 43/64-in. hole...	Two Foote - Burte 4 - spindle drill presses............	8	2	850 in 8 hr.
3. Burr................				
4. Press in bushing T-225	Ferracute press............		1½	850 in 8 hr.
5. Ream bushing T-225 to 9/16-in.............	Barnes drill press..........	1	1½	850 in 8 hr.
6. Face to 1-in.........	Cincinnati drill press........	1	1½	850 in 8 hr.
7. Drill 5/32-in. cotter-pin hole............	Allen drill press............	1	1	850 in 8 hr.
8. Burr...............	Barnes drill press..........	1	½	850 in 8 hr.

STUB-AXLES, R AND L—T-203-204

Op. No. Name of Operation	Name of Machine	No. of Spindles	No. of Men	Time of Operation
1. Chamfer............	Barnes drill press..........	1	1	6 sec.
2. Drill one 5/8-in. hole..	Inverted driller (4).........	16	4	3 min. 25 sec
3. Line ream 11/16-in....	Foote-Burt special (2).......	12	2	58½ sec.
4. Center.............	Ford—Two machines.......	4	2	16 sec.
5. Rough-turn spindle...	Reed-Prentice lathes (5).....	5	5	58 sec.
6. Finish-turn spindle....	Reed-Prentice lathes (3).....	3	3	30 sec.
7. Face to length.......	Cincinnati drill press (2)....	2	2	14 sec.
8. Drill one 5/32-in. cotter-pin hole..........	Allen drill press (3).........	3	3	20 sec.
9. Drill one 47/64-in. hole	Foote-Burt (1).............	4	2	54 sec.
10. Face both sides 47/64-in. hole.............	Barnes drill press (1)........	1	1	12 sec.
11. Ream 3/4-in.........	Barnes drill press (1)...	1	1	9 sec.
12. Counterbore 45 degrees	Barnes drill press (1)........	1	1	9½ sec.
13. Thread 3/4 by 16-in..	Ford special (3)............	3	2	33 sec.
14. Mill washer slot......	No. 2 Pratt & Whitney milling machine (two machines)................	2	2	10 sec.
15. Fillet hole for body bushing.............	Ford special...............	1	½	5 sec.
16. Press in bushing T-223	Ferracute press............		1	6½ sec.
17. Line ream..........	Cincinnati drill press........	1	1	11 sec.
18. Face bushing to length	Barnes drill press..........	1	1	13 sec.

Two forms of drillers are used for drilling ⅝-inch holes with Celfor drills in the stub-axle hubs, one form having the drills below the work, while the other form, not shown in the illustrations, has the drillers above the work, both forms being used with flooded soap-and-water lubrication, which is more effective for the slightly greater depth with the drill above the work than with the drill below the work.

In point of fact, however, these Celfor drills work dry in steel drop-forgings, heat-treated for maximum strength and toughness, which means also maximum resistance to drilling.

The Celfor drills, ⅝-inch diameter, are driven at 430 revolutions per minute.   The length of hub is 4½ inches, and from 30 to 70 hubs (from 135 inches to 315 inches length of hole) are drilled dry for once grinding. The drills hold their cutting edges to the last instant of work; then the edge goes, the drill clearance is instantly snubbed off, the drill point is blued, and in some instances the outer drill-edge corners are rubbed off for as much as ¼ inch; generally the corners are gone for about ¹/₁₆ inch. The drills are not re-ground past the bluing, but only far enough to bring the corner into good form.   Ordinary twist drills give so much trouble in this job that were it not for the Celfor drill the forms of drilling machine used would not serve.

STEERING CONNECTING-ROD BALL—T-226

Op. No. Name of Operation	Name of Machine	No. of Spindles	No. of Men	Time of Operation
1. Center ball..........	Ford special..............	1	1	4 sec.
2. Turn ball	Reed-Prentice lathe.........	3	3	58 sec.
3. Drill 43/64-in. and ream .1116...........	Foote-Burt................	4	1	900 in 8 hr.
4. Burr................	Barnes drill press...........	1	1	4,000 in 8 hr.

Spring Hangers—T-246, T-91½

The front- and rear-axle spring hangers are nearly alike, the rear-axle hangers being longer to take the wider spring. For good reasons the rear-spring hanger, T-91½, and front-spring hanger, T-246, operations are here listed together, total production 6,400 per eight-hour day.

SPRING HANGERS—T-246, T-91½

Op. No. Name of Operation	Name of Machine	No. of Spindles	No. of Men	Time of Operation
1. Drill one 23/64-in. hole	3-spindle Allen drill press....	3	3	5 sec.
2. Countersink.........	1-spindle drill press.........	1	1	1⅛ sec.
3. Center.............	Ford special..............	4	4	6 sec.
4. Rough turn.........	Five Reed-Prentice lathes...	5	5	9 sec.
5. Finish grind........	Four Landis grinders........		4	12 sec.
6. Punch..............	Ferracute press............			9,000 per day—8 hr.
7. Face to length.......	Two Cincinnati drill presses..	1	2	5 sec.
8. Drill one hole 5/32-in..	Allen drill press...........	1–2 sp. 3–1 sp.5		11 sec.
9. Drill one oil hole and one pin hole..........	Three Allen drill presses..... Three Leland drill presses...	6	6	9 sec.
10. Burr...............	Barnes drill press...........		1	6,400 in 8 hr.
11. Thread end.........	4-spindle Geometric machine.		2	10 sec.
12. Tap...............	Garvin Machine Tool Co....	2	2	
13. Spot face...........	Barnes drill press...........		1	5 sec.
14. Case harden........				

One floor inspector, half time—one final inspector, full time.

STUB-AXLE CONNECTING ROD—T-213

Op. No. Name of Operation	Name of Machine	No. of Spindles	No. of Men	Time of Operation
1. Drill, ream and bore..	Warner & Swasey turret machine.................	1	1	2,400 in 8 hr.

FRONT RADIUS-ROD ASSEMBLY—T-263

1. Assemble T-228 to T-224.................	Hand.....................		1	3,000 in 8 hr.
2. Punch..............	Ferracute press.............		1	3,000 in 8 hr.
3. Drill 1/8-in. air hole..	Barnes drill press...........	1	1	3,000 in 8 hr.
4. Braze studs.........	Brazing fire (four).........		8	2,500 in 8 hr.
5. Assemble T-214 to T-244.................	Hand..................		2	1,400 in 8 hr.
6. Drill and drive brazing pin.................	Barnes drill press (two).....	2	2	1,350 in 8 hr.
7. Braze..............	Three brazing fires.........		5	1,500 in 8 hr.
8. Grind	Grinding machine..........	1	½	1,500 in 8 hr.

FRONT RADIUS ROD STUD—T-228

1. Center tube end......	Ford Special...............	1	1	2,000 in 8 hr.
2. Turn tube end.......	Le Blond lathe..............	2	2	1,700 in 8 hr.
3. Center hanger end....	Ford Special...............	1	1	2,000 in 8 hr.
4. Turn hanger end......	Le Blond lathe	4	4	1,800 in 8 hr.
5. Drill one hole 5/32-in.	Allen 2-spindle drill press...	2	2	1,800 in 8 hr.
6. Chamfer	Geometric threading machine	1	½	1,800 in 8 hr.
7. Threading	Geometric threading machine	1	½	1,800 in 8 hr.

STUB CONNECTING-ROD TUBE ASSEMBLY—T-268

1. Assemble T-213-226-227-260.............	Rack and pinion press — Greenerd.............		1	850 in 8 hr.
2. Drill 1/8-in. hole.....	Two Barnes drill presses.....		1½	1,200 in 8 hr.
3. Brace..............	1½ fires.................		4	1,400 in 8 hr.
4. Thread..............	Landis bolt cutter, two machines.................	4	2	1,200 in 8 hr.
5. Hand ream.........	Hand.....................		⅔	1,500 in 8 hr.
6. Tap 7/16 by 20 in.....	Garvin tap machine.........	1	1	1,000 in 8 hr.
	Inspect 1269			

FRONT-SPRING PERCH, LEFT—T-222½

1. Drill one 39/64-in. hole	Two Foote-Burt, 4-spindle...	8	2	1,200 in 8 hr.
2. Ream one 5/8-in. hole.	Cincinnati drill press........	1	½	1,200 in 8 hr.
3. Drill 43/64-in. hole...	Two Foote-Burt, 4-spindle...	8	2	1,200 in 8 hr.
4. Ream 11/16-in. hole..	Foote-Burt, 4-spindle.......	1	1	2,000 in 8 hr.
5. Face and burr........	Foote-Burt, 4-spindle.......	1	1	1,200 in 8 hr.
6. Center.............	Two Ford special machines..	2	2	2,600 in 8 hr.
7. Finish turn..........	Five Le Blond lathes........	5	5	2,000 in 8 hr.
8. Drill 5/32-in. hole....	Allen drill press............	3	3	2,400 in 8 hr.
9. Thread.............	Two Ford special machines..	2	1	2,000 in 8 hr.
10. Press in bushing T-230	Ferracute press.............		½	4,000 in 8 hr.
11. Chamfer bushing.....	Barnes drill press...........	1	⅔	4,000 in 8 hr.
12. Ream bushing to .5635.	Cincinnati drill press........	1	1	4,000 in 8 hr.

FRONT-SPRING PERCH, RIGHT—222

Op. No. Name of Operation	Name of Machine	No. of Spindles	No. of Men	Time of Operation
1. Drill one 39/64-in. hole	Two Foote-Burt, 4-spindle...	8	2	1,200 in 8 hr.
2. Ream one 5/8-in. hole.	Cincinnati drill press........	1	½	1,200 in 8 hr.
3. Drill 43/64-in. hole...	Two Foote-Burt, 4-spindle...	8	2	1,200 in 8 hr.
4. Ream 11/16-in. hole..	Foote-Burt, 4-spindle.......	1	1	2,000 in 8 hr.
5. Face and burr.......	Foote-Burt, 4-spindle.......	1	1	2,000 in 8 hr.
6. Center.............	Two Ford special machines..	2	2	2,600 in 8 hr.
7. Finish turn.........	Five Le Blond lathes........	5	5	2,000 in 8 hr.
8. Drill 5/32-in. hole....	Allen drill press............	3	3	2,400 in 8 hr.
9. Thread.............	Two Ford special machines..	2	1	2,000 in 8 hr.
10. Press in bushing T-230.	Ferracute press.............		½	4,000 in 8 hr.
11. Chamfer bushing.....	Barnes drill press..........	1	⅔	4,000 in 8 hr.
12. Ream bushing to .5635	Cincinnati drill press........	1	1	4,000 in 8 hr.

Final inspection—1267

FRONT AXLE BODY 56-IN. T-202

Inspect for straightness—1268

		No. of Spindles	No. of Men	Time of Operation
1. Mill spring perches...	Ingersoll turret milling machine (Ford design).....	4	2	1,450 in 8 hr.
2. Mill fork bosses......	Various machines to make up production............			2,450 in 8 hr.
3. Drill and ream, counterbore spring perch and fork bosses.......	Six Foote-Burt, 4-spindle....	24	6	135 axle bodies to 1 machine in 8 hr.
4. Burr...............	Hand operation............		1	800 in 8 hr.
5. Countersink .505 hole 3/8-in. deep..........	Cincinnati drill press........	1	1	800 in 8 hr.
6. Tap...............	Cincinnati drill press........	1	1	800 in 8 hr.
7. Hand line ream......	Hand....................		1	800 in 8 hr.

Ops. 1 and 2 change cutters once in 4 hours.
Operations in natural sequence.

Final inspection—1257 Fig. 10

Preliminary inspection of form.
Operations 1 and 2 are performed on same Ingersoll milling machine.

FRONT RADIUS-ROD BALL—T-214

		No. of Spindles	No. of Men	Time of Operation
1. Center ball.........	Ford special..............	1	1	4 sec.
2. Turn ball...........	Reed-Prentice, three lathes..	3	3	8 sec.
3. Center two arms.....	Special Ford machine.......	1	1	12 sec.
4. Turn two arms......	Two Reed-Prentice lathes...	2	2	36 sec.

STEERING-BALL-SOCKET CAP—T-254

		No. of Spindles	No. of Men	Time of Operation
1. Punch two holes......	Toledo press..............		½	2,000 in 8 hr.
2. Disk grind...........	Gardiner disk grinder.......	1	1	2,400 in 8 hr.
3. Spot...............	Barnes drill press..........	1	1	2,400 in 8 hr.
4. Ream for T-226......	Barnes drill press..........	1	1	4,000 in 8 hr.
5. Cherry ream........	Cincinnati drill press (Two)..	2	2	1,600 in 8 hr.

STEERING-BALL CONNECTING-ROD ASSEMBLY—T-289

Op. No. Name of Operation	Name of Machine	No. of Spindles	No. of Men	Time of Operation
1. Assemble T-253-258...	Hand......................		2	1,600 in 8 hr.
2. Drill two 1/8-in. brazing pin holes.........	Two Allen 2-spindle drill presses...............	4	2	1,000 in 8 hr.
3. Rivet both ends......	....		1	1,000 in 8 hr.
4. Braze..............	Special rotary brazing machine................		3	1,400 in 8 hr.
5. Cherry ream........	Two Cincinnati drill presses..	2	2	1,000 in 8 hr.
6. Tap two holes 3/8-in. by 24-in.............	Cincinnati drill press, special attachment Garvin tapping machine..........	3	2	1,000 in 8 hr.

STEERING-BALL SOCKET—T-253

1. Drill two letter "Q" holes...............	Special Cincinnati drill presses, 2 working spindles...	4	2	2,000 in 8 hr.

STUB-AXLE CONNECTING-ROD YOKE—LEFT T-248

1. Straddle mill........	Kempsmith milling machine —180 deg. fixture......	1	1	950 in 8 hr.
2. Drill 13/32-in. hole...	Allen drill press............	1	1	1,200 in 8 hr.
3. Drill 41/64-in. hole...	Foote-Burt special..........	4	1	900 in 8 hr.
4. Countersink 13/32 in. hole................	Barnes drill press...........	1	1	900 in 8 hr.
5. Spot face...........	Barnes drill press...........	1	1	900 in 8 hr.
6. Drill 35/64-in. hole and ream 9/16-in.........	Cincinnati drill press........	3	3	1,050 in 8 hr.
7. File................	Hand......................		1/2	900 in 8 hr.
8. Countersink........	Cincinnati drill press........	1	1	900 in 8 hr.
9. Mill 3/32-in. slot.....	Pratt & Whitney No. 2—hand milling machine........	1	1	900 in 8 hr.
10. Tap 7/16 by 20-in. hole	Garvin tap machine........	1 half time		900 in 8 hr.
11. Tap 11/16 by 20-in. hole................	Foote-Burt, 4-spindle taps drop through............	4	1	900 in 8 hr.

STUB-AXLE CONNECTING-ROD YOKE—B-227-T

1. Mill...............	Kempsmith milling machine.	1	1	950 in 8 hr.
2. Center...........	Ford special machine.......	1	1/3	1,200 in 8 hr.
3. Turn...............	Reed-Prentice lathe........	1	1	800 in 8 hr.
4. Drill two holes and ream..............	Foote-Burt special drill press	4	2	800 in 8 hr.
5. File................	Hand......................		1/2	800 in 8 hr.
6. Counterbore........	Cincinnati drill press........	1	1/2	800 in 8 hr.

FRONT RADIUS-ROD TUBE—T-244

1. Ream and countersink	Cincinnati drill press........	1	1	1,200 in 8 hr.
2. Disk grind..........	Gardiner disk—2 disks......	1	2	4,800 in 8 hr.
3. Drill 31/64-in. hole...	Foote-Burt 4-spindle drill press	4	2	1,800 in 8 hr.
4. Ream 1/2-in. hole....	Foote-Burt 4-spindle drill press	4	1/3	1,800 in 8 hr.
5. Spot face...........	Barnes drill press...........	1	1/2	2,400 in 8 hr.
6. Drill 1/4-in. hole.....	Barnes drill press...........	1	1/2	2,400 in 8 hr.

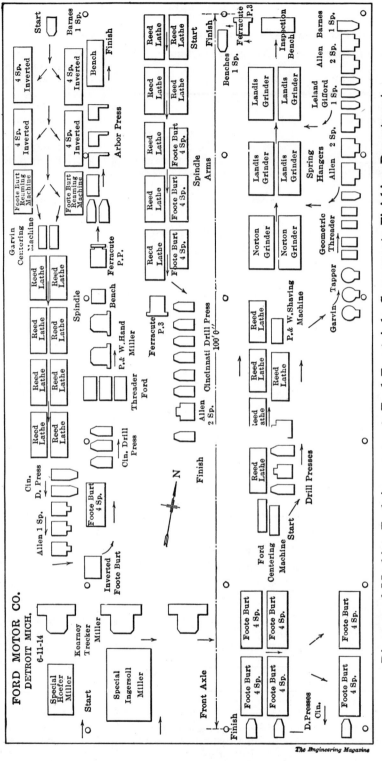

Diagram of Machine Tool Arrangement, Ford Front-Axle Components Finishing Department

Completed on the opposite page. The two parts of the floor stand to one another in the exact rotation and relative position here shown

FRONT-AXLE COMPONENTS FINISHING DEPARTMENT

July 9, 1914, this department was working about 375 men, graded according to efficiency in four grades, numbered 1, 2, 3 and 4, grade No. 1 being of lowest efficiency and No. 4 of highest efficiency. The grade number of a man does not determine his hour wage. A No. 1 man, lowest-efficiency grade, may be paid $5.00 for 8-hours work, and a

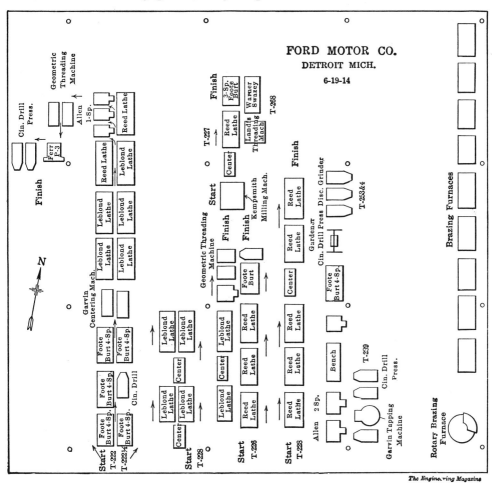

Continuation of Front-Axle Components Finishing Department

No. 4 man, highest-efficiency grade, may be paid $2.80 for 8-hours work. Again, in reducing department force of workmen, the ordinary management would, of course, prefer to keep No. 4 men and let No. 1 men go. Under the present arrangement of affairs those men having most individuals dependent on their wages for a living are given most pay, regardless of efficiency rating, and in letting men go those having the

FORM 915

PRODUCTIVE TIME TICKET
K-17 FRONT AXLE PARTS   Dept. C

Empl. Name_____

D JUL 9 - 1912 91-   Empl. No._____

Prod. Order Number	Part No.	Operation Number	Number of Pieces	Hours

O. K.

_____   Total_____
Foreman

Form 915.   Production Time Ticket

more individuals to support are likely to be retained, regardless of efficiency standing.

The front-axle components finishing department is in charge of one foreman, who has two assistant foremen, three clerks, and one "straw boss" for about every 20 workmen, besides tool-setters who are machinists of intelligence, experience, and all-round reliability. The foreman is, of necessity, a competent mechanic and a competent administrator.

The department records are kept on three form blanks; Form 915, Production Time Ticket, Form 552, Report of Stock Machined, and Form 858, Individual Workman's Production Record, an index-card form.

PRODUCTIVE TIME-TICKET, FORM 915

Form blank 915 is a stiff manila card $3^{11}/_{16}$ inches wide by $6^7/_{16}$

REPORT OF STOCK MACHINED

Final   M. Banta   DATE 6-25-14 91-

REQ. NO.	SYM. NO	B-1-Shift	NAME	B-2-Shift	AMT
41		1400			
91½		3725		3720	
152		685		820	
153		663			
191		720			
193		760			
202		504			
203		750			
204		1260			
213		1200			
214		2075			
217		2635			
222		548			
222½		253			
226		757			
227		653			
228		1582		1367	
246		2700		1602	
248		410			
253		1325			
254		782			
263		736		930	
268		204			
270		889			
282		440			
289		188			
862		842			
867		818			
1557		903			
1736		58			
2739		268			

Form 552.   Departmental Report of Stock Machined

DATE	MAN. NO.	PROD.	TOTAL PROD.	HRS.	DATE	MAN NO.	PROD.	TOTAL PROD.	HRS.	DATE	MAN. NO.	PROD.	TOTAL PROD.	HRS.
6-1	194 6 59	246		1										
	272	630		2										
6-2	" 44	1587		8										
--3	" "	1450	3873	8										

(Part Name: *Front Radius Rod Assembly.* T. NO. 263; Operation: *Assem. T 228 to T 244*; OPER. NO. 1; Date: 6-1-'14)

Form 858. Individual Production Record

inches high, printed in black and red on one side only, "K-17, Front Axle Parts, C," the date being printed in red. Each workman keeps an individual record of his own day's performance, and these records are gathered by the straw bosses and transferred to Form 915, each man's work record on an individual card at the close of each day's work, and delivered by the straw boss to the two clerks who fill forms 552 and 858 from the forms 915.

WORKMAN'S INDIVIDUAL PRODUCTION RECORD, FORM 858

This is a stiff index card, yellow in color, printed in black, ruled in red and green with the 31 lines of the workman's record, in three principal divisions, giving space for 93-days record; size 8 inches wide by 5 inches high. It is filled by a department clerk from Forms 915 with the calendar month's record and sent by the department clerk to the cost department, where labor cost and time of production totals are taken from those forms 858, which are preserved for six months and then destroyed.

The capital letter "B" in the upper left corner of the form reproduction is the work-hours shift symbol. Working one 8-hour day only the shift symbol is "B-1," contracted to "B" on card. Workmen go on at 6:30 a. m., stop 10:30, take 30 minutes of their own time for lunch, go on again at 11:00 a. m. and off for the day at 3:00, making an 8-hour day.

Working two shifts, the shift symbol for the first shift is "B-1." On this basis the men go on at 6:30 a. m., stop 10:30 a. m. for lunch, 30 minutes of their own time; on again at 11:00 a. m., off at 3:00 p. m., an 8-hour day. The second shift, with the symbol "B-2," goes on at 3:00 p. m., off at 11:00 p. m., with gift of 15 minutes, 7:00 to 7:15 p. m., for eating.

Working three shifts, the shift symbols are "C-1,"—on at 8:00 a. m., off at 4:00 p. m., with gift of 10 minutes for eating from 12:00 noon to 12:10 p. m.; "C-2," on at 4:00 p. m., off at 12:00 midnight, with gift of 10 minutes from 8 to 8:10 p. m. for eating; "C-3," on at 12:00 midnight, off at 8:00 a. m., with gift of 10 minutes, 4:00 to 4:10 a. m., for eating.

These allotments of shift working hours are made to equalize demands on shop driving-power.

Ford Special Threading Machines Threading the Ends for Cone and Nut, Stub Axles T-203 and T-204

One man works two drills, the fixture slide running to a stop which opens the threading dies. The machine spindles run continuously when in work

DEPARTMENTAL REPORT OF STOCK MACHINED— FORM 552

Printed in black, on white, thin paper, size 5½ by 12 in.

Because the "Requisition" is for the whole year round, one year after another, the "Requisition No." column is not used, and because the entire Ford shops production is "Model T" cars, the "T" is not written, and because the symbol, as "T-202," carries the component name with it, the "name" space is not filled.

Forms 552 are filled, as shown on page 182, by a department "C" clerk, from the productive-time ticket Form 915, in pencil, one original and two carbon copies, one copy being sent to the "division foreman," next above the department foreman, one to the "machine-shop foreman," next above the division foreman, and one copy to the head of the "finished stock" (components) records department. Card-index records of individual-component production are made from these forms 552 by clerks in the machine-shop foreman's office and in the finished-stock department.

From the front-axle components finishing department, work goes to the front-axle assembling department, symbol letter "A," by monorail.

FRONT-AXLE ASSEMBLING DEPARTMENT

The officials are one assembling-department foreman, one assistant foreman, one straw boss, and one clerk. The form blanks, filled by the clerk, are as in Department C.

The assembling department assembles the front axles, paints them, bakes them, paints them a second time, and bakes them a second time, using doors on the west side of the ovens, and then, through doors on the east side, removes the finished axles ready for the assembling line.

The assembling department works 44 men in each shift to turn out 800 axles, double shift 1,600 axles, three shifts, 2,400 axles.

One man is a stock handler, one man is a floor sweeper, 30 men work as

Drilling Holes for Steering Arms T-270 and T-282 in the Stub Axles T-203 and T-204

The stub axles are spotted in fixtures by the hub holes and outside ends. Foote-Burt special four-spindle drill using ordinary twist drills with soap-and-water lubrication. One man tends two drill spindles; one machine with two men drills about 1,600 steering-arm holes per day

actual assemblers, and 10 of the assemblers work on the moving-assembly line. The list of operations necessary to the front-axle assembly is as follows:

FRONT-AXLE ASSEMBLY

1. Assemble minor No. 1 and No. 2 to T-202 axle with two T-211 spindle bolts.

2. Screw in T-211 bolts to minor No. 1 and No. 2.

3. Put on two T-60 nuts, and two T-763 cotter pins to T-211 spindle bolts.

Small Globe Finishing

Small globe finishing is by a grooved tool at the back, pulled forward to a stop by screw and hand-wheel, for the rough turning. The finish turning is by a shell tool with a notch for the globe-neck. The ground internal cylindrical bore of the finishing tool has its working annular face ground to a 7 degree angle, the bore being same diameter as the finished globe. About 150 globes are finished with one grinding of the finishing tool. This cylindrical finishing tool is carried on the free end of a rect-angular body, confined in a slot in a tool-holder fixed to a cross slide, the out-end of the rectangular body being pivoted to swing up and down in the holder slot, so that the cylindrical tool has an auto-matic vertical adjustment to suit the globe vertical position. The roughing tool leaves the globe about ten thousandths oversize, and the finished product is very close to a sphere

4. Assemble minor No. 3 to minor No. 2 with one T-216 bolt.

5. Adjust minor No. 3 and tighten T-216 bolt to minor No. 2, put in one T-216 bolt to minor No. 1.

6. Put on two T-220 nuts and tighten up with two T-753 cotter pins to T-216 bolts.

7. Assemble minor No. 4 to T-202 axle with two T-242 nuts.

8. Tighten up two T-242 nuts and put in two T-82 cotter pins.

9. Tighten up two T-77 radius-rod nuts and put in two T-82 cotter pins.

10. Tighten up four spring hanger nuts T-242 and put in four T-88 cotter-pins.

11. Tighten up connecting-rod yoke bolt-nut T-8 and put in one T-82 cotter pin.

12. Paint.
13. Bake.
14. Paint.
15. Bake.

Only two of the minor assembling operations are shown in the upper picture on page 192.

In this view, the middle workman is pressing the inside ball-bearing cone onto the stub axle, using for the purpose an ordinary hand-lever arbor press.

The man at the right does not come into this story. In the right middle of the picture is seen a small machine, belt-driven, with a chuck

Landis Grinder with Broad-Face Wheel for Grinding Full Length of Cylindrical Parts of Spring Hangers T-91 1/2 and T-246

The work is on one fixed and one spring center, and is so driven that work automatically drops down when tail center is drawn away, and thus clears the machine to take the next piece. Wheel slide is run to a stop, set by the tool-setter after truing the wheel. 225 to 250 pieces are ground at one slide-setting, 1,300 to 1,400 pieces for one man and one grinding machine in 8 hours

on the spindle nose, formerly used to run the nut on T-270, T-282, after being pressed into the stub-axle steering-arm hub. The assembling of the steering arms and stub axles was formerly as follows: First, with arbor press, force arm into hub eye; next, with small machine on bench, run the steering-arm holding nut on; and third, adjust this castellated nut by hand so that the split-pin could be placed.

These three operations are now performed at one single handling, on the machine shown at the left on page 162, which is curious, inasmuch as it combines two hand operations and one power-driven operation, with marked time sav-

Inspecting Rough Axle Bodies T-202, Coming from the Heat-Treating Department

They are supposed to be delivered to the front-axle job straightened and in correct form. The first operation in machining of component T-202 is to verify form and straightness. Unsatisfactory axle bodies are returned to the heat-treating department

Inspecting Finished Components T-222 and T-222½

The inspection bench is covered with sheet metal, and the inspector drops the passed components into heavy sheet-metal boxes or trays ready for transport to the assembling lines

ing. This unique machine is a rack-and-pinion arbor press, having a fixture to take T-270 or T-282 on the press vertical-spindle bottom-end, set on a base which contains an electric motor at the bottom from which a vertical spindle on the workman's side is friction-driven, this running vertical-spindle top-end, directly under the threaded end of T-270 or T-281 held in the press-slide fixture, being fitted to take the hex-nut which holds the steering arm home in the stub-axle hub boss, so that the nut is running friction-driven when the workman, having placed the steering arm in the press-slide fixture, next places the stub axle in a fixture under the press slide, ready to take the steering arm. Next, the workman forces the arm home to the shoulder in its stub-axle hub seat, the power-driven nut being simultaneously run home on the steering-arm thread by the friction-driven vertical spindle.

The lower power-and-friction-driven nut-spindle has fixed to its top end a double-acting ratchet with a horizontal lever; the workman holds the press lever down

Testing the Brazing of Fork and Globe Wrist

Three components, the rod, the ball-wrist T-226 and the fork, T-227 are united by pinning and brazing. The globe-wrist stands at 90 degrees to rod axis, and prevents the assembly from turning when dropped into the testing-block slot. Then a heavy handled wrench is applied to the fork and moved rapidly so as to give strong torsion blows in both directions with sufficient force to rupture the brazing if imperfect

Driven End of the Front-Axle Assembling Line

All the Ford chain-driven lines use the chain and sprockets of the Link Belt Engineering Company, Chicago. The speed of each assembling line must be brought to suit exactly the work performed on it. This chain moves at a speed of 14 feet per minute. The drive is from an electric motor on the ceiling, belted to a first counter-shaft, thence to a second overhead counter-shaft, thence by a cased-in vertical belt to a pinion-shaft on floor hangers, from which the sprocket-shaft is driven by enclosed pinion and spur-gear. The floor hangers stand on sections of I-beams to bring them to height

with his right hand, the nut screwed home to the boss-end holds the friction-driven vertical spindle still, and the workman then grasps the double-acting ratchet lever with his left hand and, as shown in the picture, bends his head down and with the ratchet adjusts the castellated-nut notches to the split-pin hole in the end of the steering-arm screw thread, all in about five seconds time.

It should be here noted that in hand-work time is saved by dividing operations, while exactly the reverse is true in automatic-machine work, where time is saved by combining operations performed at one setting or chucking of the work.

The steering-arm and stub-axle assembling machine is the first to come under my observation in which power-driven and hand-made adjusting operations are combined.

West of the assembly line are two drill presses, spindle friction-driven, by which the stub-axle pins are driven into the threaded lower fork-bosses, making the axle ready for the chain-driven assembly line.

The lower picture on page 191 shows the middle part of the chain line, with a bridge over it. This bridge carries on top a full-length fixture which takes both stub axles

Milling the Fork-Lugs of Component T-248

The work is done on the Kempsmith milling machine. The turn-around fixture latches in two positions, 180 degrees apart. The workman takes out the finished piece and puts in a rough piece, while the cut is being made on the piece previously placed

and holds them in line while the steering-arms parallel-connecting-rod is placed and adjusted to length, so that both the front wheels will stand in straight-ahead running position at the same time. This bridge is elevated and its supports clear the full length of the assembled front axle.

Those axles which are to be sent to the Ford "branches," do not have the steering-arm parallel-rods fitted, as the length-adjustment of this rod would be lost in "knocking-down."

Idler End (West End) of Front-Axle Assembling Line

This picture, taken before encasement, shows the construction of gray-iron uprights or cross-frames, and horizontal channel-section and angle bars supporting the chain. This is the latest moving-assembly line installed in the Ford shops and shows a good form of construction

Axles to be placed in chassis assembly at the Highland Park shops are lifted up off the chain-line, placed on the bridge, and have the parallel rod placed as described, and are then lifted off the bridge and placed on the chain-line slides again, all as seen in this illustration.

The upper photograph on page 191 is a view of the south side of assembling line, looking west-north-

Upper View is Along the South Side and Lower View Shows the Middle of the Chain-Driven Front-Axle Assembly Line

Everything is encased with sheet metal so as to prevent a smooth surface, where the workmen's bodies or clothing touch it, and so as to form a continuous trough for small components on top between chains.

191

Assembling the Steering Arm and Front Axle

In assembling the steering arm and stub-axle there are two operations to be performed: (1), to press the arm into its seat in the stub-axle hub boss; (2), to screw the nut on the threaded end of the steering arm. The castellated nut must be turned so the split pin can be seated

Rotary Brazing Machine, Brazing T-253 to Its Rod

The work turret is revolved by hand by the workman at the left, who takes the work from the turret support as soon as the joint is brazed. The man at the right applies borax paste and places short piece of brass wire about $\frac{1}{8}$-in. diameter in drilled hole against the rod end, and then places the job on the turret supports. As the turret is revolved the braze joint passes through a gas-flame-heated arc-shaped top chamber

west. The foreman of assemblers stands at the left, attentively watching work in progress.

Page 194 shows the painters at work; 800 axles are handled off the line, painted, placed in the ovens seen at the rear, baked, taken out, painted again, baked again, ready to be removed from the far side of the ovens, all at the rate of 100 axles completed per hour.

Duplicate of Machine Shown at the Left of the Upper Picture, Page 192

A new machine; front view from workman's side with vertical spindle cover removed. The vertical spindle is driven by a bevel gear and pinion (not visible in the picture) from a motor in the machine base. The photograph shows the friction spring and friction disk above the bottom journal of the spindle and the nut-positioning ratchet lever above the top bearing of the spindle

FORMER FRONT-AXLE ASSEMBLING PRACTICE

January 1, 1913, the final assembling of the front axles, after sundry minor assemblies had been made up, was carried on by providing each assembler with a vise of his own, all final assemblers being placed at one long, sheet-metal-covered bench. The assemblers were competent mechanics and the front-axle assembling job was regarded as being in pretty good form. With 125 men, all told, 450 front axles were assembled in one 9-hour day, not painted nor baked. This was at the rate of 1,125 hours for 450 axles, or 2 hours 30 minutes of one man's time for assembling each axle.

January 1, 1914, things were better; 90 men in an 8-hour day, assembled 650 axles. The rate was 720 hours for 650 axles, or 1 hour 6½ minutes of one man's time for assembling one axle—less than one-half the January 1, 1913, time.

The moving-assembly line began working June 1, 1914, and this day, July 13, 1914, 44 men, all told, are assembling, painting, and baking 800 axles in one 8-hour day, giving a rate of 352 hours for 800 axles, or 21.120 minutes—say 26½ minutes—for one front axle. To recapitulate:

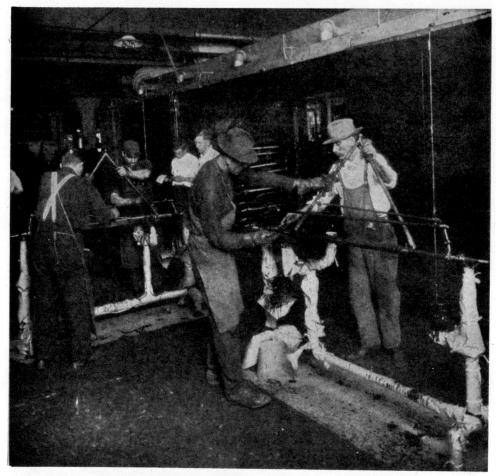

Painting the Front Axles: Baking Ovens in the Rear

The painting stands are placed close to the eastern (delivery) end of the assembling line. The axles are painted as soon as they come off the assembling line, are lifted from the painting stands and piled in the baking ovens, baked for 30 minutes, taken out, painted a second coat, and baked again for 30 minutes, and are then taken from oven doors on the other side of the ovens, directly to the chassis-assembling line

January 1, 1913, axle assembling, 150 minutes.

January 1, 1914, axle assembling, 66½ minutes.

July 13, 1914, axle assembling, 26½ minutes.

All of which shows, beyond question, that by use of a few new ideas and some hard work, machine-shop labor costs, in some instances, may be very materially decreased. While the Ford engineers cannot justly be said to be puffed up with the successes of their efforts, they are really disposed to claim having produced at least one single example of that extremely rare exhibit, a 100 per cent efficiency installation which produces the Ford Model T commutator.

This small construction does not involve the use of the moving-assembly line, but it does involve one initial feature of absolutely novel machine-shop practice, so far as my personal observation in work of this or similar character goes.

The Ford commutator construction, prefaced by one or two of the more striking 1914 work-slide installations of the Ford shops, will be described in the next chapters—certainly the most surprising labor-cost reduction data ever printed, considering the simplicity of the original conceptions which are shown to have paved the way to the incredible savings gained.

CHAPTER VII

THE CRANK-SHAFT, PISTON AND PISTON-RINGS

MANY attempts have been made to obtain a built-up crank-shaft for small multi-cylinder motors, which could be machined in separate components each having one axis only, these components being susceptible of assembling to form a crank-shaft having any number of crank-throws, set at any desired angle to each other; also many special forms of lathes have been devised for crank-shaft turning, some of which have had considerable employment.

The Ford Company, however, adheres to the simplest form of integral four-throw crank-shaft, and uses lathes of ordinary construction for finishing the crank-shaft bearings and flange, and ordinary forms of grinding machines for finishing the crank-wrists, or "pins," as they are sometimes named. The Ford crank-shaft is therefore an integral drop-forging, four throws, 2-inch crank radius, made of the highest grade of steel and heat-treated.

The Ford connecting rod is also a steel drop-forging, which has the piston pin fixed in the top eye, the crank-wrist eye being capped and babbitted, and the cap held on with two bolts. The babbitt bearing is broached, and thin brass liners, about 0.006-inch in thickness, are placed between the cap and the rod end, to permit wear take-up.

The piston pin is cut off from steel-tube stock, centered, finished, and hardened and ground, fixed in the top rod-eye and rocking in bronze bushes in the piston-pin hole. It is common practice to give the piston pin as much diameter as may be and have it bear directly on the wall of the piston-pin hole, thus avoiding the piston-pin-hole bushes altogether, but the Ford piston pin is of comparatively small diameter and works in brass bushes, as before said.

The Ford piston is a very light and accurately formed gray-iron casting, finished all over outside and having three grooves cut in it to take gray-iron, eccentric piston rings, one ring in each groove. The piston rings are of gray iron, eccentric, finished all over, outside and inside.

The gray-iron "pots," or flanged and cylindrical piston-ring blanks, weigh about 6½ pounds each as they come from the foundry and are expected to give 12 rings from each blank, or so-called "pot."

As is well known, three steel rings, cylindrical, not eccentric, can be placed in one single groove and make a perfectly tight packing having many advantages over the three eccentric rings in the way of lower cost, and giving more piston wearing surface; but the Ford engineers adhere to the usual eccentric gray-iron-ring practice, in spite of the cost and machining difficulties inseparable from that form of piston packing ring, which demands a great number of finishing operations.

Re-Striking a Crank-Shaft

THE CRANK SHAFT

All cranks of any description whatever are difficult constructions, if a close degree of accuracy is expected. When it comes to an automobile crank-shaft, where lightness, strength, elasticity and accuracy of form are highly desirable, the four or six-throw crank-shaft which fully meets the requirements of its employment becomes an extremely exacting production.

The Ford crank-shaft forms no exception to this rule. The steel stock must be the best known for the purpose. Then follows a host of problems in the way of heat-treating, straightening, centering and finishing, each one of these operations and their details demanding the very highest grade of metallurgical and mechanical skill, if the finished crank-shaft is to have the strength, elasticity, and close approximations to accuracy of form and dimensions at every point which are so highly desirable, so fundamentally indispensable, that every crank-shaft maker roundly asserts the perfection of his output, although it is well known to all competent experts that very many crank-shafts for small internal-combustion motors are constantly being made which can lay no valid claim to high-grade construction from any view-point whatever.

The Ford crank-shaft is most scientifically constructed so far as selection of material, heat-treating and quenching are concerned. This much is fully proven by the very great trouble experienced in even slightly changing the form of the rough drop forging, before the crank-shaft goes into the finishers' hands.

First there is the re-strike under a heavy steam hammer, in dies which are to crank-shaft form drawings; then, after snagging, comes the rough-straightening under a lighter steam hammer, then centering and finish-straightening with sledges and anvils, and many-times repeated gauging with the rough crank-shaft on centers, before the rough piece is in form for the first machine cut.

The many separate operations required to finish the Ford crank-shaft drop forging, as received from outside suppliers, in order of sequence, are as follows:

OPERATIONS ON CRANK-SHAFT

The operations in the Highland Park shops begin with four heat-treat operations,—A, air heat; B, heat and quench; C, anneal; D, re-strike. The heat-treating operations A, B and C are not here described. The story of the mechanical treatment of the Ford crank-shaft begins with operation D, re-strike.

In the Heat-Treat Shop.   Rough-Straightening Crank-Shafts

General View of Operation of Finish-Straightening the Shafts

As shown on page 198, the warm crank-shaft is laid in the lower half of a die of correct form and struck such blows as may be required with a 1,200-pound hammer having 36-inches fall. Three men are used in the re-strike gang, one hammer man and two tongs men, who lay the shaft in the lower half of the die. The production is about 200 re-strikes per hour, three men's time. Steam hammer by the Morgan Company.

Operation E. Tumble. Two men and two tumbling barrels tumble about 100 crank-shafts per hour.

Operation F. Snag. Five men, using five emery-wheel stands, snag about 150 shafts per hour.

The tumbling removes much of the scale produced by heating in presence of free oxygen, and the emery wheels leave the job in good shape for:

Operation G. Rough-straighten. The rough-straightener uses flat-slab stands, set with hardened-steel studs, which should touch the shafts at certain points.

In the picture shown on page 199 a rough-straightener has a crank-shaft laid on the elevated gauge slab, and is looking through under the shaft, to see where it is away from the gauge pins. The 1,000 pound steam-hammer, 21-inches lift, is seen in the rear, with the hammer man at the levers. One hammer man and three gauge men make up the rough-straightening gang, and the output is about 150 crank-shafts rough-straightened per hour. Steam hammer by the Buffalo Foundry Company.

From the rough-straighten job the crank-shafts go to the machine-shop finish-straighten gang, ten men all told—one centerer, seven finish-straighten gauge men, and three strikers, who use 18-pound sledges and strike the crank-shafts held on three anvils by the gauge men, as directed, often with a full-swing repeated in the same spot. The crank-throws often require opening, effected by standing the crank-throw on the anvil horn, and giving a full-swing 18-pound sledge blow on top of the crank-wrist. One would naturally expect to see one such blow open a throw of this slender crank-shaft half an inch or so; but no such result occurs, and often two or three full-swing blows of the sledge fall on the crank-wrist before the gauge man is suited. Indeed, it seems impossible that the Ford crank-shaft should show such indifference to heavy sledge blows as it certainly does show.

The illustration on page 200 shows a general view of finish-straightening, this page the crank-shaft centering, and page 202 a crank-shaft

Centering the Crank-Shaft on Ford Double-Ended Machine

Dead Centers and Gauges for Finish-Straightening of Crank-Shaft

dead-centers gauging stand, showing the gauges used in finish-straightening the crank-shafts.

After the hand-work operations described and illustrated, the crank-shaft finishing offers little of special interest, although every operation demands a well contrived fixture and accurate machine work. After centering, the first lathe cut is rough-turning the middle bearing. This is shown just below. Then follow in order the twenty-nine operations listed below:

Turn center bearing. Reed lathe. The crank-shaft is supported on the lathe centers, and by a long sleeve-rest is fixed to the live spindle, which supports the crank-arm next to the center bearing, and gives steadiness to carry a big chip in rough-turning the center bearing. Five Reed lathes, one man to each, 25 center bearings turned by one man and lathe in one hour.

Face the flange. Reed lathe and one man, 20 per hour. See page 203.

Turn flange circumference. One Reed lathe, one man, 65 per hour. See page 203.

Square down to center. One Reed lathe and one man, 65 per hour.

"Re-center." Should read "Deepen the center." The centers are not changed from first location. One Ford centering machine, one man, 125 per hour.

Straighten. One man and one hand-operated screw-press, 65 per hour.

Drill and ream two 0.441 spotting-pin holes. These holes are diametrically opposite each other in the flange, same radius to centers,

Rough-Turning the Middle Bearing

and serve to locate the crank-shaft for wrist-finishing by grinding. Only the crank-shaft bearings are turned with lathe tools. The wrists are finished wholly by rough-grinding and finish-grinding. One man with one two-spindle Cincinnati drill press drills and reams these two spot-holes in 40 crank flanges per hour.

Drill four fly-wheel bolt holes in flange; Cincinnati drill-press and one man, 100 per hour.

Turn two end bearings. Reed

Facing the Crank-Shaft Flange

lathe and one man, turn end bearings of 23 crank-shafts per hour.

Rough-grind middle bearing. Landis grinder and one man, 40 per hour.

Rough-grind flange bearing. Landis grinder and one man, 25 per hour.

Rough-grind front-end bearing. Landis grinder and one man, 35 per hour.

Rough-grind wrists. Landis grinder and one man, 15 shafts per hour.

Turning Circumference of Flange of Crank-Shaft

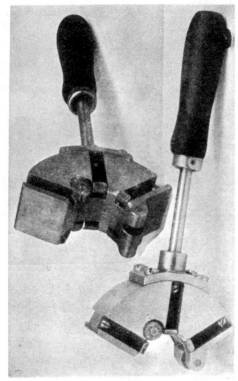

Crank-Shaft Burring Tool, Hand-Operated

Finish-turn flange. Reed lathe and one man, 25 per hour.

Face ends of crank-shaft to over-all length. Reed lathe and one man, 50 per hour.

Drill and ream one ⅝-inch starting pin hole, Cincinnati drilling machine and one man, 50 per hour.

Mill key-way. Pratt and Whitney milling machine and one man, 125 per hour.

Hand-ream starting-pin hole and burr key-way, hand operations on bench, one man, 125 per hour.

Balance; balance-disk stand and emery-wheel stand. One man, 40 per hour, close balancing.

Finish-grind end wrists. Landis grinder and one man, 12 per hour. Shown below on this page.

Finish-grind middle wrists. Landis grinder and one man, 12 per hour.

Finish-straighten. Man, dead centers, and hand screw-press, 60 per hour.

Finish-grind middle bearing. Landis grinder and one man, 35 per hour.

Finish-grind flange bearing. Landis grinder and one man, 15 per hour.

Finish-grind front-end bearing. Landis grinder and one man, 35 per hour.

Finish-grind gear fit. Landis grinder and one man, 35 per hour.

Finish-turn flange circumference. Reed lathe and one man, 100 per hour.

Finish-Grinding End Wrists of Crank-Shaft

Facing and Boring Piston, Warner & Swasey Turret Machine

Burr. Twenty-seven per hour, one man on bench. This is the old style. Now, with new hand burring tool, one man burrs over 100 crank-shafts per hour.

By the old method, with first-class vise hands using fine files of various shapes, one man could burr only a very few, not more than ten, crank-shafts per hour, and at that the job could not be any too well done, as some of the burrs were very difficult of access. The full capacity of this new burring tool, of which two views are shown opposite, is not yet certainly known. It was first placed in use about December 15, 1914, and effects a labor saving estimated at about $20.00 per day.

Two widths of this hand burring tool will be used, one for each length of crank-shaft bearing. The up-turned toothed ends of the springs scrape the burrs off at one passage over.

Final operation. Polish the crank wrists. The crank-shaft is belt-driven on its own centers. Each crank wrist takes a special connecting-rod end which closes a felt ring on the wrist, under light pressure. The free end of each rod is jointed to a vertical lever. The felt is not charged with any abrasive—simply rubs the wrist as the crank-shaft revolves. One of the wrist-polishing machines polishes the wrists of about 20 crank-shafts per hour.

The reader who follows this sketch of crank-shaft production atten-

Finishing Pin Holes in Pistons
New Britain machine

tively will fully understand that if the Ford crank-shafts are not well finished the faults cannot be charged to any lack of painstaking on the part of the machine-shop management.

THE FORD PISTONS

The Ford Model T piston is an extremely light gray-iron casting. The piston finishing is a simple job: the piston is first chucked, open and outward, in a turret machine of ordinary construction (Warner and Swasey, suppliers) and is then rough-bored and finish-bored with two tools in the turret and faced with cross-slide tools. This gives a substantial spotting surface for subsequent operations in piston-finishing.

Next the piston-pin hole, about $^{15}/_{16}$ diameter, is drilled, bored and reamed; then the piston is rough-turned and finally completed by finish-turning.

If desired, the piston-pin hole could be made as much as $1^{3}/_{8}$ inches diameter, could take a hollow piston pin $1^{3}/_{8}$ diameter, soft, which would give sufficient projected area to carry the piston pressure without displacing the film of lubricating oil lying between the pin and the walls of the piston-pin hole, and the entire piston and pin assembly weight could be brought below that of the present construction, which includes a hollow pin, hardened, and two bronze bushes forced into the pin holes in the pistons.

The use of a piston pin having sufficient projected area to prevent displacement of the oil film is not new. A good many years ago, in the shops of the first American automobile company to sell any considerable number of cars, I saw a motor, 4-inch diameter of pistons, pins 1⅜ diameter, hollow and soft, pulled down after driving its car 5,000 miles on the road. Neither the piston-pin holes nor the piston pin itself showed any signs of wear, which was proof conclusive that the oil film had not been displaced, and this, too, in spite of certain proof that the job was not true, and that the piston-pin axis did not correspond with that of the pin holes in the piston. Of course, as every machine man well knows, it is far better to use a bearing of sufficient projected area to prevent oil-film displacement than to use a bearing of such small projected area as to make brass bushings and hardened rubbing surfaces necessary to successful working, because it is better to wear out the lubricating oil than to wear out the metal of the working parts.

The Ford engineers, however, elect to use a small-diameter hardened-steel piston pin, and place bronze bushes in the piston-pin seats.

Rough-Turning and Grooving Pistons on Foote-Burt Vertical Lathes

The foundry number of the pistons is 1-418. The foundry operations are, A, molding; B, tumbling; C, rough grinding; R P, chipping. The pistons are then sent to the machine shop for the following finishing operations:

Face and bore. Warner and Swasey turret machine, rough-bore and finish-bore open end of piston with two tools in the turret, then rough-face and finish-face with two tools in the cross-slide. (See page 205.) Production, one screw machine and one man, 80 per hour.

Drill, bore, and ream the piston-pin hole. Up to about a year ago these operations were performed on some single-operation tools.

Finish-Turning of Pistons

Then the Ford Company installed three special machines by the New Britain Machine Tool Company, which are regarded as satisfactory, but have a combined capacity of only about 240 pistons per hour, 80 for one machine and one man, so that the old single-operation machines are yet used, though their work is the more costly. The special machine is illustrated on page 206.

In this adequate and well designed machine, which is automatic save for fixing and removing pistons on the four arms of the work-carrier, this fixture is automatically indexed to four positions by revolving the fixture on a horizontal axis placed lengthwise of the machine. At the right end this machine has three live spindles with independent feeds, one for drilling, one for boring, and one for reaming. The top of the four-arm indexing fixture turns toward the operator. Each arm face is offset the distance from the faced open-end of the piston to the center of the pin hole. The top of the fixture is the put-on-and-take-off station. As the fixture is indexed round, the piston first comes to the drilling station, and has the pin hole drilled. At the second station a second piston is drilled while the first pin hole is being bored. At the third station a third piston is being drilled while the second piston is being bored and the first piston is being reamed. The next movement of the fixture brings the first piston to top position, where the attendant removes it, and replaces it with another, and from thence on, so long as the attendant removes and replaces the pistons, all three operations of drilling, boring, and reaming piston-pin holes are in continuous progress, save for the time occupied by drawing the tools back and indexing the fixture from one position to the next following position.

Rough turn and groove. Vertical lathes with rocking tool carriers, by Foote-Burt. Set in banks of four-machines each, all four attended by one man. The piston is spotted on its open-end, and held by a pin in the pin hole and a tension eye-bar, shown at left, pulled down by the capstan wheel seen low down on base of the machine, a cam and a lever. Four of these well arranged machines and one man rough-turn 75 pistons in one hour. See page 207.

Press in bushings. Two brass bushings are forced into the piston-pin holes, one on each side of piston. One man and one Ferracute press place bushings in 300 pistons per hour.

The next two operations (formerly separated as K-6 and K-7) are now combined, and are performed on a line of sixteen new Reed-Prentice rocking-tool-carrier lathes. One man attends two of these fine tools. Production, one man and two of these lathes, 50 pistons finish turned per hour. See page 208.

Ream bushings; this operation is worked on the motor-assembling job. The piston department work on the piston ends with operation 7, finish turn.

THE PISTON PACKING RINGS

The Ford gray-iron eccentric snap-rings, placed one snap-ring in each of three grooves in the pistons, are certainly a job. They are also certainly the most amazing example of subservience to vogue and prejudice that ever came under my observation.

Cartwright, clergyman, of the time of James Watt, was the first one to devise a metallic piston-packing for steam engines. The Cartwright

First Operation on "Pots" for Piston Rings
Facing on Reed lathe

packing consists of three rings, cylindrical, in one groove; first a wide one, filling the groove inside, and outside of the inside ring two rings, each one half the width of the inside ring. This three-ring packing, 45-degree angle cuts, is tight, costs but little, needs but little expansion spring for small-diameter cylinders, and is in every way so exactly right for its place that it came into immediate use and is, to-day, the standard packing for small steam engines.

Mr. Ford, who had an extended personal acquaintance with steam engines before he began with gas engines, must be fully aware of the Cartwright three-ring piston packing and its many virtues, and yet the Ford motors use eccentric snap-rings, with holes straight through them, one ring in one groove, each ring tested to show 18 pounds of resistance to closing to cylinder-bore size.

The "Reliance" of Detroit, used the Cartwright packing, three cylin-

Rough-Turn and Cut Off Piston Ring on Potter & Johnston Special Automatic Machine

drical rings in one groove, with entire mechanical success, but changed to eccentric snap-rings, one ring in a groove, because Reliance car purchasers preferred the eccentric snap-ring.

At the beginning of the American motor-car trade, American makers were beaten out of sight by the French and German automobile constructors, who had all the trade worth having, and presently the American builders joined in a cry of "Give the public what it wants" and

Piston-Ring Boring, Eccentric Turning, Marking and Cutting Off
Potter & Johnston special lathe, showing lathe saddle and cutting and marking tools

with one accord began copying foreign practice, the snap-ring among other details.

I do not know whether Mr. Ford ever tried Cartwright packing in a gas-engine cylinder, but I am informed by the machine-shop head that no piston packed with three cylindrical rings in one groove has been tried in a Ford motor during the eleven years of his Ford Motor Company service.

THE PISTON-RING "POTS"

These are gray-iron hollow cylinders, having a low flange at one end, from which the Ford eccentric snap-rings are laboriously carved.

The twelve finished rings expected from one "pot" weigh about 17 ounces, or $1^5/_{12}$ ounces each. Each pot as it comes from the foundry weighs about $6^1/_2$ pounds, or 104 ounces, from which 17 ounces of finished piston rings is expected to be produced—that is to say $^5/_6$ of the pot stock is wasted.

The foundry supplies the machine shop with 13,000 pounds of ring pots per day, worth, at $2^1/_2$ cents per pound, $325 per day.

The machine shop produces about 14,000 rings per day, $1^5/_{12}$ ounces

Straddle Cut on Sides of Rings, Pratt & Whitney Machine
Takes the place of grinding the ring sides

each, say 1,240 pounds of finished rings from 13,000 pounds of ring stock, 11,760 pounds of stock, worth $294 wasted for the pleasure of cutting it into chips and using snap-ring piston packing.

That is to say, $325 worth of ring-stock is supplied to the machine shop, $294 of this value is wasted, and $31 of stock value utilized in the finished work.

These figures are not favorable to low-cost piston-ring production.

The piston-rings finishing job works about twenty-two machine hands, and no less than fourteen inspectors are needed to make sure that the rings are suitable for their employment after they are finished.

The rough dimensions of the pot, a hollow gray-iron cylinder, flanged at one end, are as follows: diameter of hole, $3\frac{1}{2}$ inches, diameter of body, 4 inches, diameter of flange, $5\frac{1}{4}$ inches, thickness of flange, $\frac{1}{2}$ inch. Length over all, $6\frac{7}{8}$ inches.

Breaking the Rings

The operations on the piston rings are as follows:

Face. The pot is chucked in a Reed lathe, flanged end out, is faced off, and the flange edge is cut to about a 20 degree angle, large diameter outside. This gives the holding surface for the Potter and Johnston automatic operation of boring, eccentric turning, marking thin point and cutting off. One Reed lathe and one man face 112 pots in one hour. See page 210.

Facing and beveling the pot flange. In specially designed Potter and Johnston automatic machines the pots are chucked by the flange on the face plate, cylindrical part of the pot in the air. See page 210.

This tool has a frame, supporting a tool carriage which has an automatic feed and slides on top of the frame. This carriage carries a heavy boring bar, cutter set in advance of the turning tool, which bores out the inside of the pot as the carriage is fed towards the head stock. The carriage also carries a cross-slide, moved by a crank action making even turns with the head-stock spindle, which moves the turning tool towards the work center and draws the tool away from the work center, both motions, once to every revolution of the pot. This gives the ring-blank its eccentricity.

Widening the Break

The frame supports a head-stock at the left-hand end, carrying a live spindle to which the pot is chucked, while a horizontal rock-shaft placed along the back side of the lathe carries a rocking tool-holder, automatically moved to cut the rings off successively as the carriage moves towards the head-stock, the rocking tool carrier having 13 parting tools fixed in it, the tools being set at different heights so as to cut the entire pot body into 12 separate eccentric rings by the combination of automatic agencies specified.

The illustration on page 211 gives an enlarged view of the carriage and the rocking tool carrier of this highly ingenious Potter and Johnston automatic piston-ring rough-turning and cutting-off machine, and shows the

Placing Piston Rings on Arbors, Ready for Finishing the Ring Circumference

rocking head of cutting-off tools, the front right two or three rings cut off and hanging on the boring bar, with the crank-moved eccentric turning action carried in a horizontal cylindrical cross-slide housing extending to the left. It is needful to know the exact thin point of the ring, and a spring striker, seen above the eccentric action slide, carries the center punch at its end and marks each ring at the thin point as the turning and cutting-off proceeds. Two machines and one man, 300 rings per hour rough-turned and cut off.

Straddle face the ring-sides. Pratt and Whitney machine, with expanding collet in live spindle, and ring receiver in hand-lever-moved tail-spindle. A notably clever machine design, shown on page 212.

The workman places one ring in the tail-spindle receiver, pulls it over the collapsed expanding head-stock collet (which is milled on the holding surfaces) expands the arbor, withdraws the tail spindle, and then with two tools faces both sides of the ring at same time. One man and one machine, 300 rings faced on both sides per hour. The rings are not ground on the sides.

"Break" slot. Cut the ring open at exact thin point, 45 degrees angle punch and die cut in Bliss press. See page 213. One man and one press, 1,062 rings per hour.

Mill slot. On small hand milling machine, having a mill of right width on the arbor in the live spindle, the rings are hand-lever clamped in a 45-degree angle receiving fixture and the "break" is widened to width of mill by hand-movement of cross-slide. See page 213. This operation finishes the ring 45-degrees angle cut to final width. One man and one machine, 650 per hour.

Put on arbor, rough turn, take off arbor, put on arbor, finish turn, and take off arbor are sufficiently illustrated by page 214. When an eccentric snap-ring, rough turned, is pushed into a cylinder it does not touch the cylinder wall at all points. To obtain rings bearing at all points the rings are placed

Inspecting Piston Rings for Closing Resistance

inside of receiving cylinders of tool steel, hardened and ground. The receiver stands on a flanged gray-iron base with top-end open, and first takes six rings, laid one on top of the other, thin sides and thick sides alternating. Next is placed a finished steel collar about ½ inch thick, then on top of this collar, six more rings, similarly disposed. Then the filled receiver goes to the arbor man, who passes a flanged arbor, fitting the receiver, through the inside rings, places a finished collar on top and screws a nut down on the collar, hard. Then the receiver and arbor go to the arbor-press man who presses the arbor out of the receiver, with the rings and collars firmly clamped in place by the arbor nut. Then the filled arbor goes to a hand on a Reed-Prentice lathe. The reader will understand that the ring's circumference is not, at this time, a true circle, but has high and low points, because an eccentric ring will not touch a confining cylinder at all points without special fitting. The lathe man now proceeds to rough-turn the rings with a cut just deep enough to clean their outside surfaces. One man and one Reed lathe, 12 rings on an arbor, 1,050 rings turned per hour. Next the rings are taken off the arbor and are then again packed in receivers, the same as before, and now stand very much less away from the containing cylinder than at first, but yet not touching all round. Once more the arbor is put through the rings, is pushed out of the receiver, goes to a lathesman, who takes the finishing cut over the rings, again barely enough to clean the surface.

The entire ring rough-turn and finish-turn gang, as shown in the illustration, can rough and finish-turn, with two Reed-Prentice lathes and two lathe hands, about 2,100 snap-rings per hour.

Rings Inspection

The fourteen inspectors on the ring job, two-thirds as many inspectors as there are workmen, inspect the rings constantly in course of finishing. The final inspection is for 18 pounds of ring resistance to closing to cylinder diameter. Several forms of closing-resistance testing-machines are used, the latest, in use but a short time, being shown on page 215.

The ring under test is seen close to right of the inspector's right hand, cut to front; the reader's left (workman's right) of the inspection machine, is fixed. The inspector lays the ring down flat on the testing-machine surface and pulls the ring towards him, left side of ring against the fixed abutment, ring passage resisted by a lever on right side, weighted to 18 pounds. When the ring resistance is 18 pounds the lever makes an electrical contact which rings a bell. If the inspector pulls the ring through with no ringing of the bell, the ring is a waster, and some lots of rings show 20 per cent of failures in standard pressure-resistance. As a general rule, however, the failures do not go above about 5 per cent. of total number of rings subjected to test.

Chapter VIII

THE COMMUTATOR PRODUCTION AND ASSEMBLING JOB

THE Ford commutator consists of a case, contacts, and rotor fixed to the end of the cam-shaft, geared to make one turn to two turns of the motor crank-shaft.

This rotor hub, T-4446 (see the plate on page 218, showing rotor components, fiber insulation ring and hand-nuts) has two short parallel arms on one side, forming a clevis, adapted to have pivoted therein a swinging arm, T-672, this T-672 having also two arms forming a second clevis adapted to take the hardened tool-steel pin, T-476, and hardened tool-steel roller, T-673, extending from one side and a spring-tail extending from the other side.

The rotor hub, T-4446, has also a spring tail extending in an opposite direction to the clevis arms, and a close-wound, coiled, steel-wire spring, T-469, has its ends hooked into the two spring tails specified, all so that the spring tension constantly tends to swing the hard-steel contact roller, T-673, away from the hub of the rotor, T-4446, as the rotor revolves with the cam-shaft.

The rotor is surrounded by a vulcanized-fiber insulating ring, T-4447, forced into the case, T-4439, page 219, and afterward milled with four sinking cuts, to take four contact assemblies, T-462-B, with their hand nuts, 90 degrees apart, all as shown in two views, symbol T-4443, on page 219.

The commutator case is revolubly seated on its large end concentric with the cam-shaft, placed to make the four contact-head faces match the rotor roller for height, so that as the rotor revolves the roller will contact with the four fields successively.

COMMUTATOR OPERATION

The four contacts are wired to four coil boxes, each coil being wired to the fly-wheel magneto so as to be supplied with electric current so long as the motor fly-wheel revolved at 25 or more turns per minute; but

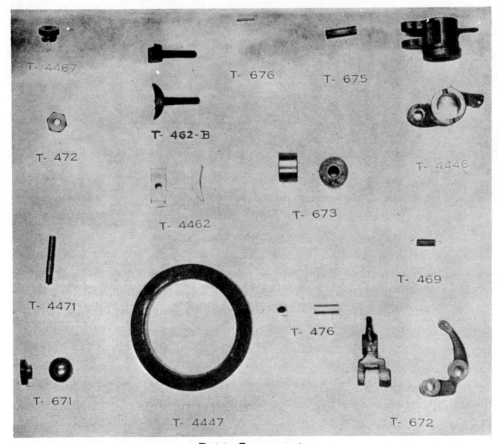

Rotor Components

These are the fiber ring T-4447, the contact-stud insulation T-671, the nuts T-467 and T-472, and the coil-spring T-469. The last three are from outside suppliers

as the contacts are insulated in the fiber ring pressed into the case, there can be no ignition-spark-creating discharge of electric current until the rotor roller touches a contact and so grounds the electrical circuit.

The case can be rocked by its integral control-rod arm, so as to cause the contact to occur earlier or later in the rotor revolution, thus advancing or retarding the ignition-spark production time.

A constant spring pressure is maintained on the small end of the case to hold the case to its seat.

In the illustration on page 219 an oiler is shown seated opposite the case control-arm, which placing of the oiler makes the case right-hand control. If the oiler is moved round 180 degrees, and seated in the center and hub there placed, next to the control-arm, then the case is left-hand control.

The outside diameter of the finished case is 3 inches, inside diameter

$2^{13}/_{16}$ inches, total height 2 inches, and the weight of the case aluminum casting, rough, is $4^1/_2$ ounces. The weight of the complete case assembly T-4443, is $6^1/_4$ ounces. The weight of the complete rotor assembly, T-4481, is 3 ounces. The combined weight of the case assembly and the rotor assembly is $9^1/_4$ ounces. The retail selling price of the commutator, case and rotor complete, is $1.50.

Sixty men, total, produce 1,750 of these Model T commutator and rotor assemblies in one 8-hour day, 480 hours total, a production of one Model T complete commutator for something less than $16^1/_2$ minutes of one man's time, as

Commutator Case Assembly (T-4443) and Rough Aluminum Casting for Commutator (T-4439), Snagged

against 24 minutes 18 seconds, Jan. 11, 1914, before the commutator job was first moved to the fourth floor, and of 23 minutes 41 seconds of one man's time per commutator completed, March 31, 1914, after the commutator job was moved to the fourth floor and before the case-foundry was installed there.

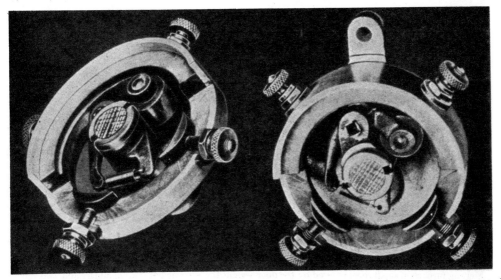

Commutator Assembly (T-4443) Showing Contact-Seating and Contact-Stud Insulation

Gas-Fired Aluminum-Melting Furnace of Ford Construction in Small Room Shown at the Left in the Picture Below

The charge is given as 168 pounds pure aluminum and 32 pounds of alloy, consisting of equal parts by weight of aluminum and copper. This gives a trifle over 8 per cent of copper in the melt

The commutator job is such as to make the best relative placing of the machine tools and benches a matter for trial after the job was moved to the fourth floor, and the placing of the work-slides was not completed March 31; hence the small labor-time reduction shown from Jan. 11 to March 31, 1914. Now, August 12, 1914, everything except the brass castings for the rotor is in pretty fair form. These brass castings were made outside, the Ford shops having made their first brass casting Aug. 10, 1914, and a hand-hammer operation is required on the rotor-hub spring-tail. The Ford shops are now making new pat-

Aluminum Foundry, North End of Commutator-Job Machine Floor

Melting furnace in small room entered by the door seen at the extreme left; two moulders and two moulding machines inside the low concrete enclosing wall, and one helper outside; concrete floor throughout

terns for the rotor brass castings which will bring them right, and will somewhat lower the present labor-time of $16\frac{1}{2}$ minutes of one man's time for each commutator produced.

The sixty men on the commutator job are divided as follows: One head, one foreman, two tool-setters, one straw-boss, one clerk, three men in the screw-machine department, one of whom hardens and tempers the tool-steel rollers and roller-pins, and three hands in the foundry.

Operation B. Snagging Case Castings (T-4439)

At the right a workman at the grinding wheel; in front, boxes of case castings; in the rear, two sheet-iron annealing chests, partly filled with gray-iron chips used in annealing the contact assembly T-462-B; in the left background the annealing furnace with chain hoist in front of it

The workmen's routine for shop entering is: ring up on time clock, take work card from clerk's desk, go to tool crib, take out tools, leaving checks at tool crib, remove street clothing, and be at their places ready to work at bell time 6:30 a. m.; lunch, 10:30 to 11:00 a. m.; start at 11:00 a. m. and work until bell time, 3:00 p. m. After the 3:00 p. m. bell, each worker cleans his machine, then fills his production card, and on his way with his tools to the tool crib leaves his production card at the

Operations 3, 4 and 5 on Commutator Case
Bore and Turn Fiber Insulating Ring

In the left-hand picture operation 3 is performed on the drill at the extreme left, operation 4 on the tap at the right. The boring and turning of the fiber insulation ring ready to force into the case is done on two Warner & Swasey turret machines shown in the right-hand picture. The men were taken off the Garvin tapping machine and the Ferracute press (operations 4 and 5) to show the tools. The commutator machine floor is so filled with machines and men that photographing is difficult

Operation 1 on Commutator Case   **Operation 2 on Commutator Case**

Operation 1 consists of boring the inside diameter and facing. Two men on two Warner & Swasey turret machines. Time 19 seconds for one case

clerk's desk, and then leaves his tools at the tool crib and gets his checks back again.

Checking all tools into the tool crib at quitting time makes it certain that all tools will be ready for the workmen at starting time next morning, or for the workmen in the following shift.

Each workman takes his production card from the clerk's desk at starting, when he obtains his tools from the tool crib, the clerk's desk and the tool-crib window being close together.

The form-blanks used in the commutator department are the workmen's time card, the non-productive time ticket, Form 759, the productive time ticket, Form 915, and the report of stock machined, Form 552, all of which, with their uses, have been already shown and described.

ROLLER AND PIN HARDENING

The contact rollers, T-673, and their pins, T-675, are of tool-steel, and are hardened by being heated to 1,400 degrees F., quenching in a caustic-soda bath, and are tempered in a bath of Atlantic tempering oil, kept at a temperature of 400 degrees F.

The pins and roller holes are not ground.

The rollers are placed on an arbor and ground to uniform diameter.

The commutator life is about five years, ordinary car-duty; hence, as there are now over 500,000 Model T cars in use, the commutator replacements are over 100,000 per year, and the replacement requirements are constantly increasing.

The vulcanized-fiber insulation is of the yellow-gray variety, which is much stronger than the red-colored sort, and is very hard on cutting-tool edges.

SPECIAL MACHINE-TOOL CONSTRUCTIONS

The only unusual special machine-tool adjunct used on the commutator job is a drilling-machine spindle addition, Ford design, carrying three drilling spindles, for drilling T-4446 and T-672, all three holes at one time.

DRILLING JIGS

These are of ordinary forms, leaf and stationary bushes.

The great number of illustrations given with this commutator story, together with the brief description of the commutator itself, will give the reader a fair idea of the Ford commutator department.

Operation 1 on Commutator Contact Head, T-4462
With a gang mill, cut 10 pieces at once from a crescent-section steel bar

FORD SHOPS "PROGRESSIVE" TOOL-PLACING

Ford engineers are fully aware that the lowest costs cannot be had save by placing all the tools and men used in one assembled-component production close together and in operation sequence, so that each component shall have the shortest possible line of travel, with the fewest handlings.

PLACING A FOUNDRY IN THE MACHINE SHOP

To carry out fully the foregoing proposition the aluminum foundry for producing the commutator case T-4439, is placed at the north end of the commutator machine-tool floor. The watchman starts the aluminum-melting furnace gas-fire at 5:00 a. m., and thus makes the metal ready to pour at 6:30 a. m., starting time. Three men, two machine moulders and one pourer, shake-out, and furnace man, produce the rough casting aluminum cases, hour by hour, as they are required by the finishers, about 1,800 per 8-hour day, maximum.

We are so thoroughly accustomed to the entire separation of the machine shop and the foundry that most shop men have never given a moment's thought to the advantages gained by making the foundry a part of the finishing floor, even when using a low-heat-melting metal.

In the present case there is no requisition made for case castings, and no handling and transportation of case castings between the foundry and the stores room, nor between the stores room and the commutator department. No writing, nor records needed, save weight of pig melted.

The case castings are simply in the boxes, ready to hand, as if they grew there or blew in at the window. No one has to pay any attention to the rough-case supply, because the supply begins automatically when the starting bell rings and continues until the quitting bell rings; every hour so many cases moulded, knocked off the gates, and placed in the boxes ready for snagging.

Operations 2 and 3 on Commutator Contact Head

Tumble in the Ford tumbler surrounded by a wire cage at the left, and drill in a 10-spindle Langelier Manufacturing Co.'s revolving-head 10-spindle semi-automatic drilling machine at the right. The workman arranges the head blanks against the flange of a horizontal revolving table, an automatic finger places each contact head in proper position in the revolving head, and the machine then automatically drills and discharges each piece

In a word, the commutator-case production starts at 100 per cent efficiency, an impossible condition if the case-foundry were not placed where it is, on the machine-shop floor, where it forms the first element of the commutator-production plant, as it should and must, if 100 per cent efficiency is to be made possible.

See views on page 220, aluminum foundry on machine-shop floor, for producing the commutator case, T-4439. The small moulding floor has a shake-out grating, not shown here, inside the concrete low wall which separates the moulding floor from the machine-shop floor. The founding equipment includes two Berkshire Manufacturing Company's Model E moulding machines, with match plates for the cope in one machine and for the drag in the other machine, followboards and flasks, and one moulder to each moulding machine. The aluminum-melting furnace is housed in the small room at the left, with open door, as seen at left extreme. The furnace is of Ford construction and is attended by the workman at the left, who also pours the moulds and shakes out

Brown & Sharpe Automatic Single-Spindle Screw Machine Making the Contact Stud, T-4471

the work, ten cases, T-4439, to each flask, and knocks the cases off the runner with a mallet as seen in picture. Time required to put up the cope, 1 minute 33 seconds, drag 1 minute 42 seconds. These three men, two moulders and one helper, turn out about 1,800 cases, T-4439, per 8-hour day.

The picture on page 220 shows the aluminum-melting furnace, "Industrial" construction; capacity about 200 pounds of aluminum alloy. The furnace is gas-fired, and gives metal ready for pouring in about 80 minutes after the burners are lighted.

SNAGGING CASES, T-4439

The photograph on page 221 shows at the right a workman at an emery wheel, snagging cases, T-4439; time of snagging, 4 seconds; front, right, and left, boxes of cases. Two annealing chests,

Tap Commutator Contact Head
Two men, two single-spindle drilling machines

Ford Machine with Gronkvist Chuck, Friction-Driven, in the Middle

The man at the right screws the stud into the head; the man at the left with vise and hand-brace tightens the stud in the head. Operation 1 on T-242-B

partly filled with gray-iron chips, the chests having hinged covers, all of sheet iron, show at the middle left, with annealing furnace and chain hoist above. This view is at the north end of commutator machine floor, on which tools are placed for commutator finishing in operation sequence.

The progressive finishing operations upon the cases and other components making up the complete commutator assembly are given in the following pages in a condensed description which covers the main points of the nature of each job, the machine or tool used, the time taken, and any points of special interest attaching to the work or the equipment used. The illustrations follow in close parallel to the text and are referred to by number as the point they show particularly is taken up.

FINISHING THE COMMUTATOR CASE, T-4439

Operation 1. Bore inside diameter and face: chuck and bore on two Warner and Swasey turret machines, two men. Time 19 seconds. The times here given are stop-watch from actual operation time of workmen. The pictures are flash, actual work, no posing. See page 223.

Operation 2. Turn outside diameter and center. Page 223, two Reed and Prentice lathes, two men. Time on one case, 18 seconds.

Operation 3. Drill one $^{11}/_{32}$ hole, time 6 seconds. One Allen drill press, one spindle, one man.

Same Machine Shown Above

It is equipped with the same friction-driven Gronkvist automatic chuck and used for the same operation, but equipped with triple-operated leather-faced double-lever brake. Pressure on the pedal holds the chuck shell from revolving and releases the work. This leaves both the operator's hands free at all times and permits much faster work

Operation 4. Punch one $^{15}/_{64}$ hole, time 3 seconds. Ferracute press.

Operation 5. Tap $^{11}/_{32}$ hole, $^{1}/_{8}$ pipe tap, for oiler; Garvin tapping machine; time 7 seconds. See page 222.

Operation 5. Makes the case ready to have the fiber insulating ring, T-4447, forced into its inside.

MACHINING THE FIBER RING, T-4447

Operation 1. Bore out inside. One Warner and Swasey turret machine, one man, time 11 seconds.

Operation 2. Turn outside, 1 Warner and Swasey turret machine, one man, time, 10 seconds. See page 222.

MACHINING THE CONTACT HEAD, T-4462

The contact head is cut, ten pieces at once, from a bar of crescent-section steel, with a gang of mills in a Pratt and Whitney hand milling machine. The time required to cut ten pieces from the bar is 53 seconds. One machine, one man. See page 224. This constitutes operation 1.

Operation 2. Tumble, Ford tumbler.

Operation 3. Drill one No. 19 hole in middle of contact head, Lang-

Operation 2 on T-462-B; Welding

elier Manufacturing Company's special driller. This driller has a spindle head, carrying ten vertical spindles and revolving at constant speed on a vertical axis. The work is automatically fed up to the drill-spindles. This is an elaborate semi-automatic machine-tool, rapid and precise in action.

The contact heads are placed by hand on a horizontal, revolving circular table, flanged at the edge, against the flange. Then an automatic finger pushes each head-blank into a receiver in the bottom part of the revolving drill head, and the heads are drilled and ejected as the drill head revolves. See page 225. One man and one machine drill ten contact heads in 18 seconds.

Operation 4. Tap holes in contact heads, T-4462. One Barnes drill press with one man, and one Allen drill press with one man; long-shank taps in drill spindles, taps 10-32; taps are run through until the shank length is filled with contact heads, then the chuck is released and shank cleared of heads. One man taps six contact heads in 33 seconds. See page 226.

COMMUTATOR CONTACT STUD, T-4471

See pages 218 and 226.

Operation 1. Thread both ends and cut off. Brown and Sharpe automatic screw machine, single-spindle, as shown on page 226; also, same piece, T-4471, on Acme four-spindle screw machine, no illustration. Time, one stud, Brown and Sharpe machine, 10 seconds. Acme four-spindle machine, 6 seconds.

T-462-B ASSEMBLE CONTACT HEAD, T-4462 AND STUD, T-4471

See page 227.

Operation 1. Assemble head and stud, Ford machine in middle, one spindle, constant speed, with friction driven "Gronkvist" automatic chuck. While the chuck is running, a stud is slipped into the chuck, which automatically tightens when the head is held in hand pliers by the man at the right, and applied to running stud, held in the friction-driven, self-tightening chuck. This screws the stud, T-4471, into the contact head, T-4462, as far as the friction will drive it. The workman then grasps the chuck-shell, which releases the stud, and the workman then drops the assembly into a tray on the bench. Time for 10 assemblies, 48 seconds (man at the right). The workman at the left takes the assembly from the tray, grasps the stud in a vise, and with hand brace turns the head down hard on the stud. Man at left keeps pace with man at right. Two men complete assembly of ten pieces, T-462-B, in 48 seconds.

The "Gronkvist" automatic drill chuck is extremely rapid and convenient in action, is self-tightening, and is made to release with very small muscular exertion.

With a production of 1,750 commutators in 8 hours, 7,000 of these contact head and stud assemblies are used in 8 hours, and speedy production of this T-462-B assembly is highly important. At first the T-462-B assembly was made an integral drop-forging, and the stem was milled with a cup-mouth mill, which also shaped the convex side of the contact head; this method had the fault of leaving the outside of the head curved, which made it needful to cut the contact seat in the insulation ring, T-4447, with a curved-face mill, and these objectionable features led to the present satisfactory construction with the head and stud separated, screwing them together, then electric welding the stud to the head, and finally annealing the assembly because the electric welding produces hard spots.

Operation 2. Electric weld T-462-B. One man, Winfield Electric Welding Machine Company's welding machine. Time, 3 seconds. See page 228.

Operation 3. Anneal T-462-B. 5,000 components T-462-B are packed for annealing as follows: the annealing boxes are of gray-iron with covers, as shown on this page. A rough tray of sheet iron, about half an inch smaller all round than the inside of the box, corners merely cut out and sides and ends folded up, is provided to hold, say, 5,000

Annealing T-462-B

The workman is shown completing the luting of the annealing box and cover-joint with fire-clay. In the middle at the rear is seen the Industrial Furnace Co.'s gas-fired annealing furnace with chain hoist in front and pyrometer box on the pillar at the left. The sheet-iron cooling box is at the extreme left

contact assemblies. Half an inch of gray-iron fine chips is spread over the annealing box bottom, then the sheet-iron inside tray is set on the chips, the 5,000 assemblies are put in, and then the whole inside is packed with gray-iron chips, the box cover is laid on and luted with fire-clay, and the box is placed in the "Industrial" furnace, cold, and the gas fire turned on, heating everything gradually for from 2 to 4 hours, until the pyrometer shows 1,600 degrees F. Then the box is withdrawn from the furnace and buried in gray-iron chips in one of the large sheet-iron cooling chests, where it is let lie for 24 hours, at the end of which time the box is cool enough to handle. The labor time charged against these 5,000 pieces of annealing is 30 minutes of one man's time, for packing in annealing box.

L. H. COMMUTATOR CASE ASSEMBLY, T-4443, OPERATION LIST

Operation 1. Press fiber ring, T-4447, into case, T-4439, by use of one No. 3 Grenerd arbor press, one man, time 7 seconds. See picture adjoining.

Operation 2. Mill four sinking cuts in the fiber ring for seating contact heads, drill for four contact studs, and counterbore for four stud insulations, T-671, page

Operation 1 on Commutator Case

Pressing the fiber ring into the case. No. 3 Grenerd arbor press

218. Contact heads seated 90 degrees apart in ring; two Pratt and Whitney hand milling machines and two men. Time for one case, 1 man, 26 seconds.

Two belt-driven drilling and counterboring spindles are journaled in this fixture, in the plane of the milling machine spindle, and the central part of the fixture frame is bored to take the round fixture in which the case assembly is fixed; the round fixture is revolubly seated and can be hand-indexed in two positions, 90 degrees apart. The milling-machine spindle carries a shank-mill, same radius as outside of the contact head.

Action. The case and fiber-ring assembly is clamped in the fixture, which is on a slide, and with the fixture indexed in one position the slide is moved both ways to stops, which cuts the contact-head seats and drills and counter-bores the case on two sides, 180 degrees apart. Then the fixture is indexed 90 degrees and the slide is again moved to the same stops, both ways; total time of one man and one machine for making the four contact cuts in one case, 26 seconds only.

Operation 3. Burr fiber ring and clean out contact stud holes, hand operation on bench, as shown on page 235. Time, 6 seconds. Operation 3 is performed by the middle man on the left side of the sheet-metal-covered bench, who drops the cases as burred and cleaned on the bench at his right front, convenient to the left hand of the first man on the right side of the bench, who performs Operation 4, placing a contact assembly (T-462-B) in each one of the case four contact seats, and then drops the cases at his right, ready to be picked up by the second man on the right-hand side of the bench, who performs Operation 5, placing four contact-stud insulating-fiber bushes (T-671) in their seats in the case, around the contact studs, and then drops the case on the bench at his right. Next, Operation 6, the case is picked up by the man at the extreme left of the bench, who uses the Ford machine shown on page 235 for performing Operation 6,

Operation 2 on Commutator Case
Mill, drill, and counterbore T-4447 and T-4439 to take the contacts and contact-stud insulation T-671

running a brass hex nut (T-472), on each one of the four contact studs. This Operation 6 machine has a belt-driven spindle carrying on its nose a friction-driven hex-nut socket, in which, while running, the operator places a hex nut, and then pushes a contact stud against the nut which is then friction-driven up against the fiber bushing. After running nuts, Operation 6 workman drops the case on the bench from his left hand in front of the third man on the left of the bench, who performs Operation 7, tightening up each of the four contact-stud hex nuts, by hand, with a box hex-wrench, bringing the nuts to a good solid bearing on the fiber bush, T-671, and making sure that the contact head is fairly placed in its seat in the inside fiber ring, T-4447, and thus making the case ready for Operation 8.

The operation times are: Operation 3, 6 seconds; Operation 4, 10 seconds; Operation 5, 10 seconds; Operation 6, 12 seconds; and Operation 7, 11 seconds.

Operation 8, page 236. Bore out inside diameter; time, 64 seconds. Five Reed-Prentice engine lathes, with Ford hand-revolved and latched, four-tool, four-position turrets. Two lathes are shown on page 236. This operation takes a finishing cut to exact inside diameter over the fiber ring and contacts, and also on top and bottom of fiber ring and contacts. From these lathes the cases go first to the chip cleaner, shown at the right of the lower view on page 236, and then to the inspector, page 237. It is important that all boring chips be removed before testing, because of a possible current-circuit. The chip-cleaner stands near the tall-stock end of the right-hand lathe.

Operation 9. Inspection of case, including insulation test. The inspector examines the case to see that it is free from chips, gauges the outside diameter, and places the case on an insulation test block, wired to a bank of four lamps, which light if insulation is defective. See page 237. One inspector only for each shift.

Milling Machine Fixture Used in Operation 2

The hinge clamp is partly open. The drill-spindle belts are seen, one at the right, crossed, the other at the left, open. These two drill-spindles carry the drills and counterbores for seating the contact insulation T-671 and the contact stud. The little mill which makes the sinking cuts to take the contact heads is in the center inside the fixture. This is shown more fully in the drawing on page 234

T-671 COMMUTATOR-STUD INSULATION-FIBER BUSH

Operation 1. Stock is gray fiber rods, $9/16$ diameter by 68 inches long. The bushes, T-671, are made on two Warner and Swasey turret machines, two men, one operation time, 4 seconds. Page 238.

In ordinary screw-machine practice, the turret would carry one stop, to fix stock length out of the chuck, and one drill, to drill the bush-hole, and the cross-slide tool-post would carry a cutting-off tool, moved by the cross-slide screw, and the fiber bushes, when cut off, would drop

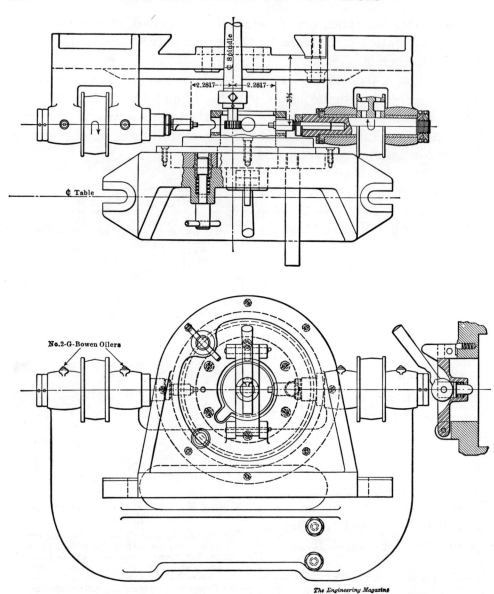

Construction Drawing of the Ford Fixture Used on Pratt and Whitney Milling Machine for Operation 2

Front elevation of the fixtures below, with cross section of the index at the right, and plan and partial section above

down into the chips and have to be picked out by hand, somewhere about 7,000 of them for every 8-hour day's work.

CHANGES MADE IN T-671 PRODUCTION MILLING MACHINE

The head of the commutator department at first made these fiber bushes, T-671, by the foregoing ordinary routine, but has since doubled

Above, North End of South Bench, Disassembling Outfit. Below, Operation 6, Assembling Contact-Studs and Hex Nuts

The Ford machine used in operation 6 carries on its spindle a friction-driven hex socket to take T-472 and drive it on the outside end of the contact-stud up against the fiber-insulation bush T-671. The lower view shows the right-hand end of the bench appearing in the upper picture. In the lower picture the man at the left is on operation 7, the man on the Ford hand-running-on machine is on operation 6, and the man at the extreme right is cleaning out the chips after lathe operation 8, the last thing done to the case assembly before final inspection

Operation 8 on T-4443; Boring Inside Diameter and Facing Both Edges of Fiber Insulation and Contacts

The middle figure, at the tail-stock end of the right-hand lathe, is an inspector

the per hour production by making the following list of changes. The cutting-off tool is shouldered on the head-stock side, so that by moving the cross-slide inward to a stop the small diameter of T-671 is made on the next bush about the same time a finished bush is cut off, in a well known manner.

See page 238. The cross-slide screw is taken out; an arm, 1, is fixed in the turret and has fixed to it the slot-piece down-hanger, 2; the slot takes a stud fixed in the cross-slide and projecting upward, the slot head-stock-end leading to front in the illustration, all so that as the turret slide is moved forward towards the headstock, the cross-slide is moved outward, away from the work.

The turret is locked to the slide and does not revolve at all.

The turret stock-stop is chambered to be an easy fit on the small diameter of T-671, and also has fixed in it a twist drill projecting more than the total thickness of T-671 beyond the stock-stop flat face.

A thin sheet-brass spring is fixed to the top end of a stud projecting upward in front of the cross-slide tool-post, this spring being bent into a quarter circle at its inside end, all so that, as the finished bush is being cut off, the brass spring will press against the bush front side, and when the bush finally breaks off the spring snaps the bush against the flanged top-incline of sheet iron, seen above the work-catching box, top of page 238, so that the bush drops into the box, instead of dropping into the chips.

BURRING, T-671

The cutting-off and shouldering tool of course raises some burrs on the work and on the stock, and it is common practice to remove these burrs with a hand-file, float-cut, a hand operation which uses both of the operator's hands and so takes considerable time, say $1^1/_2$ or 2 seconds, to remove hands from levers, pick up the file, remove burrs with the file, lay the file down, and again grasp one lever with each hand.

In these T-671 producing machines, a spring-lifted file-block, double-ended, float file-cut top and bottom, is placed underneath the work, at 4, page 238, so as to hold the top file-cut surface constantly up against the under side of the stock and work and burr the job, so the operator need not take his hands off the levers. This file-block is lifted by a very weak spring and has a long life; those now in use have worked for a year, one end only, and the teeth are yet good.

Operation 9. Case Inspection, Showing Insulation Test Block

The bank of lights glows when the case is placed on the test block if the insulation is faulty; four lamps, one for each contact in the case

Both the flip-over spring and the spring-lifted, float-file-cut-block are new devices to the writer; the flip-over spring saves picking 7,000 bushers, one by one, out of the fiber chips every 8 hours, and the spring-lifted automatic, file burring-block saves 5 movements of each of the operator's hands for each one of the 7,000 pieces produced per 8-hour day, 35,000 movements of each hand of the workman per 8-hour day, 70,000 motions total: viz.:

(1) Take both hands off levers;

(2) Pick up file in both hands;

(3) With both hands file off burrs;

(4) Lay file down;

(5) Re-grasp levers, both hands.

This little story of little things shows in a very striking manner the labor-cost-reducing value of seemingly insignificant minor inventions.

This is a device new to the writer, and applicable to any small piece of turret-machine work; it saves picking the 7,000 bushes out of the chips every 8 hours.

Because of moving the cross-slide by the rigid slotted-bar fixed to the turret, the operator can keep his right hand constantly on one bar of the capstan which moves

Making the Stud Fiber-Insulation Bush, T-671

Turret Tools and Turret-Machine Modifications

The changes made by the head of the commutator department doubled the production per hour of the two turret machines making the bush T-671

the turret slide; if the turret is moved away from the head-stock the cross-slide is moved inward; if the turret is moved toward the head-stock, the cross-slide is moved outward. The operator keeps his left hand constantly on the live-spindle chuck-lever. The stock is ratchet-fed toward the turret in the usual manner.

OPERATION

Having cut off one T-671, the operator pulls the chuck-lever towards him and pushes the turret-slide lever away from him, keeping the end of the stock against the stop drill-point, until the capstan lever stands about horizontal; then

Operation No. 2. on T-4446.   Drilling Two Holes

lever away to draw the turret back, the cross-slide and cutting-off tool meanwhile being moved inward by the slotted piece fixed to the turret and moved with the turret slide, until the cross-slide reaches its stop, cutting off the new T-671 and forming the tit on the next T-671, the brass spring flipping the new T-671 into the box as soon as it is cut off.

This novel scheme of turret machine and tools construction and handling permits the operator to keep one hand on the feed-and-chuck lever and the other hand on the turret-slide capstan-lever, and to produce twice as many of T-671 per hour as by ordinary practice; and it also places the finished pieces in the box away from the chips, so that picking them out of the chips is avoided, and is here

the operator moves the chuck-lever away from him, to grasp the stock lightly, and pulls the capstan lever until the turret-slide, moving towards the head-stock, reaches its stop, the hole in the next T-671 being drilled and the T-671 tit entering the stock-stop counterbore and the stock-stop flat end pushing hard on the next T-671, the cross-slide meanwhile moving outward; when the turret-slide meets its stop, the workman pushes the chuck-lever away from him to full chuck-tightening position and holds it there while he pushes the capstan

Operation No. 1. (Straddle Milling) on Rotor Body, T-4446

Operations on Commutator Roller Clevis Brass Casting, T-672

The picture on the left shows operations 1 and 2, which consist of straddle milling, and straddle milling a 5/16-in. boss. This is done by two men on two hand milling machines. The picture on the right shows the drilling of two 3/64-in. holes on a Ford 3-spindle drilling head. One drilling head is shown working with two drills only, and another drilling head is seen at the right lying on the driller table

described at length as something new and extremely useful in turret-machine operation.

COMMUTATOR ROTOR BODY, T-4446

This piece is a brass casting.

Operation 1. Straddle-mill ends on Pratt and Whitney hand milling machine; one man, time 5 seconds. Illustrated on page 239.

Operation 2. Two men on one Allen two-spindle driller, and two Allen single-spindle drillers, altogether three men, drill and ream large hole in the hub of rotor body, T-4446. Operation time, 30 seconds. See page 239.

Operation 3. Smooth and burr, Ford rotary files; float cut, on

Operation 7 on Roller-Clevis Brass Casting, T-672

Drill one hole 1/16-in. diameter in spring tail to take one end of the small coiled spring T-469

Operation No. 3. On T-4446

Smoothing and burring on Ford machine and Ford rotary files

Ford machine. Makes fine brass dust; two men wearing nose protectors. Operation time, 15 seconds; this page.

Operation 4. Ream to $9/16$. Langelier driller; operation time, 7 seconds.

Operation 5. Cut $1/8$ slot. Pratt and Whitney hand milling machine; operation time, 9 seconds.

Operation 6. Drill $1/16$ hole in rotor spring-tail. Burke bench driller; operation time, 5 seconds.

COMMUTATOR ROLLER CLEVIS, T-672

This is a brass casting.
Operation 1. Straddle mill.

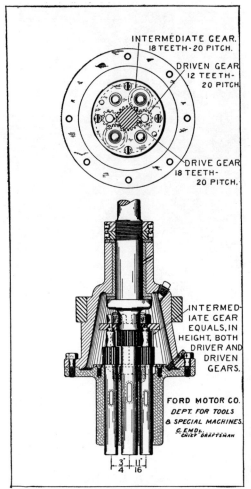

Construction of Ford Special 3-Spindle Drill Head

This head made for drilling three holes at once in T-4446 is now used for two holes only because of faulty castings, but will be used for three drills when the castings are made right

Pratt and Whitney hand milling machine; operation time, 7 seconds.   Page 240.

Operation 2.   Straddle mill $5/16$ boss; operation time, 6 seconds. Operations one and two are shown on page 240.   Pratt and Whitney milling machine.

Operation 3.   Drill two $13/64$ holes, Ford special three-spindle head on one spindle of an Allen two-spindle drill press; operation time, 2 seconds.   See page 240. The two drillers, single spindle, at right, are Burke one-spindle drillers, set close together, so as to be used as a two-spindle machine, and are also used for operation 3.   A Ford special three-spindle drilling head is shown at left, working, and at right, lying down on the drill-table.   These special heads are made to carry three taper-shank drills each, drills $3/4$ and $11/16$, center to center.   This Ford special three-spindle drilling head is of interest, and a section and plan are shown in the construction drawing reproduced on this page, as likely to be of service to readers who can save time by placing the drill spindles very close together.   The peculiar feature of this construction is the making of the intermediate gear long enough to cover both the driving and driven spindles, which gives the largest possible drill-spindle diameter for a given center-to-center distance. See page 240.

Operation 4.   Ream one $11/64$ hole.   Burke drill press; operation time, 2 seconds.   Page 240.

Operation 5.   Drill one hole, No. 32 drill, Burke drill press; operation time, 3 seconds.   Page 241.

Forming the Tool-Steel Contact Roller on Three Acme 4-Spindle Screw Machines
The man in the middle is picking up soldering coppers after dressing them on the emery grinder at the
extreme left; this work does not belong to the commutator job. The Barnes drill press at the
right is working on operations 2 and 3 on the contact roller

Operation 6. Flatten spring-tail with hand-hammer. Operation 6 is due to faulty castings. No time is given.

Operation 7. Drill one hole, $\frac{1}{16}$ diameter. Burke drill press.

Operation 8. File, Ford rotary file. Page 241.

CONTACT ROLLER, TOOL-STEEL, T-673

Operation 1. Form on three Acme four-spindle screw machines; time for one roller, 37 seconds. Shown above.

Operation 2. Ream, Barnes drill press; time, 6 seconds.

Operation 3. Burr, Barnes drill press; time, 2 seconds. See the illustration above. Barnes drill press at right.

Operation 4. Harden. Time of operation 4, 15 minutes to harden 75 rollers. The roller and roller-pin hardening and tempering are briefly specified in the early part of this article. Furnace heat, 1400 degrees F. See page 245.

Operation 5. Temper in oil bath, constant heat, 400 degrees F.; time, 20 minutes to temper 900. Same illustration.

Operation 6.   Grind on two Landis grinding machines, on arbor; time, 22 seconds, each roller.   See page 246.

Roller-Pin, T-675, Tool-Steel

Operation 1.   Cut off, on Acme automatic screw machine; time, 10 seconds.

There are three men in the screw-machine department of the commutator job.   All the screw machines are automatic.   See page 243.

Operation 2.   Drill one cross-hole with No. 50 drill, Allen drill press; time, 11 seconds.

Operation 3.   Burr.

Operation 4.   Harden.

Operation 5.   Temper in oil.   See the illustration on page 245, for these three operations, 3, 4 and 5.

Clevis Pin, T-476

Operation 1.   Cut off and bore one end.   Acme screw machine; time, 16 seconds.

Operation 2.   Countersink the other end.   Allen drill press; time, 10 seconds.

Roller-Pin Locking Pin, T-676

Operation 1.   Cut to length from wire coil, on automatic wire-cutting machine; time, 268,000 pins cut off in 8 hours.

Commutator-Roller and Clevis-Pin Assembly, T-4474

Operation 1.   Fit one T-675 pin in one T-673 roller.

Operation 2.   Assemble one T-672 clevis and one T-673 roller with one T-675 pin to match up holes in T-672 and T-675.

Operation 3.   Place and rivet one T-676 pin to complete assembly T-4474.

Commutator Rotor Assembly, T-4481

Operation 1.   Assemble one roller, T-4474 and arm assembly with one rotor hub, T-4446, and one clevis pin, T-476, and rivet.

Operation 2.   Line up roller and adjust.

Operation 3.   Assemble with spring, T-469, to complete T-4481.

Operation 4.   Inspect.   See page 247.

These assembling and inspecting operations are made on the long metal-covered bench, marked "Assemble T-4474 and T-4481," page 248, floor plan, beginning at the south end and ending with the inspection bins at the north end. The illustration on page 247 is a view of the north end of this assembling bench, with inspection bins in fore-ground. Inspectors are taken away to give a view down the bench, looking south.

COMMUTATOR DISASSEMBLING

See page 235. Many worn-out commutators are handled. In this picture the left-hand man, on Ford machine, is unscrewing hex-nuts, T-472, and taking out contacts. P is a Ford machine for pulling the fiber ring, T-4447, out of the case. The vise is for general repair work.

The reader, technical or non-technical, who has looked through this Ford commutator story will find it difficult to believe that 60 men can produce 1,750 Ford commutators in one 8-hour day —16 minutes and 27 seconds of one man's time producing one complete commutator, including the case founding; and the underlying factors of this surprising efficiency should undoubtedly be displayed in detail.

How Ford Shops Make a Commutator in 16 Minutes and 27 Seconds of One Man's Time

(1) By minutely subdividing labor operations. The actual stop-watch time of each operation is

Roller and Roller-Pin Hardening and Tempering Plant; Ford Construction

given, and can be referred to by the reader in connection with the pictures that show the operation performances. Some of the operations are done in as little as 2 seconds of time. Many of the operations are the work of automatic tools.

Minute division of operations is effective in labor-cost reducing in two ways: first by making the workman extremely skillful, so that he does his part with no needless motions, and secondly by training him to perform his unvaried operation with the least possible expenditure of will-power, and hence with the least brain fatigue.

(2) The work hours are short, 4 hours at a stretch only, so that workmen in good form can, and do, stand in their tracks, working with the regular production of an automatic machine.

(3) Work-slides, successive-operation men and successive-operation tools and appliances, are so placed that one man drops a piece when his part is done, either where it is ready to the next man's hand or where the gravity work-slide will carry the piece to the next man's ready reach.

Operation 6 on Grinding the Roller Circumference

Two Landis grinders with roller on the arbor

(4) Placing the case foundry on the machine floor, close to the machine tools, is a very great time-saver. Not only is the rough-case supply thus made certain, but the castings are perfectly moulded and come to the finishers in best possible form, with least possible thought, travel, and labor, both of the head and the workmen.

(5) All operations requiring heat, melting, annealing, hardening and tempering, are performed in furnaces so located, and so grouped where more than one heating is needful, as to save all possible time expenditure.

(6) While the machine tools used are all regular commercial productions, the fixtures used with them are most elaborate, carefully designed to save movements as far as may be, and are well made, so that the workman need exercise no care or scrutiny in operating and working them.

(7) In three instances the special tools and fixtures used are unusual; the two turret machines which produce T-671 have been so ingeniously changed as to produce more than double the work that could be turned out by ordinary handling of a turret machine, as described in detail herein.

The three-spindle drilling head, also fully shown, is a marked time-saver.

North End of the Assembling Bench, Showing General View of the Machine Floor South of the Annealing Furnace. Inspection Bins in Front

The contact-seat milling and drilling fixture is very clever, and enables twelve cuts to be made in the commutator case and insulation ring with great rapidity, and perfectly to gauge, so long as the mill which makes the sinking cut in the fiber insulation remains sharp. The life of this mill is very short; the fiber is hard to cut and the mill-diameter must always be nearly the same; these mills often work only one hour for once grinding, and can be ground only a few times before they become too small in diameter. This fixture is fully shown.

(8) Constant supervision of workmen, constant work inspection, and constant watching of tool-cuts by the two tool-setters, give skilled overlooking to the work of every man on the commutator job. Many of the machine hands, though not regular machinists, are highly skilled and grind and set their own tools. Every workman is perfectly aware that he is under constant observation, and that he will be admonished if he falls below the fast pace of the department.

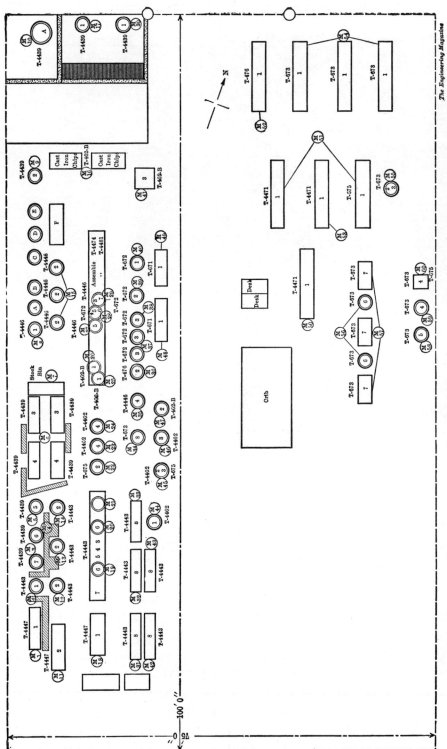

Floor Plan of Commutator Plant Machine-Tool Placing, Foundry, Desks and Tool Crib

For key to machine tools and operations see footnote on opposite page

(9) An automatic drill chuck, the "Gronkvist," can be handled more rapidly than anything ever seen previously by me, and saves much time.

(10) The workmen are suitable for the performance of their operations, and for their environment and working conditions. They are docile, and yet the physiologist will seek in vain for weak chins and narrow heads in the portraits of these workers, who are, without exception, mentally capable of concentration and determined effort, having well defined, firm chins, wide jaws, and wide heads.

After reading the foregoing summary of Ford labor-cost reducing elements, the Commutator Department Head asserted its correctness, but added as follows:

"I depend largely on my tool-setters for my production. The tool-setters know exactly what I want, and as long as the tool-setters have plenty of newly-sharpened tools on hand, all ready to go into the machines as soon as tools in use show loss of smooth-cutting edge, I have no trouble in keeping my production up to the 1750 per 8-hours mark. But if there is even a very small delay in replacing a cutting tool which does not work exactly right, trouble begins."

Undoubtedly this post-script is of first importance in this 16 minutes and 27 seconds achievement.

The commutator job is regarded by the Ford shop heads as being in as nearly satisfactory condition as any department of the entire plant, and the low labor-costs therein reached fully warrant the minutely detailed and profusely illustrated story here printed.

EXPLANATION OF DIAGRAM ON OPPOSITE PAGE

Figures without enclosing circle are operation numbers.
Letter "M" and figure inside of a single circle mean "machine" of the number given in following list.
The double-line circles mean machine tools, and figures inside of double line circles are the operation number of the operation performed on that machine.

1—No. 4 Warner & Swasey.
2—No. 3 Grenerd Arbor Press.
3—Auto Tapper.
4—P2 Ferracute Punch Press.
5—Allen Single Spindle Drill Press.
6—No. 4 Warner & Swasey.
7—Ford Stock Bin.
8—No. 2 Pratt & Whitney Hand Miller.
9—No. 2 Blount Column Grinder.
10—Ford Melting Pot.
11—No. 4 Warner & Swasey.
12, 13, 14—No. 2 Pratt & Whitney Hand Miller.
15—Foote-Burt Three Spindle Drill.
16—Ford Stock Box.
17—Model E Berkshire Hand Squeezer.
18—No. 4 Warner & Swasey.
19, 20—Ford Nut Tightener.

21—Ford Fiber Puller.
22—15″ Barnes Drill Press.
23, 24—Allen Single Spindle Drill.
25, 26—Ford Nut Tightener.
27—Langelier Sensitive Drill.
28—No. 1 Burke Bench Drill.
29—Ford Rotary File.
30—Pridemore Rockover Moulding Machine.
31, 32, 33—14″ x 6′ Reed Engine Lathe.
34—Leland-Gifford Sensitive Drill.
35—No. 2 Pratt & Whitney Hand Miller.
36, 37—No. 1 Single Spindle Allen Drill.
38—No. 2 Two Spindle Allen Drill.
39, 40—No. 2 Pratt & Whitney Hand Miller.
41—No. 203 Industrial Furnace.

42, 43—14″ x 6′ Reed Engine Lathe.
44—No. 2 Pratt & Whitney Hand Miller.
45—Ford Tumbler.
46—Special Carousel Drill.
47—Winfield Electric Welder.
48, 49—No. 2 Warner & Swasey.
50—No. 0 Brown & Sharp Auto Screw Machine.
51, 52—No. 52 Auto Screw Machine.
53—No. 57 Auto Screw Machine.
54—No. 53 Auto Screw Machine.
55—15″ Barnes Drill Press.
56—No. 2 Grenerd Arbor Press.
57—No. 1 Landis Plain Grinder.
58—Ford Oil Drawing Furnace.
59—Ford Quenching Tank.
60—Ford Gas Furnace.

CHAPTER IX

SHEET-METAL WORK

IT is a characteristic feature of Ford practice that if there is anything to be done, it must be done in the quickest and easiest way consistent with good work. Even in the smallest details this most important underlying common-sense principle of true efficiency is found.

It was not until the beginning of 1914 that the Ford engineers became fully aware of the very great saving in labor cost which could be had by the avoidance of shop-floor transportation of parts in the process of finishing, but at the time of this writing, February 1, 1915, the importance of short lines of work in progress and in travel, and of starting the travel at the best place, and delivering it at the best place, is fully comprehended.

No end of thought has been given to the placing of all tools or appliances in the best possible position. Instead of putting a battery of presses, or washing machines, or drying ovens by themselves, and carrying the work in progress to them, it has been found that the working time for the full process can be very materially reduced by grouping all the machines, tanks, drying ovens, tables, and trays into as small a space as possible consistent with the necessary "elbow room."

Even such a detail as "cleaning stock" has not been treated with the usual superficial "lick and promise" process found in other shops, but special machines have been devised which will perform this work well and quickly.

For instance, a very good example of the completeness and value of such grouping is to be found in the Ford running-board manufacturing process.

Placed just to the east of the main crane-way in the general machine shop, where the sheet-steel stock can be easily delivered, this department occupies a space of approximately 1,200 square feet.

How the Ford Metal Running Boards Are Made

The steel is delivered in rectangular blanks of the required size, and is first passed through the cleaning machine seen in the foreground below. An endless-chain conveyor in the table carries the stock under a wire brush which cleans the surface thoroughly and prepares it for rolling. As it comes out on the other side, it is transferred to a nipping press, where the two entering corners are clipped off, passing

Special Ford Design Steel Stock-Cleaning Machine Equipped with Revolving Wire Brush and Endless-Chain Conveyor

thereafter through six sets of rollers which emboss two parallel beads on the surface, turn up the edges, and flatten the metal against itself in such a way as to form a strong rectangular reinforcement along the edges.

During this process the metal and rollers are constantly flooded with soda water, which is pumped up and over the work by a centrifugal pump driven from the main motor shaft above.

The rolling machine just described stands at right angles to and about four feet to the west of a large drawing press, which performs with one stroke the next two operations, those of embossing the surface and perforating eight holes in the body of the running board. The trade mark name "Ford" is carried in the central part of this embossing die.

Rolling the Ford Running Board

At the left of the upper picture is shown the large press in which the final finishing and embossing operation is performed. The lower picture shows the other side of the large press, and the entrance to the Blakeslee self-feed automatic washing machine

Clipping Off the Corners of the Running Board Blank Preparatory to Feeding It into the Rolls

So close are the rollers to this press that the workman who handles the job needs only to turn slightly from one to the other.

A metal table set in the space directly in front of the rollers receives the work waist high, so that there is no necessity for stooping or taking any unnecessary steps.

Immediately after the drawing operation, another man, standing on the opposite side of the press, withdraws the board and inserts it into the north end of a self-feed automatic washing machine, equipped with an endless-chain conveyor which carries it through boiling water and steam, thoroughly cleaning it and heating it so that it is practically dry when it reaches the other end of its 25-foot travel.

Approximately two minutes are required for the board to go through the rollers, press, and washer.

It is then taken out, stacked up, and allowed to dry on a rack. It is now ready for enameling. Here again, Ford efficiency is evident.

Instead of carrying the metal to an enameling oven, the "mountain comes to Mahomet." The first drying oven is only the length of a running board away, so that by tilting the board up slightly it is within the reach of another man standing in front of the enameling tank.

This man stacks the boards on end in the tank, inserts a special handle in one of the perforated holes, and passes it over to another man who completely immerses the board in the enameling liquid, and immediately after hangs it to dry on a cross rod of a double traveling-chain traversing a draining room set parallel to the washing machine.

It takes approximately 45 minutes to complete its journey through this draining and drying enclosure. Twenty-four boards are hung on each cross bar. Placed at the north end of this drying box, and setting at right angles to it, is one of the new vertical Ford japanning ovens, equipped with a patented enclosed-flame burner. As will be seen in the illustration, the desired baking travel is secured, a great saving of floor space effected, by the introduction of this new style oven. So practical and so efficient have these ovens been found, that they are rapidly displacing the old types throughout the Ford factory.

Only one man is required to transfer the running boards from the

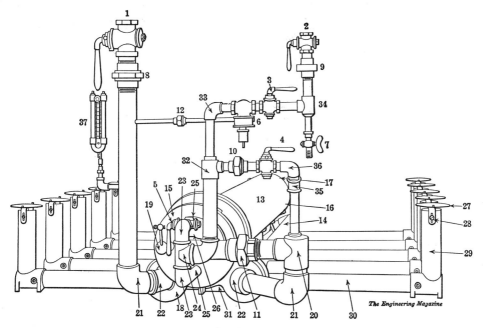

Gas Burner for Japanning Ovens

Made by Oven Equipment & Mfg. Co. Parts of burner: 1, main air cock; 2, main gas cock; 3, gas-control cock; 4, air-control cock; 5, upper burner gas shut-off cock; 6, automatic cut-off valve for gas; 7, lighter cock; 8, main air union; 9, main gas union; 10, air-mixture union; 11, lower main air union; 12, automatic valve air union; 13, generator pipe; 14, side air pipe and back connection; 15, front head; 16, back head; 17, cap screws; 18, generator and air-pipe collar; 19, peep-hole cover; 20, main air reducing tee; 21, main air ell; 22, main air 45 degrees ell; 23, gas-burner ells; 24, gas-burner tee; 25, gas-burner pipes; 26, internal air pipe; 27, air cap and bolts; 28, air-cap lugs and screws; 29, lateral ells (short ells now being used); 30, lateral heat-distribution pipes; 31, generator support and heat-distributing tees; 32, mixture tee; 33, main gas-supply ell; 34, gas-supply, lighter cock tee; 35, air-mixture 45 degrees ell; 36, air-mixture ell; 37, air-pressure gauge and connections to main air pipe

dripping and drying enclosure to an upward-moving endless-chain conveyor traversing the baking oven. Twenty-four minutes after, they are extracted by a man on the other side entirely finished, ready for transportation to the third floor, where the step bolts and under blocks are added.

Thus it will be seen that what might be a long, tedious process has been condensed into a compact, continuous, efficient process, requiring

The Enameling Tank, Drying Enclosure and Vertical Enameling Oven

Attention is called to the manner in which the hook handles, which are used for hanging the running boards on the conveyor in the draining and baking ovens, are returned to their initial position ready for use again. The enameling tank is here shown covered. When this department is in operation, this cover is pulled up out of the way

the services of only a total of eleven men, including a foreman, a sub-foreman, and nine workmen to complete 2,500 pieces every eight hours. Such is Ford efficiency.

THE FRONT-FENDER JOB

The Ford front fender is made up of seven parts—the peak, the body, the apron, the ribbon, two pieces of wire, and the fender bracket.

MAKING THE FENDER PEAK

Starting with steel which is really scrap from the fender body operation, operator No. 1 blocks out the general form of the fender peak, "V"-ing one edge ready for the wiring operation performed later. This work is done at one stroke in an ordinary punch press, and presents no unusual features.

A waist-high pedestal tray at the workman's left hand receives these blanks, from which they are taken by a second man who performs the second operation, that of turning up one side and bending down the other. Operator No. 3 in turn removes them from a similar tray and by inserting them into another press bends the wiring edges still further around.

They are now ready for wiring. This is done in a special Ford wire-rolling machine. The peak is then delivered to another press where the wiring edge is bent over so as to form a shoulder, and another insertion in a similar press flattens this edge and finishes the peak, after which it, along with other stamped parts, is thrown upon the belt conveyor running in an easterly direction between the presses. From this it is picked off by a sorter at the proper point, piled in rows, and conveyed to the fourth floor, where the final assembly of front fenders is effected.

Section of Fender Ribbon Produced by the Ribbon-Rolling Machine

This department employs seven men and has a capacity of 2,500 fenders every eight hours. Shifts work from 7 a. m. to 3.30 p. m., and from 3.40 p. m. to 12.10 a. m.

THE FENDER RIBBON

Starting as a ribbon of steel, from a coil at the end of a ribbon roller, the metal composing the fender ribbon passes through six sets of rollers, which in one continuous operation form it into its finished shape, as shown by the section illustrated.

By means of an automatic stop of special Ford design, co-acting with a punch press, this steel is cut off in required lengths and deposited in a metal box from which it is picked out and placed on hand trucks for transportation to the Ford ribbon-bending machine, which sets just to the west of the ribbon roller. This ribbon-rolling machine is made to take two ribbons at once, and by the use of two punch presses one set can be cut for the front fender and one for the rear.

The manner in which the ribbon is rolled into shape is unique.

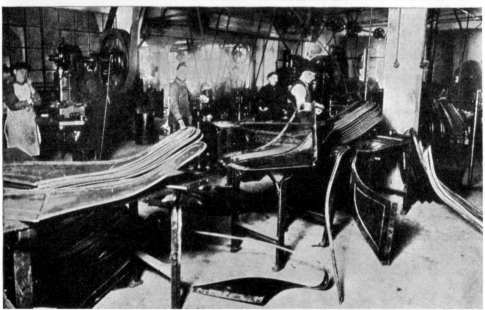

Two Views of the Ford Fender Department

The upper one is taken looking toward the fender department from a position in front of the fender-ribbon-bending machine. Note in the foreground the special rolls used for crimping and wiring the edges of the fender apron. Just beyond, with their backs toward the camera, are two workmen operating the welders for fastening the peak and apron and peak and ribbon together

The lower view shows the other side of the fender department. The large press at the left will be recognized as the same one shown on the right of the upper picture. In the foreground, on the floor, and leaning up against the bench, will be seen two views of the ribbon, peak and apron. On the bench at the left is a finished fender body, while on the one in the center, directly in front of the welder, is an unfinished job showing the apron partially tacked to the body ready for treading

258

Showing One End of the Ribbon-Rolling Machine

The Other End of the Ribbon-Rolling Machine, Showing Cutting-Off Punches

Here again Ford ingenuity asserts itself. Not satisfied with the old tin-shop methods of hand-shaping, Ford engineers have devised a very clever and ingenious combination of rollers and levers, which accomplish the required result quickly and simply.

As will be seen from the photograph, the metal is fed into two sets of two pairs, right and left. The operator, by throwing up two cam-operating levers, pulls down two through-bolts which grip the metal tightly. By moving the large lever, he brings the eccentric-mounted top

The Ribbon-Bending Machine

The rolls carried on the large "U" lever have just started on their downward course

rollers down into position against the metal. The power is then turned on and the top roller, which is carried on a U-shaped lever and compelled to follow a circle whose radius is the width of the ribbon greater than the foundation segment beneath, bends the metal in accordance with the required form. By limiting the travel under this roller-carrying arm, or altering the position of the guide stops, the machine can, of course, be made to put this bend in any portion of the ribbon desired. A machine of like construction is therefore used for the rear-fender ribbon, which owing to its slightly different shape requires a different bend.

These two machines practically do all the work and but two men are needed in this department, one for tending the ribbon-rolling machine, the other for operating the bending machine.

Die Used for Blanking and Notching Operation

Operation No. 1, front fender body. Weight of punch about 3,700 lb., of die about 5,300 lb. All punch and die sections, guide pins and guide-pin bushings are of tool steel, hardened and ground

Special Ford-Designed Bracket Die for Bliss Press

A clever arrangement by which an extension bracket die is made to produce a double-action effect, saving one press hand

The ribbon-rolling machine has a capacity of 36 feet per minute, and occupied a floor space of 1,405 square feet, including storage racks. The bending machine will handle two sets of right and left ribbon at each operation, and has a capacity of 2,800 pieces per 8-hour day.

Only a small amount of space in the so-called bridge between the new and old buildings is occupied by these two machines, and because they are only slightly removed from the fender assembly, the product can be quickly delivered where needed.

The Front Fender Body

The blanks for the front fender body are cut and notched on one of the large presses in the general machine shop, and afterwards carried to the fender department on the fourth floor, where they are placed in piles on the floor at the left of the workman who operates a press on which the next two operations are performed. The first forms a bead following the outline of the piece, turns up the edges, and perforates five holes. As soon as this operation has been completed the workman standing on the opposite side inserts the end of the fender body under an extension arm press shown in illustration, which noses up the fender at the next stroke of the press.

Photograph Showing Three Successive Operations on the Fender Apron

The manner in which the part is handled, and the effect produced, are clearly shown in the photograph.

The third workman now takes the fender off the table and trucks it to the fender assembly room. Here two pieces are spot-welded on the surface, one as a reinforcement for the running board, the other to strengthen the metal around the holes cut for the bracket rivets. These two spot welders are mounted on the same bench and are so close together that the work can be passed from one man to another without any stooping or moving from their working position.

A table at the right hand of the last welder holds the work until it is picked up by the operator of a press, which breaks the edges down and folds them against the main body of the metal. At this man's right hand is a table, knee-high, on which he, in turn, deposits the part. It is then picked up and put through rolls which crimp the edge ready to join with parts of the fender. This last operation, called edging, also forms the fender body to shape.

It is now ready to take its part in the assembly operation.

THE FENDER APRON

Like the fender body, the metal for the fender apron is first blanked to shape on a regulation draw press in the main machine shop, put through a second press which turns up one edge and another down, and embosses a triangular reinforcement bead following the outline of the piece edge.

It is then carried to the first set of rollers in the fender-assembly room, where the edges are put through a special set of rollers which prepare them for wiring, which is done on two rolling machines.

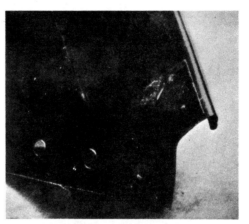

The next operation breaks the edge for attachment to the body. Progress through another set of rolls finishes this operation, putting on a shoulder by bending the metal until it is practically at right angles to the face. A reinforcement plate is next spot-welded to the lower end, after which the part is put on a high table at the left of

The spot-Welded Reinforcement on One Corner of the Fender Apron

a welder, who feeds it right into a press which "breaks down" the edge into proper shape for fitting to the body.

This part is then ready for assembly.

THE FENDER BRACKET

The fender bracket is made in three operations. The first blanks it out and perforates it; the second, which is a forming operation over a special die, draws the central projecting section; the third perforates the rivet holes.

How THE FRONT FENDER IS ASSEMBLED

The fender ribbon, the fender peak, and fender apron are now brought together. The ribbon is electrically welded to the peak and thrown on to a vertical frame, from which it is taken off by a workman who spot-welds the apron on the other side of the peak.

The next operation is characterized as "tacking the apron to the body," and is done on a bench by hand. With the aid of two plyers and a hammer, a small portion of the edges of the fender body and apron are united. The work is then seized by another workman who runs the work through a compressing roller which "treads down" the joints, firmly uniting the body, ribbon, peak, and apron. The fender is then dropped to the floor and shoved along to a man operating a hand breaking machine on a long bench nearby. Here the running-board end of the fender is "broken," that is bent at the necessary angle for attachment to the running board.

Working directly opposite on the same bench are a number of men, who with mallet, hammer, and templet tighten up the joints, and with

a hammer bend the apron and body to shape and draw up the job to required templet form.

Upon being adjudged satisfactorily formed, it is next deposited on a belt conveyor, passing between two men who count the fenders as they go by, and is taken off at the end and piled on a table ready for the addition of the bracket which goes underneath.

The Fourth and Sixth Operations Showing How the Fender Edge is "Broken Down"

This operation is performed by three men. The first man puts in the three rivets; the second fits the bracket and rivet-retainer clamping jig, shoving the work across the table to a man operating a riveter which finishes the job.

The work is delivered on the left to a knee-high table from which it is transferred by another man, after sanding and cleaning, to a truck. It is now ready to be taken to the glass-enclosed enameling room, which is only a few feet away. Here it is dipped and hung on an endless moving chain which carries it through a baking oven, dipped again, hung on the same conveyor, and finally delivered in a finished condition at the other end, ready for crating or assembly.

An example has been made of the front fender because in its manufacture a number of ingenious machines have been used, which have very materially simplified the work and improved the character of this hard-to-make, irregular product. Bent or formed sheet-metal work is difficult to do, and frequently required many makeshifts and hand operations to bring it to its final finished shape. The attention of the reader

Still Another View of the Fender Department

This photograph was taken still farther to the left and shows the treading rollers, the finishing bench, and the endless belt conveyor, which carries the fender back to the end of the room where the brackets are riveted on. At the extreme right may be seen the white walls of the enameling room

is therefore called to the absence of hand operations and the manner in which power-driven machines have been substituted for clumsy hand methods. The special ribbon-rolling machine, the bending machine, the manner in which the parts are wired, the joining in the final assembly, all show clearly the enormous amount of time and money that have been spent by the Ford Motor Company in solving these problems. They have standardized the product so that they are able not only to control the accuracy of all the operations, thereby making fenders which are absolutely interchangeable, but they have made the process continuous and therefore easily controlled.

The placing of spot welders, rolling machines, power presses, and hand hammering benches at the proper places in the process line, have so cut down the time required that they are able to produce, under normal conditions, more than 2,500 front fenders per day, or 50 fenders to a man, a most unusual showing when the difficult character of the work is considered.

Three Interesting Drawn Jobs

Although there are innumerable interesting metal-forming jobs performed in the Ford factory, which would no doubt prove interesting to the readers of the literature of metal working space, limitations have

Blanking Operation of the Steering-Column Flange

led me to confine myself to three rather unusual ones, namely, the forming of the steering-gear quadrant, the steering-gear column flange, and the fan-belt pulley.

THE STEERING-GEAR QUADRANT

The steering-gear quadrant is that piece of metal which will be found fastened to the steering post just under the steering wheel, the part upon which the throttle and spark levers rest.

As will be seen in the picture on page 268 it is of irregular outline, containing three holes. The manner in which this interesting part is formed is as follows:

After shearing the stock to size, it is put into a D. A. G. press, which in one operation blanks and draws the metal into rough shape. It is then transferred to another press which draws the projection still deeper, pulling the sides in. On the third draw the general form is finished, and the bottom perforated. It is next trimmed outside on another press, after which the two slots are perforated.

The burrs are then ground off and the face polished on a rag wheel dressed with emery, after which the teeth are embossed by the stroke of another press.

This last operation also turns up the two projections on each side of the quadrant and gives the piece its final form, after which it is ready for conveyance to the steering-gear department, where it is plated and brazed onto the column.

As now manufactured in the Ford machine shop, this part requires two operations for blanking and drawing, but it is expected in the very near future these two operations will be combined so that one stroke of the press will do the work. The total time required to finish the product is five minutes.

Steering-Gear Column Flange

On account of the second operation, where the metal is really turned inside out, the steering-gear column flange presents an excellent example of unusual steel-drawing practice.

How This Piece Is Made

The first operation is a combination blanking and drawing operation. It leaves the piece in a shape shown on the next page. The second draw, which is known as the inside cut, is performed on the other side of the metal and draws the steel cup inside out. The next process gives

Second Drawing Operation on Steering-Column Flange

Photograph Showing Successive Changes in Form of Steering Column Flange
Note that between picture two and three the metal is turned inside out

this projection an oval shape drawing it out still farther. The next forms it and punches out the bottom, after which the outside is drilled and the bolt holes are perforated on another large press.

A good understanding of the successive operations may be gained by careful examination of the accompanying photographs.

The Fan-Belt Pulley

This job is perhaps one of the most interesting drawn pieces which has so far been made in the Ford factory, and for that reason its manufacture will be described in detail.

The Ford Steering Quadrant
Finished shape

Starting on a large press, in the general machine shop, the stock is first put through a combination operation of blanking and drawing. It is then transferred to a tray at the right hand of another press operator, who submits it to a second draw. He, in turn, passes it on to another who draws it farther. At the fourth operation it is given its final draw and the center perforated.

It is now ready for annealing. This is not considered a separate operation, because the same man who operates the press which performs the fourth operation also does the annealing. A small annealing furnace placed just at his left hand makes this possible.

After passing through the annealing furnace, the part drops out into a metal barrel. As soon as it has cooled sufficiently, it is put through a press which turns up the metal around the edge, forming the face of the pulley.

The job is now flattened and half crowned, and turned over to a

Forming and Perforating the Steering-Column Flange

Final Forming and Trimming Operation, Steering-Column Flange

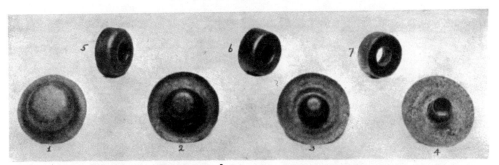

Seven Successive Stages in the Production of the Fan-Belt Pulley

screw-machine operator, who trims it up. This screw machine is so near the presses that there is no trucking whatever required.

The hub is next seized and the crown finished on another press, after which the inside diameter is reamed to size and the holes drilled out on two spindle drills mounted on a special double-headed lathe of Ford design. After drilling, the holes are burred on a drill press near by, and the job is finished.

All this work takes place in an inconceivably small space. The presses, annealing furnace, screw machine, lathe and drill presses are so close together that one can hardly squeeze between, yet each workman seems to have sufficient room to do his part easily and well.

Furthermore, the job is delivered in its finished condition at a point where it can be tossed onto the endless-chain conveyor, so that no trucking is necessary and the men are never disturbed by the moving of trays, barrels, or trucking racks.

What at first glance seems to be a confused mass of machinery, placed without any underlying plan, really reveals itself, upon careful examination, as a wonderful instance of common-sense arrangement, finally arrived at after a painstaking study of operations, handling, and delivery.

It is such a thing as this that mirrors best the mechanical genius and co-operative organization that have made the Ford Motor Company what it is today—unquestionably the marvel of the metal-working world; an institution where brain and brawn have been successfully harmonized in the solution of one of the greatest problems of modern civilization; "individualized transportation" at low cost—the Ford automobile.

Chapter X

CONVEYORS, WORK SLIDES AND ROLL-WAYS

EVERY square foot of every workshop carries a certain and inevitable overhead charge, and is hence a debtor to the plant. The only possible way in which any square foot of any factory floor-surface can be made to pay its existence debt to the plant at large, is to make this square foot of floor surface support a profit-earning load.

There must be shop-floor lines of travel which cannot be infringed upon by direct-profit-earning agencies, there must be floor-spaces which support rough stores only, other floor-surfaces which carry finished components only, and in the great majority of industrial exploitations there must be floor areas of considerable extent which carry merchantable finished product only, this merchantable product being subject to certain fixed charges for every day of its housing before it finds a purchaser.

This last form of unproductive floor-load is almost wholly avoided at the Ford Motor Company's Highland Park plant, where 90 per cent of the entire production is loaded into railway cars and shipped to cash purchasers as fast as completed, and the only finished-product stores space is the open surface of John R. Street.

Otherwise, the Ford shops are subjected to the previously specified indirectly-productive floor-space over-charges, which cannot be escaped by any manufactory whatever.

But there is another and hitherto unmentioned occupation of factory floor-space, which may be relatively large or small in direct proportion to the intelligence, ingenuity, and resourcefulness of the factory manager —that of shop-floor occupancy by components in process of finishing. This particular form of indirectly profit-earning factory-floor-space occupancy is commonly regarded by factory managers as an inevitable and unrelievable source of added overhead costs of factory product, and one which must certainly be augmented as the factory production is increased.

An increase of total production for a given time must bring more components in process of finishing into the factory; these components in progress must have floor-space to rest upon because they certainly cannot be suspended in the atmosphere between successive operations; there is no place for work in progress support save the factory floor; and consequently, since the ultimate limiting factor of production must always be the floor area available for the placing of direct-production agencies—the workmen and the benches and tools used by the workers— any increase in factory production per day must always result in decrease of factory·maximum-production limit. That is to say, the more work in progress, the less the floor-space available for doing the work.

Perhaps not one factory economist in a thousand will find any fallacy in the foregoing summary of factory-floor unavoidable occupancy by components in process of finishing; yet it does contain an error, so glaringly obvious as soon as it is pointed out as to make it seem impossible that even the most conservative of factory managers could fail to perceive it instantly, to recognize its economic significance, to bear this significance constantly in mind, and to exert all his mental powers to avoid limiting his maximum-production possibilities by needless placing of non-paying loads upon his factory floor-space.

The error mentioned lies in the assumption that components in progress of finishing cannot be carried in the air between factory operations, but must, of necessity, be supported on the shop floor.

The enormous increase in the Ford-car demand very early forced the Ford factory management to place workmen and machine tools as closely together as possible on the floor; but it was not until the beginning of 1914 that it was found that, in some special instances, the convenience of the workmen could be served by the installation of gravity work-slides, usually inclined sheet-iron troughs, so placed that the workman upon completion of his own operation could drop the component into a trough, so inclined as to carry the piece by gravity to within the easy reach of the workman who was to perform the next succeeding operation on the component, instead of dropping the partly finished piece into a box or can and having this box or can carried, pulled, or pushed by a laborer to the next workman, and thus become an occupier of non-paying floor-space—with the transporting laborer's time added to floor-space overhead charges, to increase needlessly the finishing costs.

It was at once discovered that not only were the production labor costs greatly reduced by work-slide installation, but that the floor was cleaned up, making room for more tools and workmen where it was thought the limit of close placing of productive agencies had previously been reached.

Perception of these facts brought instant activities of the Ford engineers to the front in the endeavor to reduce production costs by gravity slides, endless belts, endless chains, gravity roll-ways, and overhead carriers, each one of which as soon as installed produced unbe-

Two Lathes and Power Press for Finishing Large Thrust Washers of Babbitt Metal

At left, inspector and two lathe hands. The lathe hands face each other, and the tail-stock ends of the lathes are set close to the power press. The lathe hands take washers as they come down the slides, with outside and inside edges finished, from the press, face the slides and cut a spiral groove in each side, and then drop the finished piece into the short slide marked 4, seen between the lathe men. The washers slide to the end next the inspector, who stacks them on his table for inspection

lievable labor-cost reductions, so that, at the date of this writing, October 6, 1914, these means of transporting components in process of finishing through the air instead of on the floor, are the most surprising feature of the Ford shops interiors.

Broadly speaking, it is safe to say that anything in the way of a work conveyor which keeps work in progress off the shop floor, will be found to effect a large saving in direct-labor costs, and to increase the factory maximum-production capacity.

LABOR-COST REDUCTIONS GAINED BY GRAVITY WORK-SLIDE INSTALLATION

Surprising labor-cost reductions invariably follow the placing of work-slides, although the first gravity slides were installed merely with a view to the advantages gained in the way of transportation of components in process of finishing from one operation location to the next; but, as before mentioned, it was at once made plainly apparent that gravity work-slides vastly increased each worker's efficiency. In every instance of work-slide placing there was a gain of from 30 to 100 per cent in the production volume, with the same methods, machines, small tools, and men; seemingly nothing done to decrease labor costs, yet large savings shown immediately.

The labor savings were due, as is now fully understood in the Ford shops, to giving the workman a fixed place of reception for work leaving his hand, and a fixed point within his easy reach where he could pick up the next piece, thus avoiding thought, delay, and fatigue of the workman caused by breaking into the volition routine of his movements.

Same Job and Tools as shown on page 273, Different Workmen

Showing work slides from press to left hand lathe on page 273, and inclined slide for finished work between the two lathe hands. The sheet iron trough slides are same for each lathe. Slide 1 delivers to slide 2, which opens to tray 3. Finished work-slide between the two lathe hands is marked "4." Press hand not visible

Piston Gravity Slide from Four Drilling Machines to Piston, Pin, and Connecting Rod Assemblers

The four machines are retained for emergency use, but three men now ream as much work as formerly required four, and the work of two truckers is also saved. 4,000 pistons with bushes, total weight about 12,250 pounds, come to this reaming station in cans holding 112 pistons each, every 8-hour day

Where a workman can perform absolutely similar successions of movement, he very soon gains great skill combined with great rapidity of muscular action; but if the routine of the workman's movements is broken, he must inevitably call his brain into action to find the best means of bridging his troubles, and must lose some time in devising and executing his unusual line of procedure.   All of this seems too obvious to demand detailed specification, but it is certain that in very many factory operations great time losses are the rule rather than the exception, while it is also certain that a very large part of these time losses can be avoided by the placing of work-handling conveniences of insignificant cost.

These conveniences fall into the following classes, which will be shown and described in the order of mentioning:

1. Gravity work-slides.
2. Gravity roll-ways.
3. Slides on which work in progress is moved by hand.
4. Endless belts, power-driven.
5. Endless chains, power-driven.

My attention was first drawn to the labor-saving powers of gravity work-slides by the example shown on pages 273 and 274, front and side views of a group of three power-driven machines, a press and two engine lathes, employed in finishing a babbitt friction washer, now obsolete. The machines were placed as closely as possible—so closely that the work-slides placing seemed an absurdity. The three workmen, one press hand and two lathe hands, stood close together; the washers (babbitt-metal castings) were first passed through a die working against a spring plunger die and ejector in the bolster, this operation finishing the washer hole and the washer circumference, and leaving the washer about $3^3/_4$ inches outside diameter, hole $2^1/_4$ inches, and were then faced in the two lathes to about $^3/_{16}$ inch thickness and had spiral oil grooves cut in their sides.

Before the work-slides were placed, the regular production for the three workmen and three machines was 800 washers per 8-hour day; this rose to 1,100 washers per 8-hour day—or $37^1/_2$ per cent increase—as soon as the work-slides were used.

On page 275 are shown gravity slides which take the pistons from four drillers on which four men ream the piston-pin holes in about 4,000 pistons per 8-hour day, doing away with two truck men.

Many more gravity work-slides might be shown, as these transportation facilities appear in every direction in the Ford shops, but one or two examples are enough to direct the attention of the intelligent and aggressive shop manager to these cost-reducing agencies, since every installation of this character is a job by itself and copying is not feasible. It is enough to say that the best placing of any gravity work-slide must be preceded by a careful motion study of the movements of the workmen who are to make use of it, that most men are wiser after the fact than before it, and that no competent workshop official will hesitate to change his own work if he thinks he sees a way to better it.

GRAVITY ROLL-WAYS

Gravity-operated roll-ways for moving components having finished circular outlines are very much used in the Ford shops, and have the very desirable feature of moving work with but little roll-way inclination. Work-slides in general—mere sheet-iron troughs which do not fit the individual pieces which they are called upon to move—must have considerable "slant"; but a roll-way which is fitted to carry a certain finished piece can be built up from rough angle-iron bars so that the work will travel surely with only a very small drop of the delivery end below the level of the receiving end.   An example of such a construction, used for transportation of a flanged sleeve, is shown on this page, end view, showing how two widths of angle bars are combined with a sheet-iron bottom to produce a roll-way to fit.

Three illustrations of a roll-way for handling the Ford Model-T fly-wheel are here shown, with particulars of savings gained.   The Ford fly-wheel is a comparatively large and heavy component and has a large number of holes drilled and tapped in it to take the fly-wheel magneto.

THE FORD FLY-WHEEL FINISHING LINE OF TOOLS

Weight of Ford Model-T motor fly-wheels, T-701, gray iron: rough, 41 pounds; finished, 35 pounds. Finished by 16 operations.

See pages 278, 279, 280.   The general specifications of the Ford fly-wheel, T-701, finishing, here follow, with three illustrations of the roll-way which reduced the fly-wheel finishing time from 31 minutes to less than 20 minutes.

The 16 finishing operations on the fly-wheel and the machine tools used in performing them, were as follows:

Example of a Roll-Way for a 2-Diameter Component

Operation 1.   Rough-turn, finish-turn, face engine side complete, ream two diameters, and finish.   Machine tools used are Potter and Johnson automatics.

Operation 2.   Face transmission side, on Reed-Prentice lathe.

Operation 3.   Face transmission side of hub on Reed-Prentice lathe.

Operation 4.   Drill six holes on Foote-Burt, one-spindle driller with Foote-Burt spindle head, to drill six holes at same time.

Operation 5.   Ream two .436 holes on Cincinnati drill press, one spindle, with Ford head to ream both holes same time.

Operation 6.   Counterbore three .6755 to $5/16$ inch, on Foote-Burt, three-spindle head; counterbore three holes at once.

Operation 7. Drill three $^{41}/_{64}$-inch holes on Foote-Burt, same as operation 6.

Operation 8. Ream three .6755 holes on Foote-Burt, same as operations 6 and 7.

Operation 9. Drill sixteen $^{21}/_{64}$-inch holes for $^3/_8$-inch diameter, 24 per inch tap, on special Foote-Burt; drill sixteen holes at once.

Operation 10. Drill sixteen No. 6 holes, for 14 tap, 24 per inch, on same as operation 9.

Operation 11. Counterbore sixteen holes, $^1/_4$-inch diameter, on same as operations 9 and 10.

Operation 12. Counterbore sixteen holes, $^3/_8$-inch diameter, on same machine as operations 9, 10 and 11.

Middle Section of Fly-Wheel Roll-Way
Piping uprights and steel-channel and angle-bar construction

Operation 13. Tap sixteen holes at same time, $^3/_8$-inch, 24 per inch, on special Foote-Burt tapping machine.

Operation 14. Tap sixteen holes, 14, 24 per inch, on Foote-Burt machine, same as operation 13.

Operation 15. Tap four holes, $^7/_{16}$-inch diameter, 20 per inch, on Cincinnati single-spindle driller with Ford four-spindle head to tap all four holes at once.

Operation 16. Balance on Rockford Tool Company's balancing machine.

This fly-wheel finishing line is 120 feet long, and includes 27 separate machine tools. The roll-way covers full length of the line, but is in three sections; first, north to south, page 279; middle one, page 278; south section, page 280. Number of men when full-handed, eighteen; some men attend more than one machine. Before placing the roll-ways the best one 9-hour day production was 350 fly-wheels, with two truckers, 20 men, total, on the fly-wheel job. With roll-ways, the production was 460 per 8-hour day, with no truckers, floor cleaned up.

Before the roll-way placing two truckers were kept busy in transferring the fly-wheels in process of finishing from one machine to another and piling them adjacent to the next operation machine, never in the best place for the workman's convenience.

North End of Fly-Wheel Roll-Way
Showing the commercial bar steel construction

The tools were closely placed and the piles of fly-wheels at each machine and the constant journeys of the two truckers made the fly-wheel job a place to avoid if possible. Worst of all, the straw boss could never nail, with certainty, the man who was shirking, because of the many work-piles and general confusion due to the shop floor transportation.

As soon as the roll-ways were placed the truckers were called off, the floor was cleared, and all the straw boss had to do to locate the shirk or operation tools in fault, was to glance along the line and see where the roll-way was filled up. As more than once before said in these chapters, mechanical transit of work in progress evens up the job, and forces everybody to adopt the pace of the fastest worker in the gang, and the roll-way had the expected effect of reducing the labor-costs by better than 33⅓ per cent.

SLIDES ON WHICH WORK IN PROGRESS IS MOVED BY HAND

Placing work in progress on a slide-way and moving components along by hand as they are placed on the slide-way after an operation completion has the same effect on pace as that obtained by the moving assembly and the gravity roll-way. All the boss has to do to spot the slow man infallibly is to seek the forward end of the congestion of units in transit. This invariably results in increased labor-hour-production, besides cleaning up the shop floor and dispensing with the trucking labor.

South End of Fly-Wheel Roll-Way
Same construction as middle part, page 278

Page 281 shows the hand-moved slide-way for supporting the aluminum-casting transmission covers, T-826, between successive milling, drilling, reaming, and tapping operations. About 1,200 pieces are handled per 8-hour day, 20 operations on each piece, 33 workmen, single shift. The tools used are one Ford Company's design special milling machine with two horizontal working spindles, one Ford Company milling fixture applied to a Cincinnati driller; twelve Cincinnati drilling machines, of which two are fitted with special Ford tapping fixtures; and four Foote-Burt special machines, two of which are fitted to drill holes in three directions, while the two others are fitted to drill holes in four directions, simultaneously.

This was one of the first slide-ways to be installed in the Ford shops, and it has now been in use about one year. Previous to the use of this slide-way, 594-hours work finished 1,000 covers. Now, with no change in machines nor small tools, but with the slide-way, 264 labor hours produce 1,200 finished covers, thus more than doubling the labor-hour production, with no change in tools, method, or class of labor employed.

Transmission Cover Slide-Way. Early Construction, Built Up of Steel Tubes and Regular Fittings

Work-ways constructed of pipe and fittings have proven objectionable because, in case of changes, the pipe, cut into short pieces, remains on hand as unusable scrap. The latest construction uses gray iron uprights and angle bar steel. In case of change the uprights can go back to the cupola, and the steel bars can go back to the rack with a good prospect of speedy re-employment

This slide-way is a steel-tube construction, as were all of the early Ford shop slide-ways. The pipe construction is now abandoned in favor of gray iron supporting members and steel angle-bar sliding-ways.

Endless-Belt Conveyors

Four examples of endless-belt work conveyors are here given, with illustrations, one from the radiator job, one from the fender job, and one from the sheet-steel-working department, which takes the work from two long lines of power presses, set back to back, so that the punchings drop from the press work-slides onto this big belt and are all carried to one end, where three pickers-off and sorters place similar pieces together in receptacles for transportation to points of storage or assembling.

The fourth example of endless-belt transportation is from the motor-assembling department, and shows an overhead endless-belt carrier, close up to the roof beams, which takes components finished on the fourth floor, and transfers them through long gravity slides, to the two widely separated lines of motor assemblers, delivering components to

Radiator Job.   Three Endless Belts, Two at Right Angles to the One Shown
Belt 18 inches wide, speed 33 feet per minute. Saves work of two men with trucks

one line or the other as governed by a switch overhead, the switch being changed on signal from assembling line.

This page shows one of three belts in the radiator department, working together and placed at right angles to each other, to take assemblies made ready for soldering from a bench line of assemblers and carry them a considerable distance and then automatically transfer the assemblies to another belt at right angles, which carries them under a solderer's bench.

The belt used is sewed canvas, the same as in all the other belt-conveyor installations shown in this story. The Ford Company has purchased these canvas conveyor belts from Hethick Bros., Toledo,

Ohio, the Sawyer Belting Company, Cleveland, Ohio, and from the Gandy Company.

This page shows the mud-guard department, ten gangs of men, one gang for each one of ten "closing-down" machines, supplied by H. Collier Smith, "quick-work" sheet-metal tools, Detroit; about nine men in each gang are placed at right angles to the belt; mud-guard assembling begins at the far end, and is finished when the mud-guard reaches the belt; the last operation man lays the fender on the belt to be carried away from the job. This belt makes a direct saving of two truckers,

Horizontal Conveyor Belt Used in the Mud-Guard Department to Carry Away Completed Work

and a very considerable indirect saving by moving the fenders as soon as they are ready to move, and so keeping the floor cleaned up and the whole job in tidy shape.

Page 284 an illustration from the motor-assembling floor, and shows two gravity chutes for conveying brake bands supplied by an endless belt placed on the roof beams. The brake bands are made on the fourth floor and are dropped down chutes to the endless belt, 192 feet long, which carries the brake-bands to a switch, overhead, midway between the two lines of motor assemblers. The switch is placed by signal from the assembling lines. This belt saves one trucker, and gives far better service, besides keeping the brake bands off the floor while in transit.

The illustration on page 286 is taken in the pressed-steel department, and shows a belt placed between two lines of power presses, set back to back, to receive both work and scrap.

Work-slides from presses to belt convey all the press product to the belt as fast as it drops from the dies, and the scrap is also placed on the belt. The belt is 192 feet long, 30 inches wide, speed 80 feet per minute. Two men handle scrap, and three men sort the multiform products into receptacles at the end of the line. This belt receives the product of sixty-five presses; it was installed in December, 1913, and saves the labor of about fourteen men. Former practice was to take the press product away in barrels, by truck men, to the craneway, where the barrels were piled, to be taken out of the pile and work handled into cans and trays to go to assemblers. Scrap was collected by laborers, and piled on trucks for disposal.

Brake-Band Chute

3,000 bands used per 8-hour day. Saving of $5.00 over former hand truck delivery. Installed, August, 1914. Transmission and magneto assembly chutes are seen at middle right.

Endless-Chain Elevators and Carriers

A great number of endless-chain carriers are used in the Ford shops, some for driving assembling lines and some for elevating and carrying.

Only one example is here illustrated and described, that of the transmission and magneto assembly transfer from the finish end of the magneto assembling line to the two motor-assembling lines.

Transmission and Magneto Assembling Line

Each assembly weighs 98 lbs., 1,000 are handled per 8-hour day, 98,000 lbs., total weight. See text, below on this page

and magneto assemblies to either one of the two motor-assembling lines, according to bell signals from the lines, the one workman shown changing the switch by the pedal shown on the floor, right front, in the upper picture on this page.

The lower view on this page shows the delivery end of one of the transmission and magneto chutes. As this assembly weighs

Delivery End of Transmission and Magneto Chute

The chain seen in the picture above is used for elevating only. The delivery is by gravity and includes a brake, 300 lb. spring loaded, which retards the assemblies just before they are brought to rest against the sliding bail in front, which has about 6 ins. movement against heavy cushioning springs. A man receives assemblies and places them in racks, within ready reach of the motor assemblers

The magneto and transmission are assembled on a line located at a considerable distance south of the two motor-assembling lines. The last operation man on the transmission and magneto line places the assembly on an inclined chain elevator as shown just above. The chain serves two gravity chutes, seen close at the left of the workman's head, these gravity chutes delivering the transmission

Endless Belt Between Two Lines of Presses Set Back to Back

This belt takes product of all presses and carries to east end of line, where three men sort the product
into transportation receptacles.   See text, page 284

98 pounds, a strong brake and spring buffer are required when de-livering.

For particulars see the legends under the illustrations.   The cash saving effected by this chain elevator is about $20.00 per day, besides the indirect saving due to the removal of travel obstructions on the floor.

It is of little use to give the conveyor belt and chain speeds because in each installation there is some consideration which fixes the speed.

Chapter XI

THE BUSHINGS JOB

A "BUSHING" is a hollow cylinder, more commonly of brass or "bronze" but often of steel and sometimes of tool-steel. The diameter may vary from, say, ½ inch inside and ⅝ inch outside, up to say 2½ inches inside and 2¾ or more, outside. The length is commonly short, from one to three times the outside diameter, and often one end has a low flange.

The bush form-requirements are a truly cylindrical bore, "round and straight" in shop language, with the exterior surface exactly concentric, or "true" with the bore. The bushing is thus seen to be a simple form of production, very easily made on the engine lathe or on the turret machine when made in small quantities and with no special attention to low cost; but when bushings are required in large numbers and at a low cost they offer an extremely difficult problem, or rather several difficult problems, which the Ford engineers have solved by abandoning ordinary machine-tool practice, abandoning the turret machine and the use of reamers for finishing the bush-bore, and making several new inventions in the way of engine-lathe tools and appliances and applying multi-toothed broaches to the finishing of interior circular surfaces, in the effort to produce large numbers of components at the least possible labor-cost.

The Ford Model-T chassis requires 69 bushings, of which 30 are of gray iron, steel or babbitt metal, leaving 39 brass bushings to be made for each chassis; that is to say, with a production of 1,000 cars per day the bushings department regularly finishes about 35,000 or 40,000 bushings daily, and has turned out 52,000 bushings in one 8-hour day.

Up to about April 1, 1913, the bushings were made according to ordinary machine-shop practice, on turret machines, automatic screw machines, and drill presses and engine lathes; many bushes were made from solid round bars on hand-worked turret machines, or of castings. If of castings, these were bored and reamed on vertical-spindle machines, the bush being held in a special fixture and first rough-bored and then finish reamed, then pressed on arbors and finished to outside diameter and to length in engine lathes.

The management was well aware that the great number of bushings made every day, somewhere about 35,000, cost much more than they should; but up to about April 1, 1913, other things were of more importance and it was not until that time that the bushings production was all collected, placed under the care of one man, and made a separate department.

The first practice followed shop traditions—bored and reamed the

Bushings Job. Line of Drillers for Rough-Boring Bushings Castings. Ford Chuck on Driller Table. See Page 289 for Chuck Construction

bushings holes on turret machines, then forced the bushings onto arbors and turned them, and squared up the ends on engine lathes, placing one man with an arbor press between each pair of engine lathes to force rough bushes on arbors ready for lathe work and force finished bushings off the arbors; one arbor-press hand can keep two lathe hands going.

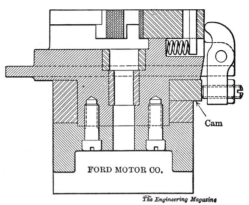

Cam

FORD MOTOR CO.

Chuck on Driller Shown in the Preceding Picture

Three jaws, spring opened, actuated by beam, shown at right, and ring carrying 3 cams. The cams are hardened and the low ends of the levers take adjusting screws with hardened ends, check-nut retained, which gives an independent adjustment for each of the 3 chuck-jaws, making these chucks easy to keep true, year in and year out, holding pieces of the one constant diameter

The first operation attacked was the reaming of the bush-holes, which gave no trouble when only a few bushings were required, and the labor cost was not seriously considered.

All kinds and sorts of reamers were tried, but solid reamers held their size only a short time, while adjustable reamers were found not to answer when production was speeded up. Finally circular broaches were given a trial, and have held their own up to the date of this writing.

FINISHING ROUND HOLES WITH CIRCULAR BROACHES

The circular broach was in use for round-hole finishing in some Detroit brass shops, though I never saw this tool before I saw it in the Ford Shops, February, 1914. The circular broach is used in power presses, is extremely rapid in action, is easily kept up to size, and makes holes which are nearly circular and beautifully smooth, but are not straight, and never can be exactly straight because the least variations in hardness of the bush sides or in the sharpness of the broach sides must infallibly deflect the broach from straight-line movement as it is forced through the bushing. The bushings-axis variation from a straight line may be as much as two or three thousandths, or as little as one-half a thousandth, but the axis is never quite straight when the hole is finished by circular broaching.

However, in some forms and dimensions of bushes the arbors used are stiff enough to straighten the bush-axis almost perfectly in course of forcing on the arbor and exterior finishing. The axis error limit is fixed

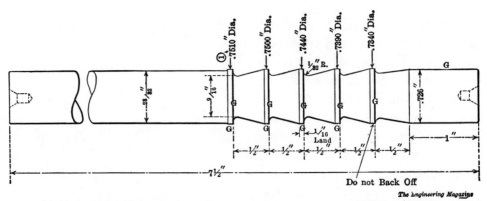

Circular Broach, Small Diameter, Simple Form, for Work in Bronze

Finishes at maximum 2,000 holes with one grinding. One man and press broach about 450 pieces per hour. Regular bushings job is to grind broaches once in 5 hours, depending on stock, however; sometimes 50 pieces will call for grinding the broach. All Ford broaches are "Star Zenith High Speed" steel

at one-half of one thousandth—not too small a limit, since the bushing is the seat of wear, and bushing errors mean working errors, if the bushing seats are straight holes and are correctly located.

The circular broaches have the one grand qualification of working faster than any other tool employed for round-hole finishing, and it is this rapid-action-characteristic which enables the circular broach to hold its place in the Ford shops.

Having found that the circular broach would finish round holes more rapidly than any other tool, the Ford engineers went at the circular-broach construction tooth and nail, and spared nothing in the

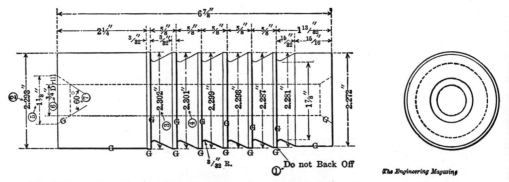

Ford Late Practice in Circular Broaches, Large Diameter, over 2¼ inches. For Brass and Bronze, March, 1914

The longer the broach, with fixed tooth numbers, and the more widely the teeth are separated, the less the power required, the less bursting stress on the work, and the less the closing of the hold after the broach passes through. Also, the longer the broach the more liable it becomes to accident in tempering, in straightening, in use and handling, the longer the stroke must be and the longer the time required. Late Ford practice favors short broaches. One man and one press broach 2,500 to 3,000 holes, about 2½ inches long, in 8 hours, bronze castings. When broaching with a power press, the length of hole makes little difference in the number of pieces per hour

way of thought, time, and treasure to make the circular broach do its very best.

Five working-drawings examples of Ford circular-broach practice are given on pages 290 to 293—one of the largest, one of the smallest diameter, and three of intermediate diameters. The circular broaches are not used for any roughing cuts on the bushings job. Circular broaches as small as $^5/_{16}$-inch diameter have been in extended use in these shops, but nothing much below $^5/_8$-inch diameter is now employed.

The Ford Company circular-broach practice probably includes more experiment that that of any other establishment, and the fact that the

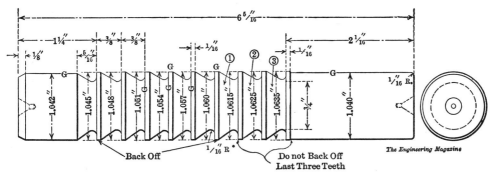

Ford Circular Broach, Current Practice, Jan., 1914.   For Work in Brass

Finishes about 100 holes in one grinding. One man and press broach about 3,000 pieces per 8-hour day Brass tube stock, requires very sharp edges. Circular broaches are very quickly ground, either on centers, or by simply holding the broach in the fingers and turning the broach as grinding proceeds. The broach sharpening emery wheels used are the "Norton Elastic," thin disks, round face, and flexible, can be readily bent with the fingers and return to flat form when released. See page 296

Ford Company, after years of use, has settled on the circular-broach employment, is conclusive proof of the advantages of this rapid working tool for certain classes of round-hole finishing, and fully warrants the placing of the illustrations here given.

Probably all circular broaches should have the teeth cut across at as many as three points, 120 degrees apart, in each circular tooth, these cross-cuts being staggered 30 degrees in each successive tooth. Some of the Ford circular-broach teeth are not so cut, with the consequence of making full-circle chips which are difficult of removal from the broach-grooves.

The circular-broach teeth are smallest in diameter at the entering end, and the last three or four teeth are made the same large diameter,[*] often in excess of the finished-hole diameter, as the outward pressure in

[*] True in case of all circular broaches, but not invariably true in case of short broaches.

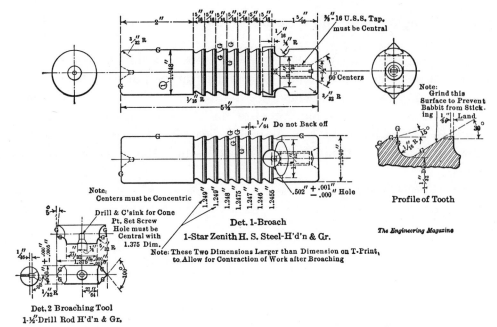

Example of Early Ford Circular Broach Practice, to Work in Babbitt Metal and to Cut Double Straight Oil Grooves While Finishing to Diameter

Used for connecting crank-wrist ends. With "gun-reamers," old practice, about 20 rod-ends were reamed per hour, with one man and one drill press; this method required one tool setter on the job constantly; only building 50 cars per day, at time of this single-tooth reamer practice. At present about 4,500 rod-ends are broached in 8 hours

circular broaching is severe, and the broached hole closes after the broach passes through the thin-walled bushing.

The largest and smallest tooth are joined by a curved line of tooth diameters, not by a straight line, so that the chips are thinnest next the broach-leaving end, and thickest at the broach-entering end, as will be seen by reference to the drawings which give the diameter of each circular tooth.

The "Zenith" high-speed tool steel, made by the Carpenter Steel Company at Reading, Pa., is used for these broaches, and for cutting tools generally in the Ford shops.

For broaching holes having key-ways cut in them to finished diameter, a 45-degree angle tool is seated in a mortice at the entering end of the broach to chamfer the key-way inside corners, to avoid turning line burrs inside the key-ways which would have to be removed by hand with a file.

The circular broaches are sharpened by grinding the leading faces of the circular teeth, which are cylindrical for about 1/16 inch in length.

The first or roughing cuts in the bushings holes are made on Cincinnati drillers, with Ford chucks fixed to the driller tables to hold the rough bushes and boring bars; twist drills, soap and water lubricated, are used for making the smaller roughing cuts, which are usually very nearly straight.

The bushings production will be illustrated and described in finishing-operation sequence. The bushing "Ford bronze" castings are now made in the big Ford foundry, and are brought to the bushings department cleaned and ready for the finishing operations.

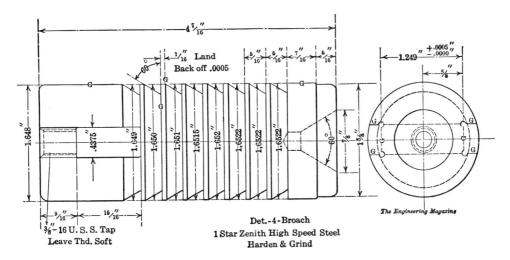

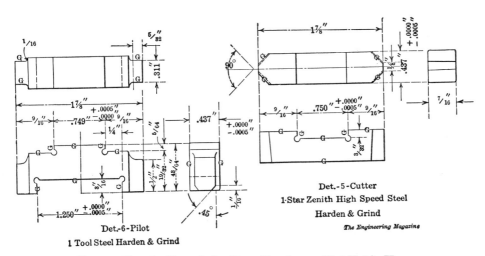

Recent Circular Broach for Drop Forgings. Not Yet in Use

This elaborate broach finishes the diameter of a hole previously splined to take two keys, 180 degrees apart. The previous splining necessitates the pilot, lower left hand, to guide the chamfering tool, lower right-hand action. In assembling this 4-component tool, the pilot leads, the chamfering tool follows, and both are retained by the thrust screw. In operation, the broach is first entered in the work, by hand, then the job is placed in the press and the broach is forced through

The finishing operations, considered in their regular order, are as follows:

Operation 1.   Rough Bore, Ford chuck.

Operation 2.   Broach, broach grinding included.

Operation 3.   Place on arbor, or otherwise hold for turning, and force off arbor.

Operation 4.   Turn, square ends, or cut in two.

Finally, The forming of bushes from flat strips of metal in power press, cut off and form one bush at each down stroke of the press slide, will be shown and described.

ROUGH-BORING BRONZE BUSHES

The tools used are 21-inch Cincinnati drillers, fitted with Ford universal three-jawed chuck, shown on page 289.   See caption for chuck construction.   The chucks are fixed to the driller tables, concentric with the driller spindles.   See the illustration on page 288.

The preferred boring tool is a boring bar, with a screw-retained, double-end cutter, the bottom end of the bar being steadied in a hardened and ground bush seated in the chuck-body.   For small-diameter holes rough boring is done with twist drills.   The lubrication is flooded soap and water, circulated by a two-pinion pump.

For large-diameter bushings the cutter is ground about once for every 100 bushings rough-bored.   The broach seen standing on its end at the right side of the driller table, Figure 15, is used for the rough-bore gauge.   About 900 bushes of the largest diameter, something over $2\frac{1}{4}$ inches, are bored per 8-hour day.   Small bushes are rough-bored with a twist drill, 1,800 per day, one man and one machine, 8 hours.

A special machine for bushings boring is now under construction, and is expected to reduce the labor cost of bushings boring very much.

The Ford special three-jaw chuck is shown on page 289 and described in the caption.   These chucks are simple, hold strongly, are extremely durable, and have an independent screw and check-nut adjustment for positioning each chuck jaw.

BROACHING BORE TO FINISHED DIAMETER

Although the Ford shops had a circular broach in successful use for some years, finishing the connecting-rod wrist-eyes, in babbitt metal (and was having plenty of trouble in finish-boring the bushes) no bush bores were broached before about April 1, 1913.   It is difficult to work babbitt without tearing the soft surface, and babbitt-cutting tools must

have keen edges to produce smooth work.   This keen edge requirement
for babbitt broaching discouraged the Ford engineers in the matter of
sizing bronze bush holes with circular broaches, possibly.   At all events,
broaches were not tried on the bushings until after everything else had
been tried for the job, with no satisfaction.   Broached holes in brass are
invariably smooth, but sometimes spring to oval form where the
broach drops through and are never exactly straight;   sometimes

Finishing Bush Bore with Circular Broach, under Ferracute Power-Press Slide

Broach Grinding, Norton Elastic Wheel $^1/_{16}$ to $^1/_8$ inch Thickness, Broach Held in Both Hands

Grinder built by Greenfield Machine Company, Greenfield, Mass.

to within half a thousandth of straight and sometimes as much as two or three thousandths out of straight. Speaking generally, the circular broached holes may be said to be round and smooth, but not straight.

The action of the broach is extremely rapid, and broached surfaces in brass are smooth; the great use of the circular broach in the Ford shops is enough to warrant a trial of broaching by any shop which wants to finish holes up to $2\frac{1}{2}$ inches diameter, in brass, in large numbers and at low cost.

BROACHING BUSHES

The broaching is done on geared Ferracute presses, "D. G.—54," 8 inches stroke, one man only to each press. Operations are: pick up bushing with left hand; pick broach out of tray under press bolster, with right hand; enter broach in bushing, both hands; hold bushing in place under press slide with right hand; depress clutch treadle with right foot (the broach shank is made long enough to carry broach teeth all the way through the work, so that the broach drops down into the pan); finally, with right hand, place broached piece in tray.

By using two men on a press, one helper to pick up the bush and enter the broach, the press output can be increased, but the one-man work cannot be doubled.

The least 8-hour number, large holes, is about 2,500 pieces broached.

Sixteen holes broached per minute is about top speed. Regular production of medium-size work, 4,000 bushes broached in 8 hours, with one man and press.

BROACH GRINDING

With difficult stock the broach may have to be ground once in half an hour. With the best stock the broach may hold up to size for 8 hours. Regular practice is once in 5 hours.

From 12 to 24 broaches of each size used are kept on hand in the tool crib.

Breaking of small broaches is rare, and is caused by uneven seating of the bush on the press-bolster. The large broaches never break.

Broach grinding is rapid. The broach is not placed on centers, but is held in both hands up to an "Elastic" Norton wheel, $1/16$ to $1/8$ inch thickness and 6 or 8 inches diameter, and it takes only two or three minutes to sharpen any broach.

Ferracute Power Press

Forcing arbor out of bush at the same time that it forces another arbor into another bush. See page 298 for details.

Placing Bushes on Arbors, and Forcing Arbors Out of Bushes; Simultaneous Operations.   See also Page 297

Forcing Arbors Into and Out of the Bushings

The hand-worked arbor-press, first used for forcing arbors into and out of bushings, is not so fast as press work for the same operation, shown on pages 297 and 298.   The former view shows the press man holding a finish-turned bush on its arbor upright with his left hand, and an un-turned bushing with arbor entered upright in his right hand on the press bolster, under the press-slide.   When the press-slide comes down the arbor is forced out of the left-hand bush at the same time that the arbor is forced into the bush held in the workman's right hand. The forced-out arbor drops into the trough, S, page 298, and the press man drops the finish-turned bush into the slide at his left, page 297, at the same time that he drops the bush and arbor held in his right hand on a slide, not seen, leading to the lathe lines in rear of the press. The press man has a helper standing at his right, shown idle in this posed picture, who picks the arbor out of the trough, S, page 298, and enters it in another bush. The press hand takes the un-turned bush with its entered arbor in his right hand, and with his left hand picks up a finish-turned bush on its arbor and completes the cycle of his movements by standing

Lines of Bush Turning Lathes. Arbor Presses in Middle Distance at Right. Hand Arbor Press on Lathe Bed at Extreme Left

both assemblies on the press-bolster, as shown on page 297, ready to repeat.

Two men and one press handle about 16,000 bushings and arbors in 8 hours, place 8,000 bushings on arbors and push the arbors out of 8,000 bushings.

One man collects the turned bushings on arbors from the lathe lines and places them in the tray at the extreme left in the view on page 297,

Page 298 shows a detail view of the press-bolster and slide. At left front, on the bolster, is a turned bushing on the arbor, arbor flattened end for lathe-driving in front. At middle left, in a raised boss on the bolster, stands a bushing ready to have its arbor forced out; immediately above, down-hanging from the press-slide fixture, is the round driver, marked "A," of smaller diameter than the arbor, which forces the arbor down all the way out of the bushing.   To the right of "A" is the short plug "B," which drives the arbor into the bush, standing on the bolster at right middle.   At right front, a bush, with an arbor entered ready for driving in, lies in the bolster.

TURNING THE BUSHINGS

See page 299, double line of bushing-turning lathes, by Reed-Prentice Co.   Extreme left, man at rack and pinion arbor press, old style, who can handle from 900 to 2,000 bushes on and off the arbor, both operations, in 8 hours, according to the length of the bushings.   With the power press the length of the bushings does not count, long bushings being handled on and off the arbor as rapidly as short ones.

The arbor presses are seen at right middle distance.

DRIVING AND TURNING BUSHES

See page 302, which shows the lathe ready to take an arbor with bushing on it ready for rough- or finish-turning.   Bushings ends are not faced in this operation.

LATHE CENTERS

The live center is fitted to slide to a shoulder in the head-stock spindle, and is pressed outward by a light spring.

Multi-Toothed Bush Turning Tools

Round nose for roughing, square nose for finishing.

The tail-center has a taper socket fit, usual style, in the tail spindle, which has no tail-screw, the tail-spindle being forced forward by a spring heavy enough to close the live-spindle-center coiled spring; tail spindle has usual clamping screw.

The live spindle is fitted with a floating driver to take and drive the flattened arbor end, and a stud fixed to the lathe carriage impinges the tail spindle front end, below the center, so that the tail spindle can be forced back against the spring pressure by turning the lathe-saddle hand-wheel.   This cut shows 20-tooth circular turning tools used for bush-turning, and these peculiar tools are also shown on page 302. These multi-tool cutters are believed to have originated with the Ford engineers. The first one used was taken from a Fellows gear-shaper; afterward these tools were tried in cylindrical form with both straight and spiral teeth, but have now become standard, on the Ford bushings job, in the form shown on page 300, a truncated cone, 2 inches outside diameter, holes $\frac{7}{8}$, thickness $\frac{7}{8}$, 20 teeth, taper about 10 degrees on a side, 20 degrees included angle, with 30-tooth V-form retaining ratchet on bottom end. The teeth are round-nose for roughing and flat-nose for finishing. The finish tools are set to clear on the following side. As there are 20 cutting teeth and the holder retaining ratchet has 30 teeth, the cutter holder is fitted with a retention screw adjustment which must be varied when a change is made from one cutting edge to the next one. These cutters are ground on top at the big end, and one grinding gives 20 sharp tools in one piece. The cutters have milled elevating hand nuts on screws under them.

TURNING BUSHES OPERATION

The live spindle runs continuously. With the lathe as shown in cut on page 302, the live center is forced outward by its light spring. The lathe man takes hold of the lathe-carriage wheel with his left hand, pushes the tail spindle back with stud on lathe tool-post fixture, takes arbor with bush on it in his right hand, applies the flat driving end of arbor to live center, guides the arbor tail end and lets the tail spindle spring force the live center to shoulder, the arbor flat entering the floating live-spindle driver, tightens the tail-spindle clamping screw, and proceeds at once to run the cut over the bush with hand-wheel carriage feed. As soon as the cut is over, the workman picks up another arbor with bush on it in his right hand, then releases tail-spindle clamping screw with right hand, then moves right hand to bushing and arbor on centers and pulls the top of hand wheel towards him, pushes the tail-spindle back, drops the unturned bushing and arbor down on his fingers, and grasps the turned bushing with thumb and forefinger of right hand, lifts right hand enough to put fresh job on centers, moves hand wheel enough to let tail center go forward and push the arbor flat end into the driver, tightens the tail-spindle clamping screw with right hand, and then drops the finished bush and arbor into the trough; as soon as the tail spindle is clamped the workman starts the cut with the hand wheel and picks up the next job with his right hand about the time the short cut is made, and so on. The workman's left hand does not leave the hand wheel and the live spindle is not stopped.   Each workman turns about 2,000 bushes per 8-hour day.   One lathe makes the rough cuts and another lathe makes the finishing cuts.   Two helpers place the arbors and bushes conveniently for the lathe men, and from the finish lathe the arbors and bushes go to the "put-on" and "take-off" power press, as shown on pages 297 and 298.   The operations are performed

Bush Turning Lathe, with Spring Live Center and Spring Tail Spindle

An arbor with bush on it, ready to turn, lies on top of the tail stock in front of clamping screw.   One tool-holder, with 20-tooth circular cutter, is shown in working position, and another tool post is set on the lathe carriage, middle front of picture, to show the tool-post construction and the 20-tooth circular cutter.
See also page 303

so rapidly that it is difficult to follow the varied performances of the man's right hand.

It will be noted that the latheman has a bush and arbor in his right hand both when releasing and when tightening the tail-stock clamping screw with that hand, and also that he has a bushing and arbor in his right hand when he takes a bushing and arbor off the lathe centers, and that he drops the fresh bushing and arbor down on his right hand second and third fingers so that he can grasp the turned bushing and its arbor with his right hand thumb and fore-finger while he lifts and places the fresh job on the lathe centers, all of which seems very awkward, but is really a great saving of time and hand-travel distance over ordinary practice which would handle both the two arbors and bushes with the right hand.

These turning lathes do not square up the bush ends. Some of the bushes are made two in one piece and are cut apart and have ends squared to length by subsequent operations on expanding arbors.

The bushings department has a line of eight new special Reed-Prentice lathes, which are expected to change the entire routine of bush

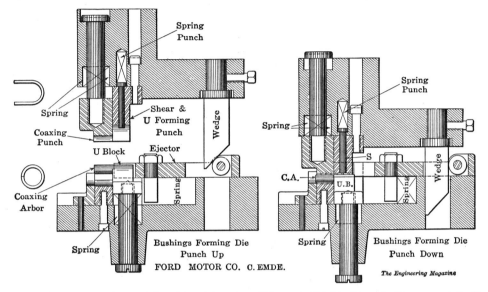

Middle Cross-Section of Bushing-Forming Dies at Right, Punch Down; at Left, Punch Up

See pages 304 and 305. and text.

finishing; expanding arbors are now being made, and practice is not fully determined. No illustrations are given of this new line of lathes.

BUSH-FORMING DIES

On pages 303, 304 and 305 appear views of a bush-forming **die,** which cuts off lengths from flat strip stock, steel or brass, and forms **up** a complete bush at each down stroke of the slide of a single-acting power press. Formerly many bushes were made by cutting lengths from steel or brass tubes.

The flat strip is fed by hand, between side gauges, to a stop. The punch descends, first cutting the blank to length, and then continuing to move downward forms the blank U-shape, at the end of the punch down-stroke. The punch then rises, and the ejector, spring-forced outward, is released by rising of the wedge fixed to the punch and pushes the U-blank outward so that it hangs on the "coaxing" arbor; see section of punch and die, open and closed, on page 303.

Front View of Bush-Forming Punch and Die, in Place in Press, with Strip of Stock Ready for Press Slide Stroke

An inverted U-form bushings blank is seen in front of stock-strip, hanging on the "coaxing arbor," see page 303. Note three stages of bushings lying and standing on the press bolster

Next the strip is fed as before, and the descent of the punch cuts off a second blank and forms it in a second U-blank, at the same time forcing the first U-blank hanging on the coaxing arbor downward, the inverted U-ends striking the die semicircle, and forming the first U-blank into a cylinder, which is ejected when the punch next rises.

The coaxing arbor and the U-block are integral, and are set on a lifting spring retained by a down-hanging shoulder screw, so that the coaxing arbor and U-block can go down together and be returned together as the punch rises, until stopped by the underneath shoulder screw.

When the punch rises the second time the ejector pushes the second U-blank outward, which forces the completely formed bush off from the coaxing arbor, thus making room on the coaxing arbor for the second U-blank.

SPRINGS AND SPRING PLUNGERS

The shearing blade is fixed to the punch body, and is cut in the middle of its under side to a half circle, to form the top of the inverted U-bend. A spring plunger is fitted in the middle of the half circle, which acts as an ejector when the punch begins to rise, to force the inverted U-blank to lie down close on the U-block.

OPERATION

See "Punch Up," in the illustration on page 303. In descending, the punch wedge moves the ejector to the right, so that the ejector-fork ends at the left barely clear the blank as the punch forces the blank downward after shearing the blank from the flat strip stock, and forms the blank to inverted U-shape at the same time (save in starting stroke) forming the inverted U-shape to a perfect cylinder around the coaxing arbor.

Left Hand End of Bushings Forming Punch and Die, Punch Up

Note bushings on front end of bolster

When the punch begins to rise the small spring plunger marked "S," in "punch down," holds the inverted U-blank on the "U-block" up to the time when the "ejector" begins to move the inverted U-blank to the left, pushing the completely formed bush off the coaxing arbor to give the U-blank place on the coaxing arbor.

This bush-forming die is given space because it is new, and can make 62 bushes per minute, completely formed, and hence may be of use to the trade at large.

The stroke of the press slide is $3\frac{1}{2}$ inches; similar dies make bushings from diameters $\frac{9}{16}$ and $\frac{11}{16}$ by $1\frac{1}{2}$ inches long to diameters $\frac{3}{4}$ and 1 inch by $1\frac{1}{4}$ inches long.

In April, 1913, 984 hours were required to equal present production of bushes.　Now (October, 1914) the bushings department performs this work in 480 labor hours, at about one-half the cost.

What the cost will be when the press-formed bushings are placed wherever they will answer, and when the eight new lathes are working up to expectation, is a subject for conjecture only, but may, possibly, split the present cost in half.

Chapter XII

SPECIAL MACHINES AND FIXTURES

THREE years ago, I heard a story about the Ford Tool Designing Department. I have not attempted to verify the incident, but judging from observations, made during the past few months, I am satisfied that it could have easily happened. It seems that one of the representatives of an eastern concern had been called into conference with the Ford engineers, regarding the design and building of a machine for a certain purpose. In going over the drawings, the Eastern Manufacturer suddenly pointed to the blueprint and said, "This is evidently a mistake. You specify an output of 200 per hour—this, obviously, is wrong; you mean *per day*." "No, I think that is right," said the Ford man. "The designer of this machine rarely makes a mistake, and if he says 200 per hour, I believe he must have figured out some way to do it. You know we check things up pretty carefully here." A heated discussion ensued, in which the Eastern Manufacturer pointed out that 40 per day was considered a fair production on such a part. "Well, it is easy enough to find out," said one of the Ford officials; "just tell the man who designed this machine to come in here a minute." The man came. The output specification was called to his attention. His only comment was, "Well, what about it?" "You can't do it," said the Eastern Manufacturer. "There is no machine built that will do it. Two hundred an hour! Why, it is out of the question." "Well," said the engineer, "if you will go down into the machine-shop on the main floor, you will find a machine doing it—we built one to try it out, and it is doing what we thought it would." Needless to say, the discussion ended there.

The Ford factory is filled with such machines. During the course of the last three years, over 140 special machines and several thousand special dies, tools, jigs and fixtures have been made. Fifty machines

Mr. Faurote's description of special tools was actually written several months later than Mr. Arnold's chapter on the Ford Foundries, which follows it in this volume. The arrangement here adopted, however, brings the topics into a more logical sequence. —THE EDITOR.

and 2,500 to 3,000 jigs and fixtures are not considered an unusual output for the 55 men employed in this department.

Improvements are constantly being introduced. Hardly a week passes when some radical change is not made in the various departments. The less efficient machine is displaced by the better one. Not only the Ford engineers, but the men in the shop, are constantly trying to do things in an easier and better way.

Like most great inventions, their best machines are often the simplest —so simple that when one sees them for the first time, the same old

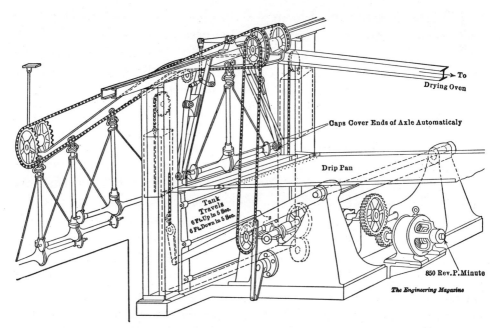

Sketch of Automatic Rear-Axle-Painting Machine

question arises—"Why didn't I think of that way before?" Of course some of the machines are complicated. They can't help but be. They are required automatically to do several different things; cam motions, toggle joints, links, automatic trips, intermittent motions, all these demand complicated looking machines, at least. In some machines the action is so complicated that wooden models are made before the design itself is completed, to test out all the motions and see that there is no locking point or other interfering element. The machines are frequently laid out full size, sometimes on a black-board, sometimes on a floor with chalk of different colors, sometimes merely a perspective drawing is sufficient.

Painting the Rear-Axle Assembly

On page 308 is shown such a sketch of a machine, just designed for automatically painting the rear-axle assembly. As explained in the chapter on painting, the rear axle was formerly dipped in a tank of enamel, by hand. It had to be handled several times and two men were required to do the work. With this new machine, it will be possible for one man to hang the rear-axle assembly on a moving chain which will carry it up over the tank. When it has reached this point, two levers will automatically thrust protecting thimbles over both ends of the axle shaft, the paint tank will travel up six feet, completely immersing the rear axle in the painting liquid, immediately returning to its former position, after which the part will proceed on its way down the track to the baking oven, as before. A complete cycle of operations will be performed in thirteen seconds; so it can be readily seen how easily and rapidly this work can be done with the new machine.

Rear End of the Crank-Case-Annealing Furnace

Showing cooling tower in process of construction. Carriers are shown on the floor in the foreground

A New Cooling Tower

Every minute that a part is not in process, it is taking up space and costing money. Therefore, the Ford engineers have, in a very common-sense way, tried to eliminate all breaks in a process line, and handle the material in such a way that it will be undergoing some needful operation at all times. For instance, immediately after the drawing operation on the crank case, it is necessary for this part to be annealed to relieve the strain set up by the very considerable draw required to form this piece. While these annealing ovens have been located near these draw presses for some time, yet a considerable amount of handling has been necessary even with this favorable arrangement. Not content with this condition, the Ford Company now proposes to erect a combination annealing furnace, cooling tower, and endless-belt conveyor which will receive the part immediately after its drawing operation, anneal it, cool it under the most favorable of slowly decreasing temperatures, and deliver it to the next press in proper condition and at a low enough temperature for its next drawing operation. Briefly, this innovation will consist of an annealing furnace with a charging door at one end and an upright chimney tower at the other.

In this tower, which acts in a dual capacity (as a means of carrying off some of the gases, and also as a slow cooling chamber for the part being annealed) is an endless-chain conveyor provided with carriers, onto which the heated crank cases are shoved through the rear opening of the furnace. The part travels up one side and down the other, where at a suitable point near the bottom, it is automatically released and slides down to its place in the pile near the next draw press. The illustration on page 309 shows the construction of this new labor-saving combination.

Some Special Radiator Machines

Up in the radiator department in the new building on Manchester Avenue, will be found another good example of the manner in which work in progress is carried through a furnace. Here, the operation is one of soldering. In the immediate back-ground of the upper illustration on page 311 will be seen a furnace with two transverse openings, an endless-chain conveyor equipped with hanging frames, and the necessary mechanism for driving it. This conveyor travels an equal distance from each end of the furnace. The work is fed in at both ends and taken out at both ends, the operation is practically continuous.

The radiators, consisting of fins and tubes, are built up, as will be described later, supplied with solder and inserted in the traveling frames. Carried along by the conveyer, they traverse the furnace which is kept at a temperature of 750 degrees. In this way, more than 1,900 radiators can be soldered every 8 hours.

The making of a radiator was formerly considered a very diffi-

Special Soldering Furnace in the Radiator Department

Punching Radiator Fins
Ford attachment to a standard press

cult operation, but Ford ingenuity has made it a very simple operation.

As is generally known, a Ford radiator is made up of a large number of transverse brass fins, intersected by 95 vertical tubes. The problem that now arises is, how to get these parts together in the shortest possible time. If you have ever tried to put 95 tubes through even one strip of thin brass, and then fit these same 95 tubes through the holes in several dozen more, you will realize how difficult it is to accomplish this operation successfully in a short length of time. Putting the pages in a loose-leaf ledger is bad enough—this is a thousand times

Making the Ford Radiator

worse. In the early stages of the automobile industry, this work
was done by hand.   Gradually, of course, other methods were adopted.
But, while the fins are racked, the tubes are still put in by hand in
some of the radiator factories.

Therefore, to see a radiator made in the Ford factory is an interesting experience; one that will not soon be forgotten.   The photograph
on this page shows how this is done.   Two types of racks are used—one
like that shown in the left fore-ground of the picture, for stacking up
the fins ready for the insertion of the tubes; the other, bearing a marked
resemblance to an old-time candle mold, receives the tubes.   Now
comes the interesting part—after these two racks have been filled, the
one containing the fins is placed on the metal table in the center; the
one containing the rods is positioned opposite it, so that the tube holes
in the fin-frame are in direct line with those of the tube mold.   Mounted
in the center of this table and moving under power in either direction,
at the will of the operator, is a ram, on both ends of which are 95 pro-

jecting rods located and spaced in accordance with the holes in the radiator molds. Therefore, after the work is all in place, the operator simply starts the machine and the tubes are shoved out of one mold into the other, completing the whole job in one operation and in a remarkably short time. The machine works in both directions so that when the ram is being withdrawn from one set of molds, it is forcing the tubes into the corresponding one on the other side. This machine has a capacity of 1,200 radiator cores every 8 hours.

In the same department is an-

Forming Solder Ribbon on the Solder-Making Machine

Side View of Hydraulic Solder-Making Machine

other very interesting Ford machine, or rather an attachment which is fitted to a standard press. It is shown in the lower illustration on page 311. It will turn out 25,000 radiator fins every eight hours. Ribbon brass is fed in from a reel on the left side of the machine. The edges are rolled up and turned over, 95 holes punched and the piece cut off automatically. It runs with an intermittent motion, affected by the use of a "Geneva cam movement." Entirely automatic, it will run continuously, with very little supervision. This machine has increased the output

Making the Ford Gasoline Tank

Blanking the galvanized-iron shell, punching filler and sediment-cup holes, and embossing the ribs

of fins from six to seven thousand per day, over the hand-operated machine formerly used. This is a characteristic example of Ford policy in increasing output and reducing labor cost.

Gasoline-Tank Rolling Machine

MAKING THE FORD GASOLINE TANK

In the gasoline-tank department there are two machines and several fixtures which are well

Rolling in Ends of Gasoline Tanks

Hand-Soldering a Gasoline Tank with Gas Flame and Wire Solder

worthy of extended mention. Not only the machines employed in forming, but the method used in soldering are unusual. The galvanized iron is first blanked out on a press shown on page 314, that turns up the sides, punches the filler and sediment-cup holes, and embosses the ribs. It then goes through a set of rolls that hems the edge and shapes the barrel on rollers, shown above, at the left, on this page.

Above: Soldering Longitudinal Seam of Gasoline Tank.
Below: Testing Tanks with Compressed Air under Water

It is then delivered to a machine designed and built by the Ford Motor Company for the purpose of "rolling in" the ends, shown in the right-hand picture on page 315. In action, it is simplicity itself, but the mechanism operating the rollers is rather complicated. Briefly, it consists of two sets of revolving spindles, upper and lower, the latter provided with a link motion which enables them to be raised or lowered at will, by means of the lever shown at the left in the illustration on page 315. This lever controls the left-hand spindle, a similar one on the other side operating the right-hand one. The machine is designed to roll in the ends of

Testing Transmission

Filleting Crank-Shaft Bearings

the gasoline tank. The operation is as follows: the workman picks up a circular disc forming one end of the tank and places it on the lower horizontal revolving plate; he then places the cylindrical body of the tank on top of this, adding another disc which serves as the other end. A swing of the floor lever elevates the whole assembly until it is securely clamped between the two rotating face plates; the power is then turned on and the upper and lower rolls, mounted on the swinging frame, gradually begin to approach the ends of the cylindrical tank. As the top and bottom discs are greater in

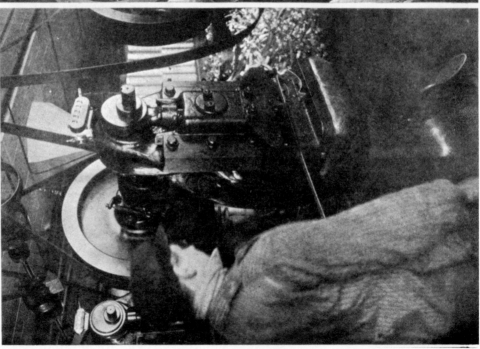

Dies for Making Tie Straps

diameter than the tank-body flange, they begin to curl over as the rollers travel toward the body, until finally both end joints are securely made. At this point the rollers are automatically withdrawn and resume their former position; the power is turned off, the floor lever thrown back, and the tank lifted out. This result is accomplished by means of a very ingenious system of cam motions. As the splash plates have been soldered in, previous to this operation, the tanks are now practically complete and ready for final soldering.

The circular joints are soldered by hand (page 315), by means of a gas torch. After the filler plugs and sediment cups are added, the tanks are tested under air pressure in water as shown on page 316.

The longitudinal seam is soldered in a novel manner on a special Ford soldering conveyer shown on page 316. A strip of solder wire cut to size is laid along the seam, soldering fluid is brushed on, and the tank, in a moving-chain trough, is carries under a six-jet gas flame which melts the solder and completes the job.

Spindle Punch - Drilling Machine for Making Wood-Screw Holes in Floor Boards

In this same department are two rather interesting die fixtures used for making tie-straps for the tanks. The left-hand picture on page 318 shows one with its finished product, performed in one operation. The right-hand picture on the same page shows the other, which carries two dies required for the forming and perforating of this piece.

SPECIAL MACHINE AND CUTTERS FOR FILLETING CRANK-SHAFT BEARINGS OF CYLINDER

Located just off the main aisle on the east side of the main craneway, are two interesting filleting machines, one of which is shown on page 317. Simple in operation and very efficient, they play an important part in

Small Filing Machines
Two of many small power machines scattered throughout the Ford shops for filing and burring rough edges from small parts

the rapid production work of the Ford cylinders. As will be noted in the accompanying photograph, the cutters are mounted on rapidly rotating shafts controlled by a hand lever which moves the cutters to the right or left. The cylinder casting, upside down, is deposited on a receiving table. When the lever is in neutral position, cutters are equidistant from the bearings on either side. A movement of the lever to the right, fillets the left-hand side of the bearings; a movement to the left fillets the right-hand side of the bearings. The operation is performed in less time than it takes to tell about it and little care is required to perform the operation perfectly, because the movement of the lever is limited in both directions so that only the proper amount of metal can be removed.

TESTING TRANSMISSIONS

While in other factories the various testing machines for trying out minor assemblies are usually grouped by themselves, in the Ford factory they are placed in the process line if possible.

Ford Machine for Forming and Quenching Spring Leaves

Cam-Shaft Grinding Machine

Special Machines Used for Testing Ford Motors

The upper figure on page 317 shows the special machine designed by the Ford engineers for testing the transmission. Mounted on a suitable connecting shaft, the transmission assembly is caused to revolve and the planetary gears which make up this unit are tested out separately.

The three lever brakes, each of which can be applied separately, make it possible to operate and test the "reverse," "slow speed," and "brake," in a very short time. This machine is located in the transmission-assembly line. The elements of the machine are clearly shown.

SPINDLE PUNCH-DRILLING MACHINE FOR MAKING WOOD-SCREW HOLES IN FLOOR BOARDS

On page 319 is shown a special attachment which has been added to an ordinary press, for the purpose of rapidly "punch-drilling" holes in wooden floor-boards. This machine requires no extended explanation, as its operation is readily understood.

POWER FILING AND BURRING MACHINES

Scattered through the Ford factory are a number of power filing and burring machines for cleaning up the edges of gears and taking the burrs off the edges of small parts. The cut on page 320 shows such a machine. Only the rotating spindle projects above the work table. Sometimes the rotating spindle is set in a horizontal position and carries a circular file face-plate against which the work is held. These machines present no unusual features, but like many others machines of like nature, add very materially to the capacity of the shop.

FORMING AND HARDENING SPRING LEAVES

Down in the north-east corner of the machine shop, a very interesting machine is being installed, which is to be used for forming, and quenching spring leaves. See the upper figure on page 321. It is entirely of Ford design and presents many novel features. It is made up of two main parts—a large steel box acting as a tank for holding the quenching oil, and a rotating frame shaped very much like the paddle-wheel on a Mississippi steamer. This rotating member, controlled by a rather complicated cam motion, has six projecting arms revolving from the front to the rear of the photograph. On each one of the "paddles," two jaws are carried; the outer one stationary, the inner moving in and out automatically. A hot spring leaf is taken from the furnace and inserted between one of these sets of jaws. Pressure on a trip pedal near the floor closes the jaws automatically, squeezing the steel to shape and causing the mechanism to rotate through an angle of 60 degrees. It stops automatically in a position so that the next set of jaws is ready to receive another spring leaf. Simultaneously with these actions, the leaves are allowed to drop out on the other side, which is the front of the picture, as shown. A tilting shelf swinging through an angle of 90 degrees automatically places itself in the proper position and at the proper time to receive the quenched leaf as the jaws release it. A further movement of the machine causes this shelf to rise to a vertical position and the spring leaf tumbles to the floor.

Cam-Shaft Grinding Machine

On page 321 is shown a cam-grinding attachment which has been designed to fit a regulation grinder. Mounted on trunnions so that it

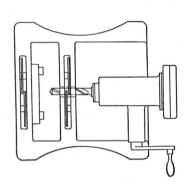

will swing back and forth in order to follow the outline of the master cams, this fixture holds the cam shaft in position in front of the grinding wheel. By moving the carriage back and forth it is possible for the workman to bring the successive cams opposite the grinding wheel. Inasmuch as the cam shaft virtually forms an extension of

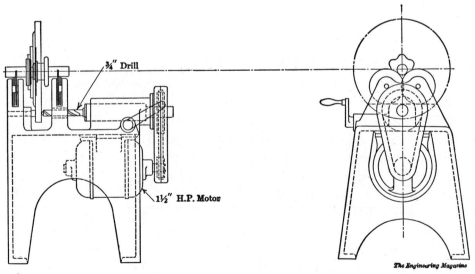

The Engineering Magazine

Balancing Machine with Drilling Attachment, for Fly-Wheel

Cam-Shaft Shaping Machine of Ford Construction

the shaft carrying the master cams, any movement of the latter is duplicated by the former. It is only necessary for the operator to move the carriage longitudinally from one cam to the other. A middle bearing prevents the cam shaft from springing out of line.

This machine has a capacity of about 115 cam shafts every eight hours, an increase of about 25 more than that secured with the former method of grinding.

Special Ford Fly-Wheel Balancing Machine with Drilling Attachment

The drawing on page 324 shows a special machine designed for balancing fly-wheels. A combination of an electrically driven drill and a wheel-balancing mechanism is unusual. It will easily be seen how such a combination of two operations, making it unnecessary for the fly-wheel to be lifted out and taken to a drill press for each drilling operation, makes for increased production.

Cam-Shaft Shaping Machine

Page 325 shows the most unusual and interesting machine to be found in the Ford shops. It is entirely of Ford design. Cam shafts were formerly cut on milling machines. It was a slow process and rather expensive. The cutters cost $8.50 apiece and one man was required to operate each machine. Therefore when it is known that this machine has increased the capacity from 90 to 275 and that one man can supervise three of these machines, it can be readily seen what a wonderful increase in production has been made by the utilization of this entirely new method of cutting cams.

In action, this machine is essentially a shaper. It carries, however, eight cutters, so that work is done on all cams at the same time. The tools are controlled by a system of master cams which bear down on the top of the cutting tools and insure a positive cut on the work. The cam shaft is driven from both ends and supported by a bearing in the center. The machine is electrically operated and the cut is controlled by means of a stop regulated by the hand wheel shown on the right-hand side of the picture. The cutters, which are held against the master cams by means of springs, move up and down in accordance with the cam outline.

This machine has a capacity of 275 cam shafts per day of eight hours. It takes about twenty seconds to load, and less than two minutes to complete a shaft.

Needless to say, in this chapter attempts to describe only a few of the many interesting machines and fixtures to be found in the Ford shops, but those selected illustrate the simplicity and directness which always characterizes Ford design.

CHAPTER XIII

THE FOUNDRIES

THE chapter on commutator production showed a small aluminum foundry located in the commutator-department machine
room to avoid needless handling and transportation of the
commutator case.

Save for the commutator-case founding, all the Ford castings are
made in one foundry, under one managerial head. This main foundry
is equipped with many novel mechanical aids to labor-cost reduction,
each one of which is here separately illustrated and described in full,
and all important particulars of the foundry practice and the labor management are given in sufficient detail to enable the reader to understand
fully all the means and the conditions which help the Ford foundries,
gray-iron, brass, and aluminum, to obtain their very low production
costs while paying higher wages than any other foundries in the world,
and paying hour rates only—no piece work, no premium scheme—to
all workmen.

Mr. Robert Thurston Kent, in a recently published article on foundry cost reductions, said that any man who said he could lower costs
in any particular foundry within six months from the beginning of his
efforts was a fraudulent pretender, and a man to be avoided, since,
even with the soundest practical knowledge, no foundry-management
expert could hope to show notable and consistent labor-cost reductions
in any foundry given into his hands for betterment, inside of two years.

Circumstances alter cases. The Ford foundries actually reduce
costs every day, all the time, continually, and no Ford foundry worker,
from top to bottom, ever shows the slightest hesitation in obeying any
new instructions whatever.

The big foundry is now working about 1,450 men, all told. Of the
moulders, about 55 men, in the "jobbing" department, are thoroughly
skilled, all-round moulders, the very best that can be obtained. Of the
other moulders perhaps 5 per cent are skilled moulders and core-setters.

The remaining 95 per cent are simply specialized laborers, many of them foreigners who had never seen the inside of a foundry and could not speak a word of English when they began; were given one piece only to put up, learned the "trade" in two days (if a man cannot learn to put up a small, plain job in two days the Ford foundry bosses pass him up as hopeless) and began to turn out a full day's work of good castings on the third day of employment.   Of the 1,450 hands on the foundry pay roll about 1,220 are receiving $5.00 or more for 8-hours work.   The remaining 230 are drawing higher hour pay than they could obtain in any other employment within their own knowledge, and,

Ford Foundry, South Side from East End, Showing Overhead Monorail

speaking broadly, it may be said that not one single man in the Ford foundries, working in any capacity whatever, knows how or where he could better his pay check.

These pay conditions make the workmen absolutely docile. New regulations, important or trivial, are made almost daily; workmen are studied individually and changed from place to place with no cause assigned, as the bosses see fit, and not one word of protest is ever spoken, because every man knows the door to the street stands open for any man who objects in any way, shape or manner to instant and unquestioning obedience to any directions whatever.

What follows should be said here, to avoid the possibility of inference that any workman, however ignorant or unskilled he may be, is ever subjected to arbitrary or inconsiderate discharge from the Highland Park shops.   First, no department head has the power to give any workman his final discharge.   All any department foreman can do is

Aluminum Foundry and Cleaning Room. Monorail Track Overhead

to notify the time office that a certain man is no longer working in his department. Before a department head rejects a man every effort is made by the department head to find a place in his own department where the man can be profitably employed. The workman's own story obtains attentive hearing, his physical limitations are considered, and every effort is made to place the workman where he can be suited himself, while he is giving profitable service. In case the department head can find no such place for a man, then the discarded worker goes before a board of higher officials, who give him a full hearing and try to place him in some other department of the plant, so that a workman must show very decided all-round incapacity before he is finally discharged. Free medical treatment is given where needed, and every man who once enters the Ford service is given every assistance, so long as there seems to be any chance of mutually profitable relations remaining.

But willful insubordination is, of course, absolutely intolerable, and Ford workers must be, first of all, docile.

The following incident gives striking evidence of the Ford consideration for workmen seriously in fault.

It is a hard-and-fast rule of ordinary factory management that when two workers come to blows in working hours both shall be instantly paid off, discharged, and put outside of the factory walls never to be taken back again.

In the foundry office my attention was attracted by a small man standing huddled in one corner with his hands in his overcoat pockets, who glowered and shook his head in emphatic negation, while a much larger man talked to an interpreter who translated the larger man's story to the foundry head; the latter said nothing, but presently penciled two slips of paper, gave them to a messenger boy, and the messenger convoyed the small man and the larger man out of the office door into the foundry.

In reply to question, the foundry head said that the small man and the larger man were second-shift core-makers, that the small man started fisticuffs with the larger man the night previous, that no certain information could be gained by cross-examination, and that he had sent one man to the cupola charging-stage for a week, and the other one to the cylinder-shake-out gang for six days, and that the fighters would both be very glad to return to their benches.

The Foundry Building

The designer of the main gray-iron foundry building achieved no great triumph in the way of a big foundry building.   The ventilation is now very far from what it should be; the air during work hours cannot be endured by any workmen save those possessing respiratory organs of the most robust description, and many visitors are unable to walk through the Ford gray-iron foundry in working hours because they cannot breathe the air.

Otherwise than in the matter of ventilation, all working conditions are of the very best.   The hours are short, only 8 of the 24, cold pure water is everywhere at hand, goggles and leather leggings are supplied by the company to those liable to accident from molten metal, and no man is worked beyond a reasonable exertion of his muscular powers.

When Mr. Kent asserted that at least two years of hard work were needed to make marked and certain headway in reducing costs in any one particular foundry, he had in view, first the inertia of the management itself, which certainly desires labor-cost reductions and just as certainly maintains a "conservative" attitude of deep respect for the traditions of its old, honorable and deservedly trusted head men.   While fully convinced that labor-costs can be and should be and must be reduced, yet from habit, the management defers to the opinion of its own men who are always opposed to the edicts of the expert cost-reducer, who thus has every man in the place against him, in his inner consciousness, though all may really desire a general betterment.   Hence the labor-cost-reduction expert must move with utmost caution to avoid a revolt against "red-tape" and "system" which will throw him out of the door in disgrace, if he puts on a front of authority at the outset of his campaign against the existing order.

The foreman and sub-foremen of the place under treatment find it hard to accept instruction; the workmen, always suspicious, never aware that the highest labor-hour production is the highest human good, object to being "speeded up," even though the speeding up may actually mean an easier day's work for themselves—all so that absolutely nothing but a long continued and wisely tactful effort can possibly bring permanent and peaceful success in labor-cost reducing.

The Ford high wage does away with all of this inertia and living-force resistance. The top men of all Ford departments know they are expected to make labor-cost reductions, that tomorrow must always better today. The workmen are absolutely docile, and it is safe to say that, since the last day of 1912, every single day has seen marked reductions made in the Ford shops labor-costs.

CAN OTHER FOUNDRIES REACH THE FORD COSTS?

In case of continued repetitions of foundry product, as in instance of farm machinery, stoves, heaters, radiators, and so on, other foundries can reach labor costs as low as the Ford costs by open shop and high-hour pay, which will infallibly secure willing obedience of day workers. Low labor-costs ensure large product sales and steady employment for day-pay men.

In case of the jobbing foundry it is probably correct to say that labor-cost reduction must be a work of time, because jobbing means uncertain sales and demands skilled, all-round moulders. Of course, as is now well known to factory managers at large, willing labor, systematically directed, will automatically effect continuous labor-cost reductions.

Mutinous labor nullifies, in large part, the gains which can be made by good management of willing labor.

The Ford foundry as first started had no distinctive features whatever, unless saw-tooth roof lighting may be so rated. The shovel and the wheelbarrow reigned supreme, everything done by hand, nothing by machinery, when, May 10, 1910, the first Ford Model-T cylinders were made from wood patterns. The early history of the foundry is of little importance in this story, which is intended to show the practice of today.

The Model-T patterns were changed to metal and placed on commercial moulding machines, some of them specialized to meet Ford requirements, but all purchased from outside suppliers to the trade and none of them demanding detailed description here.

Late in 1912, the first important novel feature of the present Ford foundry, the core-sand gallery and the core-sand mixing-stage, all on one level, with traps in the gallery floor for supplying individual mixed core-sand chutes to each core-maker's bench, were installed, thus avoiding all mixing of core sand by the core makers themselves. The endless-chain-driven mould-carriers, the second marked feature of the Ford foundry, by which moulds are now brought to one pouring field, at one end of the mould-carrier circuit, and to one chevron shake-out grating, at the other end of the mould-carrier circuit, began work in February, 1913.

With the mould-carriers, the continuous sand-handling-and-mixing endless-chain-circuit was also installed, so that the machine moulders

Sand Chutes and Moulding Machines

Sand is carried to the chutes by pushers, moving at about 40 feet per minute, in an overhead trough; the pushers go down in the vertical hollow column at the right. View looking southwest

Sand-Pushers Chain of Unit No. 4, during Installation

The view shows the pushers overhead and the descending north end of the pusher chain, with top and bottom sprockets. Pushers travel in a rectangular path which encloses both moulders and machines

were relieved of the labor of handling and cutting over the sand which they used, each machine moulder having an individual overhead sand chute which he could open to fill his flasks as needed. This sand circuit is placed over the machine-moulders' heads for supplying the individual sand chutes, with a return under the machine-moulder's feet, and an elevator at the shake-out end to a moistening and cutting-over mechanism which delivers sand ready for moulder's use to the overhead chutes, all in continuous circuit, so that the machine moulder has nothing to do save to make the mould itself.

The core-sand mixing-stage supports machines which automatically produce unvarying core-sand mixtures, and the galleries, trap-doors and core-sand chutes deliver these uniform core-sand mixtures to the proper core benches, thus making it certain that the cores will be made of the best mixture for their purpose, and also cheapening the labor-cost of core making. The Ford core-sand gallery is believed to be unique.

The mould-carriers obtain all the advantages of the moving assembly line, which has so greatly lowered the Ford assembling costs in many departments.   A machine-moulded cope and drag are two elements of an assembly finally to be completed by closing the moulds, weighting them, and pouring melted metal into them, and large savings in labor-cost can always be made by moving the assembly in progress past component supplying stations.

The core-sand gallery, the mould carriers and the endless chain core-oven—the only thing I have ever seen that ensures uniform core-baking—are the three principal factors of the Ford shops low-cost founding.

The Ford Foundry "Unit"

One "unit" comprises two circuits of mechanically-driven mould-carriers, having located midway between them a double line of moulding machines, each fitted with its own overhead sand chute, as described.

Sand Trough and Sand Pushers

Overhead sand troughs from elevated cutting-over, moistening and riddling tower to individual machine moulders' sand-chutes.   Steel vertical sand-pushers are 30 inches long by 20 inches high.   The trough is 30 inches wide inside.   The sand-pushers are driven by endless chain, running in a trough over the heads and in a sand-way under the feet of the moulders; chain speed is about 40 feet per minute.   View from the north, looking south

Pendulum Mould Carriers on Electric-Driven Overhead Endless Chain
The pendulums shown carry flasks and mould weights. Everything cleaned up, not a work-day picture

The labor equipment of each unit comprises machine moulders; mould-handlers, who take the moulds from the machines and deposit them on the pendulum shelves of the carriers, or close them on drags previously placed on the shelves; weight layers, who lay the weights on the copes of the closed moulds; pourers, who carry skimmers and skim their own hand-ladles; and shake-out men, who shake out the moulds at the grating and pile the runners together.

Wash basins are placed inside the mould-carrier circuits, together with a small table used by the "check-taker." For mould-production recording purposes each machine moulder is provided with a certain number of individually-marked, small, round, brass checks, one of which he lays upon each mould which he makes cope or drag as may be. The moulds pass the check-taker's station before closing, the checks are taken off and piled on the check-taker's table to the number of 25 for one moulder, and are then marked on a moulder's record sheet and the checks are returned by the check-taker to the moulder who owns them.

All the Model-T component gray-iron moulds except the *en-bloc* cylinders-casting moulds are produced by the units.   The cylinder moulds are taken from the moulding machines and placed on the floor, usual manner, for core setting and closing, and are poured in the usual manner, with ladles suspended from overhead electric cranes.

Drawings have been made for continuously moving cylinder-mould-carriers, but these circuits of pendulous cylinder-mould-carriers have not been constructed at the date of this writing, November 16, 1914.

POWER-DRIVEN MOULD CARRIERS

Power-driven mould carriers are old and well known in the founder's art, both continuously and intermittingly driven, though I have seen but one such installation, that in the Westinghouse Air-Brake foundry. This endless train of 240 cars (memory record) is used for producing the Westinghouse air-brake cylinder, is intermittingly driven, and has each car mounted on four wheels which run on finished metal rails.

Pouring Moulds on a Mould Carrier of No. 4 Unit

The construction of the mould carrier circuits has been changed in every one up to and including Unit No. 4, which is regarded as satisfactory.   The pendulums in No. 4 are steel tubes, while in the others they are of channel bars.   The speed of the carriers is about 12 feet per minute

One side of the chain of cars, which is run on parallel tracks connected by semi-circular ends, is used for cope and drag moulding, core setting, and closing; the other side of the train is used for pouring, cooling, and shaking-out over a shake-out grate, fitted with spiral conveyors and sand moisteners underneath which deliver the sand to an endless-chain elevator supplying the individual moulder's sand-chutes on the moulding side of the car track. Printed description of this train of mould-carrying cars was not permitted, hence the intermitting car-movement was not examined. I watched the smooth and good action of this Westinghouse train of mould-carrying-cars several times and was greatly impressed with its labor-saving virtues. As the story was told to me, this endless train of mould-carriers was invented by the foreman of the Westinghouse foundry, was patented, and patent assigned to the Westinghouse Company and held for its own exclusive use, save that a gift of a shop right was made to Crane Brothers, Chicago, Ill., who used it for valve-body moulding. I have never seen this Crane shops installation, but both the Crane and the Westinghouse mould-carriers have been seen by the Ford engineers who placed the Ford mould-carriers, and who were unfavorably impressed by the Westinghouse intermittent action but liked the Crane installation, which places the endless-chain sprockets overhead and drops pendulums down from elevated-track-carried trolleys, these pendulums having mould shelves fixed to their lower ends.

Some Mould-Carrier Construction Particulars

The diameters of the large overhead mould-carrier chain-sprockets is $121\frac{1}{2}$ inches, pitch circle. The north-end sprocket is electric-motor driven, the south-end sprocket is an idler.

The different mould-carrier-circuits have different lengths of mould-carrying shelves as well as different numbers of shelves, and have the sprocket center-to-center distances varied to suit. The principal dimensions of the No. 3 unit are as follows: conveyor sprockets, center to center, for each mould-carrier circuit are 36 feet; distance from center to center of mould shelves in the parallel sides of the circuit is $121\frac{1}{2}$ inches; distance between the circuit centers is 37 feet $3\frac{1}{2}$ inches; distance between the inner lines of the shelves of the two circuits is 26 feet. This is the width of the space occupied by the moulding machines and the moulding-machine men. This distance of 26 feet could probably be reduced to 6 feet, if one line of moulding machines was placed inside of each circuit of mould-carriers, as would be possible if the mould-carriers ran on tracks on the same level as the foundry floor.

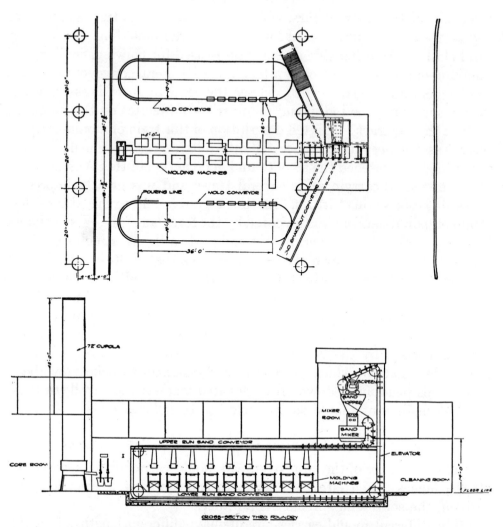

Plan and Section of Ford Foundry on February 25, 1914

The No. 4 unit has 49 mould-carrying shelves, each 23⅝ inches long by 15 inches wide.

The entire cost of one unit, exclusive of cost of moulding machines, is about $15,000.

The Ford plant mill-wrighting has been until recently charged in a lump sum to factory expense, with no detailed costs made up against individual installations, hence exact figures of "unit" costs cannot be given.

The pendulum mould-carrier has no obvious advantages, but has marked objections in the way of inaccessibility of driving mechanism and the free swing of the pendulous mould-shelves, besides greatly obscuring the saw-tooth lighting, and, the most serious fault of all, when

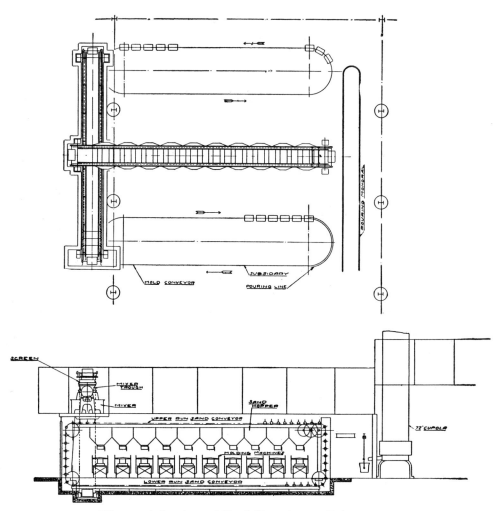

Plan and Section of Ford Foundry on July 10, 1914

the carrier is in operation it cuts off access to a large floor space which is thus made waste territory.

Unquestionably, for difficult and exact core setting, such as is demanded for the Ford Model-T cylinder, an intermitting mould-carrier-movement is highly desirable, and certainly a far cheaper continuous-movement mould-carrier installation can be had without the large overhead sprockets which drive and carry the Ford endless-chain pen-dulum-mould-carriers.

It is but justice to say that the Ford engineers are perfectly satisfied with their own installations of mould-carriers, which work steadily and smoothly, and give no trouble of any kind whatever.

Rockwell 4-Reel Revolving Core Oven.   Northwest Corner of Ford Foundry

Core-makers' benches in rear, with core-sand chutes from overhead gallery

Jobbing Core-Makers at Work under Core-Sand Gallery

Core-sand chutes from gallery, seen from the left, along rear of picture.   This gallery was devised by the
Ford engineers and is believed to be unique

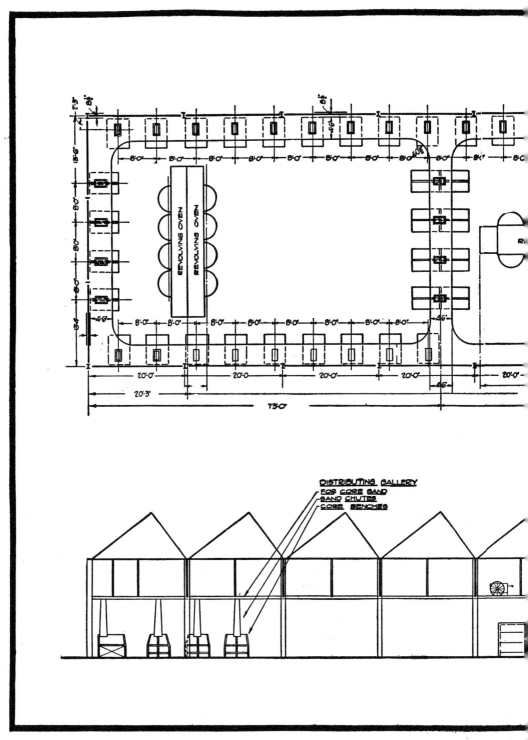

REVOLVING OVEN
REVOLVING OVEN

DISTRIBUTING GALLERY
FOR CORE SAND
SAND CHUTES
CORE BENCHES

GENERAL PLAN OF GALLERY FLOOR OV

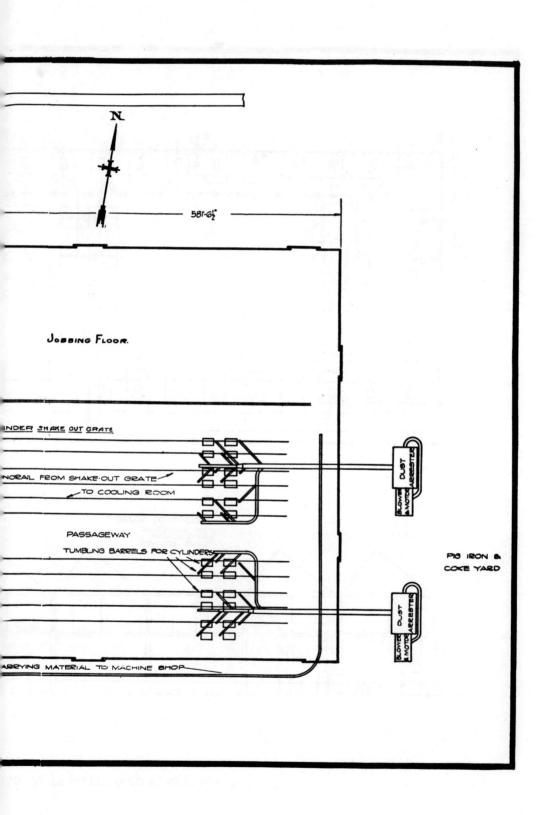

N

581'-6½"

JOBBING FLOOR.

...NDER SHAKE OUT GRATE

...NORAIL FROM SHAKE-OUT GRATE

TO COOLING ROOM

PASSAGEWAY

TUMBLING BARRELS FOR CYLINDERS

...ARRYING MATERIAL TO MACHINE SHOP

PIG IRON &
COKE YARD

DUST ARRESTER
BLOWER & MOTOR

DUST ARRESTER
BLOWER & MOTOR

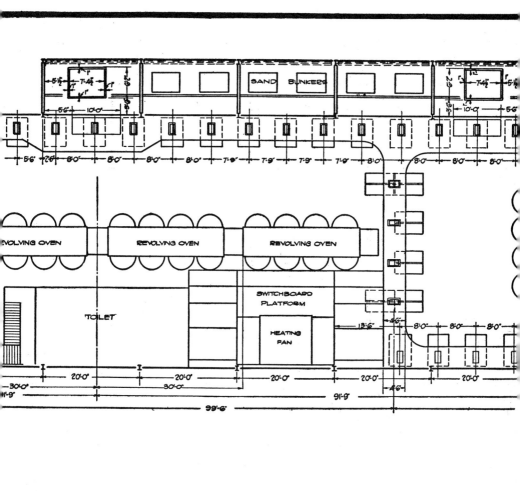

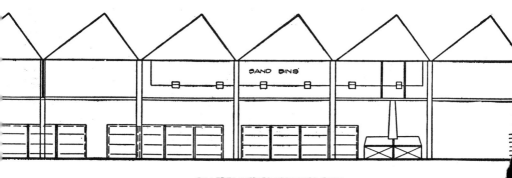

GALLERIES OVER FOUNDRY CORE ROOM
FORD MOTOR CO.,
DETROIT, U.S.A.
FEB. 25, 1914   G. A. BUCKLEY

R CORE ROOM OF FOUNDRY, FORD MOTOR COMPANY'S HIGHLAND PARK SHO

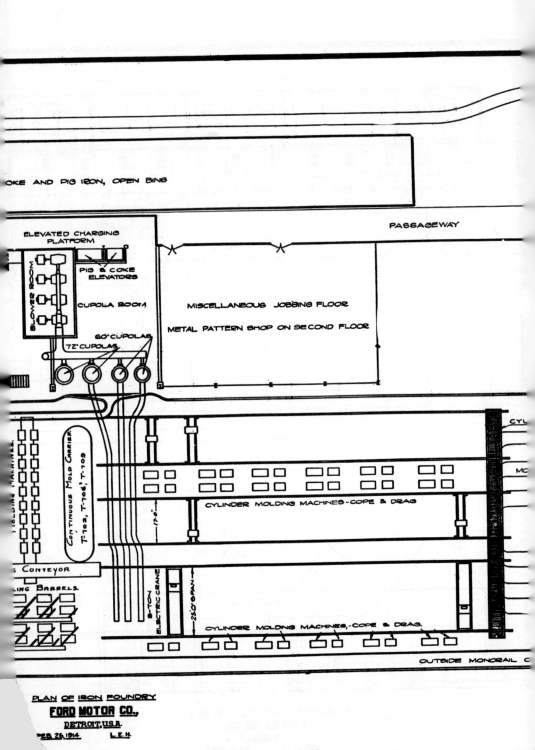

OKE AND PIG IRON, OPEN BINS

PASSAGEWAY

ELEVATED CHARGING
PLATFORM

BLOWER ROOM

PIG & COKE
ELEVATORS

CUPOLA ROOM

MISCELLANEOUS JOBBING FLOOR

METAL PATTERN SHOP ON SECOND FLOOR

60" CUPOLAS

72" CUPOLAS

MOLDING MACHINES.

Continuous Mold Carrier
T-703, T-706, T-709

CYLINDER MOLDING MACHINES - COPE & DRAG

CYL

MO

17'0"

CONVEYOR

LING BARRELS.

3-TON ELECTRIC CRANE

25'-0" SPAN

CYLINDER MOLDING MACHINES, - COPE & DRAG.

OUTSIDE MONORAIL C

PLAN OF IRON FOUNDRY

FORD MOTOR CO.,

DETROIT, U.S.A.

FEB 26, 1914   L.E.H.

THE FORD MOTOR COMPANY.   CORRECTED TO NOVEMBER, 1914

(e of gallery, see the other side of the sheet)

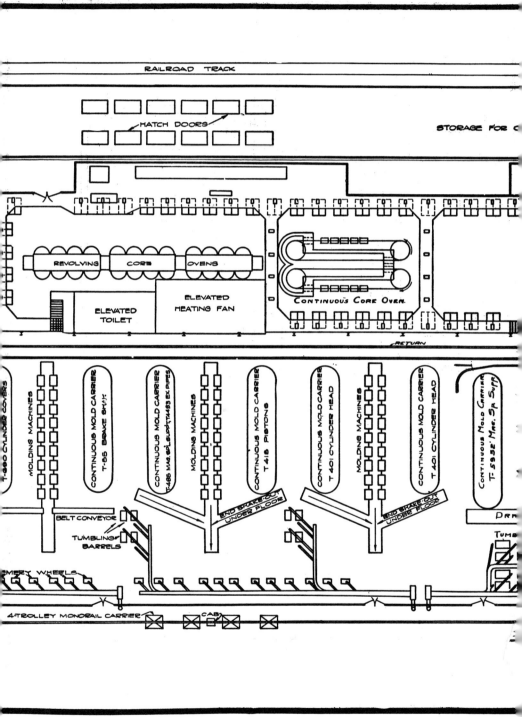

GENERAL PLAN OF THE FOUNDRY, HIGHLAND PARK 8

(*For longitudinal section a:*

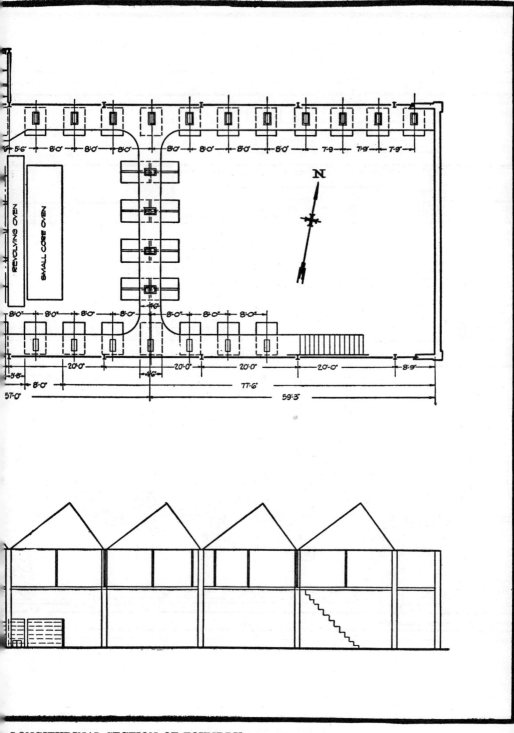

LONGITUDINAL SECTION OF FOUNDRY

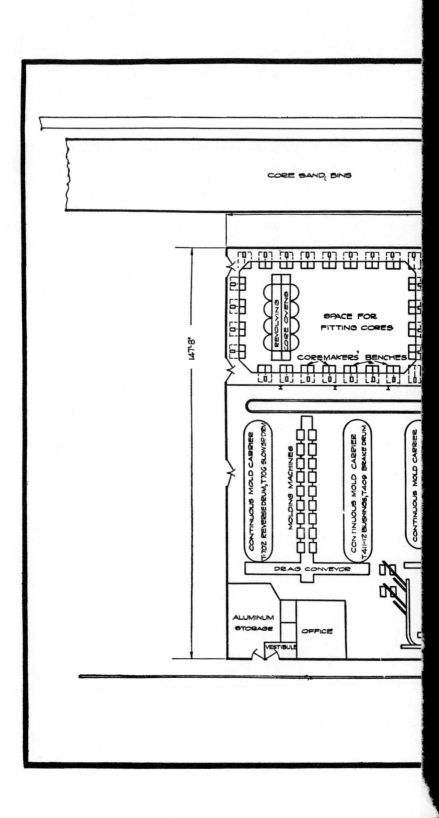

CORES, CORE DRIERS AND CORE OVENS

With core makers, as with moulders, the Ford foundry depends mainly on specialized laborers, all males. In many foundries small cores are made by females, more docile than males, and having a delicacy of touch which naturally fits them for handling fragile product.

The Ford foundry expects to transform a laborer into an efficient maker of one core only, with a couple of days' instruction, as the Ford

Top View of Double Revolving-Chain Core-Oven

The chains are driven by electric motor with worm and sprocket gearing in reverse directions, so that the inner sides of both chain-circuits run from west to east through the oven and from east to west in the return outside. Baked cores are taken off the shelves at the east end and the shelves are loaded with unbaked cores before reaching the western entrance to the oven

core makers have nothing to do with core-sand mixing, and have wires, cut and bent to suit, supplied to them, and core-oven tenders to take the finished cores from the core-maker's benches as soon as made.

CORE DRIERS

The core drier is one part of the metal core-box, often a costly piece of furniture, in which the core rests while baking. No matter what the

East End of the Double Endless-Chain Core-Oven

Taking baked cores off the chain shelves as the chains leave the east end of the oven

length or form of a core may be it lies in true form in the drier while baking, and retains its over-all dimensions perfectly after baking. The Ford Model-T cylinders are difficult productions, very complicated in form and having water-jackets only ⅛-inch thickness of wall. Hence, it is imperative that the cores should be to dimensions exactly, and the use of the core driers ensures this correctness of core measurement. The only objection is the very considerable cost of the driers, which fades to nothing in case of continuous repetitions of product.

The original installations of core ovens were the Rockwell revolving ovens, first installation in autumn of 1912, which yet remain in commission. See the upper picture on page 340.

Endless-Chain Core Ovens

The Ford engineers devised two endless chains of core-oven shelves, two circuits placed side by side and running in reverse directions, adjacent sides of the circuits running together through the oil-fired oven common to both, and returning through the open air. During this return trip the cores placed on the endless-chain-carried shelves are removed by the core takers-off. In this endless-chain core-shelf-circuit the overhead sprockets, endless chains, and overhead trolley tracks are precisely the correct thing, exactly suited to their work. Nothing could be better adapted to core-baking than this double-endless-chain arrangement, speed of chains 17 inches per minute on one side, and 12 inches per minute on the other side, so that heavier cores, placed on the outside, have the longer time in the oven. It is extremely economical of fuel, and gives a perfection of core-baking uniformity, entirely independent of the oven-tender's judgment, impossible to obtain by use of any other core oven ever seen by me.

SOME PARTICULARS OF ENDLESS-CHAIN CORE-OVEN CONSTRUCTION

The endless-chain core-oven sprockets are $80\frac{1}{2}$ inches pitch circle diameter. The center-to-center distance of the sprockets is 38 feet and 6 inches. The cross-wise center-to-center distance of the sprockets for the two chain circuits of core-shelves-carrying down-hangers is 9 feet $3\frac{1}{2}$ inches. All cores save the cylinder-barrel cores are baked in this oven. The cylinder-barrel cores are very much larger than any other Model-T component cores and require much longer time in baking, and are baked exclusively in the Rockwell revolving core ovens.

The core-oven endless-chain-carried down-hangers (see page 341, lower right hand of the picture, and page 342) are of plate-steel, 72 inches long up and down by 24 inches wide and $\frac{3}{16}$ inch thickness. The down-hangers are spaced 42 inches center-to-center, and are pierced to take 10 shelves, 16 inches wide, placed 6 inches apart up and down.

The picture on page 342 shows the eastern (exit) end of the core shelves. When this core oven was first used the eastern and western ends were alike; now, the western end has been surrounded by an outside wall extending about 10 feet eastward, thus increasing the virtual baking-oven length by that much. Taking the baked cores off the shelves is a very warm job.

This endless-chain core oven is extremely economical in points of floor space occupied and of fuel consumed in core-baking and core-handling labor, besides having the very great advantage of mechanically-determined core-baking time, nothing being left to the judgment of the core-oven tenders, thus ensuring a very close approximation to that absolute uniformity of core baking which is the first essential in the pro-

5-Ton Shaw Gantry Crane Covering the Sand, Coke and Scrap Bins on the North Side of the Ford Foundry

duction of perfect cored castings. The cost of this oven was about $4,500.

CRANES

The Ford foundry is served by nine cranes and two elevators to the cupola-charging stage. Of the cranes, one is a Shaw gantry, 5-tons capacity, working on a track north of the foundry over sand bins and scrap bins, fitted with magnet and clam-shell; six cranes by the Northern Engineering Company, Detroit, each 3-tons capacity, covering the cylinder-moulding and pouring floor, with tracks extending to the cylinder-cleaning and testing and monorail shipping floor at east end of the foundry; one Browning flat-car jib-crane, 15-tons capacity, equipped with magnet and clam-shell, and one 40-ton crane mounted on a flat car, supplied by Browning, Cleveland.

The monorail track enters the foundry at the southeast corner and takes the foundry product to the factory.

The castings cleaning (save of cylinders) is along the south side of the foundry. The cylinders cleaning is at the eastern end of the foundry floor.

BRASS CASTINGS

The Ford Company began to make brass castings in the summer of 1914, is now pouring about 2 tons of brass per day, and will soon pour

Ford Foundry, Looking West. Cylinder-Moulding Floor

Upper view shows the overhead cranes. Lower view shows the overhead trolley rail from the cupolas westward for moving ladles to and from mould-carrier circuits

Cleaning Cylinders
A Ford machine for pulling out core wires

a hand-driven core-wire-puller, Ford construction. See illustration adjoining.

The hydraulic cylinder testing is by two Ford special machines, shown in the lower picture on this page.

CASTINGS

The iron used in the cylinders analyzes: silicon 2.00, sulphur 0.06 to 0.08, phosphorus 0.20, manganese 0.65. Analysis is made daily. The cupola charge is pig, 50 per cent, scrap 35 per cent, steel scrap 15 per cent. About 135 pounds of iron in the ladle is required for each cylinder casting;

all its brass, about 11 tons per day, in a brass foundry on one of the floors in the old factory building. The present brass floor in the gray-iron foundry is a temporary affair only.

ALUMINUM FLOOR

This adjoins the gray-iron foundry west and south corner, with aluminum furnaces and cleaning floor adjoining the moulding floor.

CYLINDERS CLEANING

The tools employed are files, brushes, pneumatic chippers, and

Cleaning Cylinders
Hydraulic test for leaks

the weight of the cleaned cylinder casting is about 101 pounds each. Thirteen hundred cylinder castings are poured each day; and about 1,200 cylinders are sent from the foundry to the machine shop.

Production Per Square Foot of Foundry Floor

The daily record for Nov. 2, 1914, is given as typical:

Iron melted, 192 tons.

Weight of sand handled, 1,906 tons.

Floor space used for iron moulding, 36,324 square feet

Floor area per ton of iron poured, 186 square feet.

Total number castings made, 40,450 pieces.

Average weight of castings, 8.9 pounds.

UNIT PRODUCTION PARTICULARS

NO. 1 UNIT

Symbol	Component Name	No. sets mould-ing ma-chines	Cast-ings from each set	Total per unit	Wt. of mould	Wt. of sand	Wt. of cstng.	Wt. of flask	No. cast-ings in each mould
T-690	Exhaust end covers	2 sets	400	800	157	103	8	46	2
T-4483	Exhaust pipes.....	2 sets	280	560	231	151	14	66	2
T-702	Reverse drum.....	1 set	300	300	135	78	11	46	2
T-512	Intake pipe.......	3 sets	450	1,350	156	97	13	46	2
T-4490	Valve heads.......	1 set	400	400	156	97	13	46	40
T-411 & T-412	Cam-shaft bearings	1 set	120	120	167	101	20	46	24
				3,530					

SUMMARY

No. Moulding Machines 20—47 workmen.

No. of moulds made in Unit No. 1 in 8 hrs.........................	3,530
Sand handled by Unit No. 1 in 1 hr...............................	48 tons
Sand handled by Unit No. 1 in 8 hrs..............................	384 tons
Iron required for pouring No. 1 unit in 8 hrs.......................	21 tons
Floor space required by No. 1 unit................................	3,000 sq. ft.
Floor space required per ton of iron..............................	143 sq. ft.

Floor space utilized to complete work on castings ready for machine shop,—300 sq. ft. per ton.

NO. 2 UNIT

Part Symbol	Part Name	Sets of machines	No. pcs. per set	Total pcs. per set	Wt. of mould	Wt. of sand	Wt. of cstng.	Wt. of flask	No. castings per mould
T-55	Brake shoes.......	5 sets	450	2,250	130	76	5	46	2
T-702	Reverse drum.....	1 set	350	350	135	78	11	46	2
T-706	Slow speed........	1 set	240	240	135	83	6	46	2
T-709	Brake drum.......	1 set	180	180	142	80	15	46	2
				3,020					

SUMMARY

No. of moulds made in Unit No. 2 in 8 hrs........................ 3,020
Sand handled by Unit No. 2 in 1 hr.............................. 34 tons
Sand handled by Unit No. 2 in 8 hrs............................. 272 tons
Iron required for pouring No. 2 unit in 8 hrs..................... 10 tons
Floor space occupied by No. 2 unit.............................. 3,000 sq. ft.
Floor space required by No. 2 unit per ton of iron................. 300 sq. ft.
16 moulding machines, with 33 men.
Floor space utilized to complete all work on castings ready for machine
    shop,—510 sq. ft. per ton.

NO. 3 UNIT

Symbol	Name of Piece	Sets of moulding machines	No. pcs. per set	Total No. pcs.	Wt. per mould	Wt. of sand	Wt. of cstgs.	Wt. of flask	No. castings in mould
T-418	Pistons...........	7 sets	220	1,540	192	114	25	53	4
T-422	Piston pots.......	3 sets	125	375	248	142	40	66	4
				1,815					

SUMMARY

No. Moulding Machines—20.
No. of moulds made in Unit No. 3 in 8 hrs........................ 1,915
Sand handled by Unit No. 3 in 1 hr.............................. 34 tons
Sand handled by Unit No. 3 in 8 hrs............................. 272 tons
Iron required to pour No. 3 unit, 8 hrs.......................... 27 tons
Floor space occupied by No. 3 unit.............................. 3,000 sq. ft.
Floor space required per ton of iron............................. 111 sq. ft.
No. of men employed on No. 3 unit—65.
Floor space utilized for completing all work on castings ready for ma-
    chine shop, 191 sq. ft.

NO. 4 UNIT

Symbol	Name of Piece	Sets of mould-ing ma-chines	No. pcs. per set	Total No. pcs.	Wt. per mould	Wt. of sand	Wt. of cstgs.	Wt. of flask	No. pcs. in mould
T-401	Cylinder heads....	7 sets	190	1,330	339	216	35	88	1
T-442	Water inlet con-nections........	1 set	225	225	161	103	12	46	8
T-4483	Exhaust pipes.....	1 set	250	250	231	151	14	66	2
				1,810					

SUMMARY

No. of moulds made by Unit No. 4 in 8 hrs.......................... 1,605
Sand handled by Unit No. 4 in 1 hr............................... 30 tons
Sand handled by Unit No. 4 in 8 hrs.............................. 288 tons
Iron required for pouring No. 4 unit, 8 hrs....................... 27 tons
Floor space occupied by No. 4 unit............................... 3,000 sq. ft.
Floor space required per ton iron................................ 111 sq. ft.
Number of men employed on No. 4 Unit—64.
Number of moulding machines—18.
Floor utilized for completing all work on castings ready for machine shop—191 sq. ft. per ton.

NO. 5 UNIT

Symbol	Part Name	Sets of mould-ing ma-chines	No. pcs. per set	Total No. of pcs.	Wt. of mould	Wt. of sand	Wt. of cstgs.	Wt. of flask	Pcs. per mould
T-5932	Magneto spool....	6 sets	250	1,500	171	105	11	55	1
T-702	Reverse drum.....	1 set	350	350	135	78	11	46	2
T-706	Slow speed........	1 set	240	240	135	83	6	46	2
T-709	Brake drum.......	2 sets	180	360	142	80	15	46	2
				2,450					

SUMMARY

No. moulding machines, 20.   No. men, 65.
No. of moulds made on No. 5 unit in 8 hrs........................ 2,450
Sand handled on No. 5 unit in 1 hr............................... 35 tons
Sand handled on No. 5 unit in 8 hrs.............................. 280 tons
Floor space occupied by No. 5 unit............................... 3,000 sq. ft.
Iron required for pouring No. 5 unit in 8 hrs.................... 13 tons
Floor space required per ton of iron............................. 230 sq. ft.
Floor space utilized for completing all work on casting ready for ma-chine shop, 392.3 sq. ft. per ton.

CYLINDER FLOOR

Symbol	Part Name	Sets of mould-ing ma-chines	Pcs. per mach.	Total No. pcs.	Wt. of mould	Wt. of sand	Wt. of cstgs.	Wt. of flask	No. pcs. in mould
T-400	Cylinders........	13 sets	100	1,300	. 785	478	125	162	1

SUMMARY

No. workmen, 466.
No. moulding machines, 20; 10 sets cope and drag.
No. of moulds made per day in 8 hrs................................ 1,300
Sand used in 1 hr... 39 tons
Sand used in 8 hrs... 312 tons
Iron required per day in 8 hrs.................................... 81 tons
Floor space occupied by cylinder floor........................... 13,824 sq. ft.
Floor space utilized for completing all work on cylinder castings ready for machine shop, per ton, 320 sq. ft.
Floor space required per ton for moulding and pouring cylinders, 158.3 sq. ft.

These total production and foundry area figures are given as likely to interest foundry managers and students of foundry economies.

Every square foot of factory floor carries the same overhead charges, and the less the floor space used for a given production, the lower the overhead charges against that production are.

The cylinder sand is worked in the usual manner, moistened and cut over by hand. The machine-made moulds are set on the floor, cores are set by core-setters, copes closed on by men who do nothing but close and bank the moulds, and all the hand work is divided and specialized as minutely as may be, to reduce the duties of each workman to the lowest profitable number. Undoubtedly the total number of workmen employed on the cylinder job could be very considerably reduced by the installation of the best possible mould-carriers, moved intermittingly, so as to stand still as much more than one-half of the time as the inter-mitting driving-mechanism can be conveniently arranged to give. Perhaps 1,300 cylinders could be turned out with 250 men all told, in place of the 466 men now used, if everything was brought into the best possible form for working.

FUEL

Solvay 72-hour coke, supplied by the Semet-Solvay Company, Del-ray, Mich., is used exclusively in the Ford foundry, because of almost unvarying uniformity of analysis and its good load-supporting capacity

Lunch Time in the Aluminum Moulding Floor. Gray Iron Foundry

in the cupola. The Solvay coke is shipped to Ford plant with analysis, and is also analyzed in the Ford laboratory from time to time and is invariably found to be always very close to the following constitution,

Cleaning Aluminum Castings. Furnaces at Left. Lunch Time

Cylinders Cleaning Floor at East End of the Foundry

viz.: Volatile matter (smoke), 0.29; fixed carbon, 91.75; ash, 7.96; sulphur, 0.581 = 100.53. As is well known to chemists, it is a rare thing for the total of analysis elements to be exactly 100.

Gray Iron Analysis for Model-T Components Other Than Cylinders

From test reports of November 23, an analysis of the gray iron is: combined carbon, 0.5; total carbon, 3.35; manganese, 0.65; phosphorus, 0.455; sulphur, 0.079; silicon, 2.54.

Tensile tests and transverse tests are made on the Oleson machines, and tests for hardness are made on twelve Shore "Sceleroscope" machines, located at various points in the Ford shops, and on one Brinell and one Derihon machine in the Ford laboratory.

Cupola Charging for Model-T Components Other Than Cylinders

Toledo pig, first charge, 300 pounds; Superior charcoal pig, 300 pounds; Toledo pig, second charge, 600 pounds; "return stock" scrap (largely defective cylinders), 1,400 pounds. The Ford Company buys all the defective cylinders which can be had in this section of the country, because of their high-grade metal.

Cost of Iron in Ladle

The Ford foundry average cost of iron in the ladle is about $0.008 per pound, flat, say, including overhead, $0.016.

Core-Sand Mixing Stage

The core-sand mixing stage is supplied with sand by the Shaw gantry crane, working on the tracks over the sand-bins on the north side of the foundry. (See the picture on page 344.)

There are two machines on the core-sand mixing stage, one "apportioning" machine, sand and "compound" measurer and mixer, and one "batch" machine, both supplied by the Standard Sand and Machine Company, Cleveland, Ohio. Of course, the experienced core-maker will understand that a number of different core-sand mixtures are made, suitable for various descriptions of cores. The core-mixing stage has a working force of one foreman and five men, who mix the core-sand and deliver it to the proper core-bench chutes through traps in the gallery cast-iron floor-plates.

Cylinders Cleaning Floor. Monorail for Transporting Cylinders to Machine Shop

Sturtevant Forced-Blast-Blower Room under Cupola Charging Stage.   One Blower for Each Cupola

The "compound" or core-bond used is supplied by the Henry E. Mills Manufacturing Company, Syracuse, N. Y., for all save the cylinder-barrel cores, which are made with linseed-oil bond.   Oil "matches" are not regularly used, but find occasional employment on the jobbing floor.

FORD FOUNDRY EQUIPMENT, EXCEPTING CRANES, MONORAIL AND "CARRIER UNITS"

The monorail carries 2½-ton loads with a single car and 5-ton loads with two cars, one in front and one in rear of driver's cab.   (See the illustration on page 353.)

Two Rockwell revolving core ovens, four reels each, are used, principally for baking the 2,600 double cylinder-barrel cores required daily.

Eight "Pridmore" moulding machines are used in the aluminum foundry.   The gray-iron foundry uses Pridmore, Osborne, and Berkshire moulding machines.   Total number of moulding machines in the gray-iron foundry, 173.

Four cupolas are used, supplied by Northern Engineering Works, Detroit, Mich.   A fifth cupola, supplied by the Whiting Foundry Equipment, Harvey, Ill., is now being placed.   All of these five cupolas are 10 feet higher than "regular" for their diameters.

Each cupola is supplied with air by a No. 10 Sturtevant forced-blast blower, 8- to 12-ounces blast pressure.

Three brass furnaces, supplied by the Monarch Company, Baltimore, are used in the brass foundry. The aluminum foundry has ten "Monarch" furnaces.

Three cylinder-barrel-cores black-washing machines, each having three revoluble core-stands, of Ford construction, are used, with black-wash atomizers. Ten core-wire cutting and forming machines are worked by ten men and one foreman.

Total number of tumbling barrels in Ford foundry, sixty-two; twenty-eight used exclusively for cylinder tumbling and thirty-four for general work.

Total number of grinding and facing wheels stands, thirty. The facing wheels are "Gardners," seven in number. Thirty-four snagging-wheel stands are used, supplied by Norton.

CYLINDER MOULDING

The cylinder moulding is done under three parallel craneways, running east and west, on which electric cranes for carrying the pouring

Cylinder-Moulding Floor. Pouring Cylinders

ladles are operated.   Each pouring ladle takes about 1,250 pounds of iron.

The cylinder moulders are worked in thirteen gangs, each gang including workmen as follows: One cope rammer; one cope rammer's helper; one drag rammer; one drag rammer's helper; one drag finisher, who inspects and finishes drag half of mould and sets three cylinder cores; one cope finisher, who inspects and finishes cope half of mould and sets water-jacket core; one barrel-core setter, who sets the barrel

Cylinder Moulding Floor.   Setting the Barrel Cores

cores in mould, gives it final inspection, seals, and with aid of bankers, closes mould; two bankers, who help close mould, make runner basin and "bank up" mould.

No. 1 and No. 2 craneways, north, each serve four gangs of cylinder moulders. No. 3 craneway, north, serves five gangs. Each craneway is served by one pouring gang, including one pourer, who also operates crane, one pourer's helper, and one man who skims and assists otherwise as required. (See the cut on page 355.) The three craneways are served by one shaker-out gang consisting of one foreman and twenty-five men.

Foundry Officials

Standing, from left to right: Brass Melter; Head Cupola Man, "melter" in ordinary foundry talk;
Stock Clerk—makes requisitions and keeps record of materials received and finished castings
delivered; Pattern Foreman, in charge of patterns generally; Night Foreman; Foundry Foreman; Foundry Head (young man with sweater); Second Foundry Foreman; Head Draftsman; Draftsman; Draftsman. Office Clerk seated in center

As an instance of the Ford policy of promoting employees it may be said that the Foundry Head,
shown in the above group, was first a moulder, then a Ford wood-pattern maker, then a Ford metal-pattern
maker, and after three years of Ford service as a mechanic was made head of the foundry

Foundry and Heat-Treating Time Office Men

The head of the department is standing at the extreme right. Seated, from left to right are: First
Assistant; "Checker" for Heat Treating Department, who sees that the wearer of each badge number,
recorded as passing the time-clock, is in the department and working; Heat-Treat "Checker," same duties
as preceding. Standing, from left to right: Foundry "Checker," who is a time-taker in the foundry;
Foundry "Checker," same as preceding; Messenger; Production Record Clerk; Heat-Treat "Checker";
Second Assistant; Production Clerk; Office Clerk, and, as previously noted, the Head of the Department.
Two "Night Checkers" are not shown. Time clocks are in an adjacent small building. Picture taken
November 24, 1914

Eighty tons of sand are used on the cylinder-moulding job, about two tons of new sand being supplied daily. This 80 tons of sand is cut-over by a gang of about fifteen men, working in the second shift, who make the sand ready for the cylinder moulders; the cylinder moulders begin at 6:30 a. m. and work in one shift only, to 3:00 p. m., one-half hour out for eating, own time.

The cupolas are attended by a gang which goes on at 6:00 and iron begins to come down at 6:30 a. m.

The cupola bottoms are dropped at 3:15 p. m., sometimes as late as 3:30 p. m. for cylinder pouring.

Second-Shift Cupola Tenders

Begin 3:00 p. m., leave 11:30 p. m. Last thing, these men, who have other duties, clean up under the cupolas, making ready for five night cupola men who begin at 10:00 p. m. and leave at 6:00 a. m. These five men make the bed, charge the cupolas, light the bed, and make all ready for the day cupola men, who come on at 6:00 a. m. The wind is turned on about 6:10 a. m., and iron begins to come down at 6:30 a. m. The day cupola tenders leave at 2:00 p. m. and 3:00 p. m.

The cylinder pourers come on at 7:00 a. m., and leave at 3:00 p. m.

The management avoids working men more than 8 hours in any one shift, save the top men who, from the foundry head down, come in early, and leave when everything belonging to the day's work is cleaned up.

Metal Pattern-Makers

Of course, all patterns in regular use are of metal. The regular force of metal-pattern makers, high pay rate 87½ cents per hour, is about 63. Until very recently all of these men worked in a second floor room, about 3 feet below the cupola-charging stage, and to the east thereof; now 33 of these metal-pattern makers have been transferred to the floor east of the wood-pattern shop, these men working on new patterns while 30 metal-pattern makers are retained on the old floor in the foundry, working on metal-pattern repairs.

Ford Foundry Regular Three Shifts

Shift No. 1.   Come on at 6:30 a. m., leave at 2:30 p. m., gift of 15 minutes eating time, without leaving working stations.

Shift No. 2.   Come on at 2:30 p. m., leave at 10:30 p. m., gift of 15 minutes eating time, without leaving working stations.

Shift No. 3. Come on at 10:30 p. m., leave at 6:30 a. m., gift of 15 minutes eating time, without leaving working stations.

These regular shift hours are somewhat modified in case of men who have to do with the cupolas, as before specified.

SUMMARY

The mould carriers do for the foundry exactly what the moving assembly lines do for the machine-shop—clean up the floor, make production continuous, greatly reduce production costs and greatly increase the foundry-floor capacity.

The reader has only to compare two illustrations, that on page 336, pouring moulds on No. 4 unit, and that on page 355, pouring cylinders on the cylinder-floor, to understand fully the gains made by use of automatic mould-carriers. The former picture shows the floor clean, and everything proceeding in good "factory-form."

The latter shows the usual foundry conditions, everybody working at disadvantage in an atmosphere of smoke and steam.

CHAPTER XIV

HOW THE FORD BODIES ARE FINISHED. PAINTING, UPHOLSTERING, JAPANNING AND BAKING

PAINTING needs plenty of room and time; furthermore, it must be done by skilled men. At least, that was my belief until I saw the way that it was done in the Ford plant. But here again, one is obliged to alter preconceived conceptions and acknowledge that Ford ingenuity has triumphed.

As in the chassis assembly, described in preceding chapters, the bodies are painted and upholstered, topped and trimmed complete, on an endless-chain track conveyer. This system of finishing has been but recently introduced.

Following one after another like the successive negatives on a motion-picture film, the bodies may be seen in every stage of completion.

Like a railroad system with its stations, side-tracks, depots, and terminals, the body-painting and upholstering process line wends its way over three successive floors of the new, big, six-story building on Manchester Avenue, now running straight for 850 feet at a time, turning right-angled corners—now going down-grade to the floor below, back and across, until finally the terminal is reached—the "chassis-body assembly bridge" outside.

Starting in the east end of the fifth floor, to which the rough product is raised by means of an inclined conveyer, page 361, the bodies are thrown onto the endless-chain track and given a thorough sanding and cleaning inside and out. As now arranged, it is necessary to truck the bodies from the head of the inclined conveyer to the end of the track, but it is proposed to put in a short conveyer running crosswise of the building, which will do this work, and on this the preliminary cleaning can be done, thereby giving room on the main track (which runs a distance of 850 feet parallel with Manchester Avenue) for the first priming operation, now done in separate rooms off the line.

Driven at a speed of about 25 feet per minute the bodies soon reach the point where this first "priming" operation takes place. This is the

360

only operation, with the exception of drying, which necessitates the removal of the bodies from the track, and in all probability as soon as the cross conveyer has been put in this method of priming will be displaced by one identical with that used for the second and succeeding

coats. At the present time, however, the body is removed from the track, slid onto a truck, and shoved into one of the small painting rooms just north of the track. Here a workman wearing a mask and equipped with a giant atomizer, behind which there is a pressure of 80 pounds per square inch, gives the body a thorough spraying with a brown body metal primer which dries very rapidly. The entire surface is covered in a surprisingly short time, and with a shove, the body is sent rolling across the floor to another man who with a critical eye goes over it and with a hand brush smooths out or touches up any points which, in his judgment, need further attention.

The body is then allowed to dry thoroughly before it is placed back on the track. After being sanded, it is ready for its second priming; a blue-black coat which is "flowed on" in the following manner: standing on opposite sides of the track are two men equipped with hoses, the nozzles of which remind one of fanlike

The Conveyer Carrying the Rough Unfinished Bodies from the Unloading Dock to the Fifth Floor

vacuum-cleaner nozzles, except that the ends, instead of being entirely open, are perforated, the holes extending in a line at right angles to the direction of the flow. A large tank mounted on the floor above, and connected to the hose by means of a system of pipes, furnishes a constant stream of paint. The system is operated entirely by gravity, but by the elevation of the tank to the floor above a sufficient head is secured to insure a flow of about 6 gallons a minute.

When the body has progressed to the point where it is opposite these men, they completely shower the surface with the protecting liquid, starting at the top and working down. This they do in an incredibly short time. Some points on the back of the front seat and on the dash, which they are unable to reach easily, are afterwards done by hand, with a brush. The rear end of the body is slightly elevated by a "shield block" which prevents the paint from dripping into the track and also helps to drain the excess liquid back into the system.

On both sides of the track, and directly under the sprayers, are large galvanized-iron drip tanks which drain into a central catch tank below. Surplus paint, therefore, drips into these pans and finds its way back, after passing through screens, into the paint-supply system again. A smaller gear pump, located in the pipe line about 6 feet from the track, returns the liquid to the tank above, so that a sufficient amount can be used at all times to do the job properly, without fear of wasting it. About 2 gallons of the liquid paint is flowed on; but it has been found by computation that 1 gallon will cover 11 jobs, so it is easy to compute the amount required per body. About 200 feet of the track are required for each painting operation. The "color varnish" coats and "finishing" coats are flowed on in the same manner. After the body has traveled about 200 feet, it is sufficiently dry to be removed and stacked for drying, which requires about 24 hours.

It is then placed back on the track and "mossed"; that is, rubbed lightly with curled hair and prepared for its first color varnish. This operation is performed on a cross track running from the finish end of the priming track to the starting end of the color-varnish line, which runs back from the west to the east end of the same building, parallel with the priming track.

A similar system of tanks, piping, draining trays and strainers is utilized for this operation. About 200 feet of draining tank is here required to carry off the surplus color varnish. The body is also slightly elevated at the rear, by a cross drain board, as before.

After being allowed to drip for a time which experience has shown to be sufficient, it is removed and stacked for drying. At the end of this drying, it is again "mossed," given a second coat of color varnish in the same manner as before, and stacked to dry.

At this point the upholstering operation begins. Sets of back springs are put on the seat backs, materials needed for upholstering, including

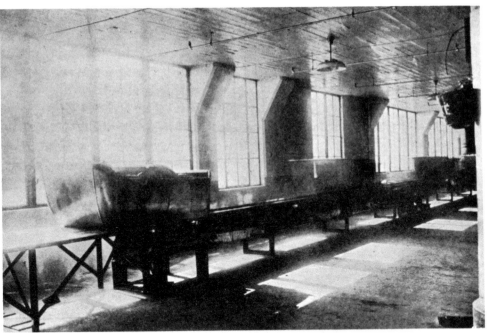

The Beginning of the Painting Operation

East end of the track where the bodies start on their way. The two at the right were running as the photograph was taken

Spraying a Body with the Priming Coat, in One of the Small Priming Rooms

Note ventilating fan in the window, and the atomizer connections. This is a posed picture, the paint spray making photography impossible under ordinary working conditions. The workman wears a mask whenever he is actually painting

partially finished "back assemblies," a big bag of hair, trimming strips, etc., are dumped into the inside of the body, just as it is shoved onto an inclined belt-conveyer which takes it to the floor below.

Here it is deposited on a metal-topped table, turned through an angle of 180 degrees, and pushed onto the "rubbing deck," where the exterior surface is given a thorough rubbing with pumice and water. The same type of track conveyer system is employed here to keep the work in progress. Instead of utilizing an ordinary "rubbing deck" where the bodies are turned up at various angles and must be handled by hand, with much labor and inconvenience, the Ford engineers, with their common-sense way of doing things, have mounted the track in the center of a concrete gutter, along which are placed, at regular intervals, water outlets and pans of powdered pumice. So conveniently arranged is everything that after the body starts on its journey across the deck, there is nothing but rubbing, washing, and polishing to be done. This work is accomplished under the most favorable conditions. The bodies are always at the proper height and in the proper position so that the work can be done without stooping or manual handling.

Flowing on the Second Coat of Blue Black

Note type of nozzle used, and drain tanks in each side of track

The pumice and water can be used freely and the work done well, in the time allowed for progress across the deck.

When it arrives at the other end, at the beginning of the two parallel upholstering lines, it is smooth and dry. At this point the work is turned through an angle of 90 degrees, divided, and started down two parallel tracks running the full length of the fourth floor.

Already provided with materials, and starting with the foundation of

springs previously fastened in place at the end of the color-varnish operation on the upper floor, the upholsterers now proceed to fasten the
made-up "cushion backs" to the body, by tacking the material firmly
to the bottom of the back of the seat, finishing it up with a strip of welt
and black-headed upholsterers' tacks.

The sides are treated in a like manner, being built out by constantly
introducing curled hair taken from the large bag of hair with which each
body is supplied. The burlap is tacked to the edge of the top of the
seat, stuffed, and sewed in place. More hair is then forced in and a big
roll made by pulling the leather over it. It is finished with the welt,
securely tacked in place.

A number of men work on the same body at the same time; some walking along the outside and some riding inside. Each man does his job and
then turns it over to the next man, so that the process is a continuous one.
The body, all this time, is moving toward the "finish varnish" room.

Finally, when the main part of the upholstering is finished, holes are

Looking South along the "Rubbing Deck"

Note the slide down which bodies come from the color-varnish department on the floor above. Back
springs put in the backs of the seats may be seen in the body coming down the incline. Photograph taken while work was in progress, as evidenced by the movement of the men

Looking North along the "Rubbing Deck" at Lunch Time

The incline shown on page 365 is in the left background. The table at the right is the beginning of the double upholstering lines. Upholstering materials may be seen inside the nearest body on the rubbing deck

Looking Down the Upholstering Lines from a Point near Their Beginning

drilled in the door frame and door, and the door straps put on.   The body is then ready to be cleaned, preparatory to receiving its final varnish coat.   This cleaning is done by two giant vacuum cleaners, which remove all the hair, bits of leather, threads, and dirt, from the interior. The exterior, in the meantime, is being wiped carefully and thoroughly by hand.

In its progress the body has, by this time, started to enter the final varnish room, through an opening in the partition extending well into the final finishing room.

On the Upholstering Line

Note the large number of men working on the body at the same time.

Here the "finishing varnish" is "flowed on" in the same manner as the other coats, and then carefully retouched by hand, in order to insure a perfect surface free from air bubbles, dry spots, bits of hair, and dust.

A metal cap is placed over the dash, so that when the body is handled it can be set upon this end without injury to the finish.

Individual trucks, fitted with draining troughs running around all four sides, are lined up along the side of the track.   When a body comes to the end, it is slid off onto a truck, shoved over to a man who acts in a dual capacity of inspector and final finisher.   He looks the job over carefully, touches it up slightly, if it needs it, and then turns it over to a man who pushes it back into the dark part of the room, where the bodies are allowed to stand until dry.

Now comes the only real break in the finishing-process line. There is, as yet, no chute or conveyer down which the bodies go after being varnished. The next operations—putting on of the windshield, top, and other equipment—are performed on the third floor, to which the bodies, therefore, are transferred as soon as they are sufficiently dry to permit of handling without damage.

In the Top Department is to be found a very interesting feature of Ford construction, because it is one of the few places where individual fitting seems to be necessary. Each Ford windshield and top is fitted to its special body. The putting on of the top and curtains is a real "custom-tailored" job.

Starting on the third floor, at the east end of the building, the bodies are again put on the conveyer track, and the windshields, which have previously been made up in the Windshield Department, and transferred in a finished condition to their proper position in the line, are now put on. Each windshield is specially fitted to an individual body.

Giving the Body Its Final Touching Up after the Finish Varnish Coat

By this time, the body has reached a point where it is ready for the top. Top bows are made in a department near by and delivered in a finished condition at proper points along the track for attachment as the body reaches that stage of completion.

From four to six workmen now begin to work on the job. One puts on the rear bows, another the front, another adjusts the brace rods which hold the bows in their proper position.

While the top bolts are being tightened up and truss rods and spreaders adjusted to proper position, the side pads are thrown over the top and nailed on; other men put on the roof of the top, which is composed of the "deck" and "quarters." The "back stays" and "back curtain"

Putting on the Tops
Note the ease with which the work is done—no stooping, good light and good ventilation

are soon added. This material is thrown on as fast as possible, waiting operators step up to the framework, quickly tack the top material into place; the back curtains and side stays are nailed to the body and to the

At the End of the Track where Tops and Curtains Are Put on
The roller platform at the left front conveys the bodies across the room to the top of an incline leading to the chassis-body assembling bridge. The body in the right foreground has its top tied down and everything movable fastened, ready for assembly with chassis

top of the back bow; the "quarters" and "deck" are then stretched tightly over the framework, drawn down, tacked and finished with a "welt" strip.

The cushions, horn, and pasteboard for the bottom of the rear seat, the mats and footboard, are then thrown in by a man who does nothing else but make up these things in a package and pass one into each body as it goes along.

The Chassis-Body Assembling Bridge

Other men are engaged in fitting the side curtains, which is another job requiring special care, because each set of curtains is cut to fit a particular body and top. The eyelets are put in, and after curtains have been "tried on" a second time, the whole job is inspected. The top is folded down and securely tied, all loose articles secured, the doors tied shut, a box of tools thrown in, after which it is given a shove onto a roller platform. This is set at right angles to the conveyer track, and carries the body to the top of the incline leading to the "chassis-body assembly bridge"—the end of the process.

This, then, is the story of the finishing of the Ford body.

The Ford factory is one of the few manufacturing establishments where the visitor is actually able to observe, within a short period of time, the successive operations involved in the finishing of any particular part. The painting and upholstering processes are especially interesting on this account.

The most impressive spectacle in the machine shop, that of the almost magical growth of a chassis, is here duplicated on the body. Groups of men slowly walking alongside the work, seem with almost

A Cushion Press in the Upholstering Department

Here the hair is squeezed down and the buttons are clinched

The Cushion Assembly Line

A chain conveyor moving about 8 feet per minute takes the place of a bench; capacity 134 cushions per hour. A similar conveyor line running 20 feet per minute is used for making backs, with a capacity of 120 backs or "trims" per hour

371

Cutting Out Material for Cushions and Backs
Note electric knife used on right-hand table

Women's Department in the Upholstering Shop
Well lighted, clean and pleasant quarters in which the sewing is done

Aladdin-like ease to transform its exterior appearance, as rapidly as the Hindu fakir causes his familiar bush to grow from the seed to maturity. They put on the paint, add the upholstering, top, and windshield, interior and exterior accessories, in an incredibly short time; so short that if you did not actually see it done before your very eyes you would declare it to be an impossibility.

The ease with which the work is handled, the almost entire absence of trucking operations, the prevention of waste of time, energy, and material, the manner in which the minor assemblies are constructed in bays along the track, so as to be near the work at the point where needed, the fact that all the men employed are not so-called "skilled laborers," but men who have received all their training in the Ford shops—all these things show the careful and common-sense manner in which problems of this character are attacked and solved by the Ford organization.

How the Cushions Are Made

As an illustration of how the "minor assemblies" are handled, it may be interesting to describe the making of a cushion. A frame upon which the cushions are built is first laid; the top of the cushion, which is plaited, is placed over this, and what is known as a "fence" is fastened around the mould. This makes a box-like framework, into which the curled hair is put. The foundation is then laid on this and the whole thing carried to a press where a "follow board" is put on. The cushion is then compressed, washers put on, and the buttons clinched. Burlap is then sewed to the foundation and cushion, the clamps taken off, and the cushion removed from the mould. Cushions are then clinched to the springs, after which the whole job is inspected and transferred to the upholstering line for assembly with the body.

The back cushions are made up in much the same manner. The process of cutting the stock is clearly shown on page 372. The leather is on the right-hand table, the burlap on the left-hand. Material is laid 30 deep and 210 jobs are cut at a time. It takes two men about two hours to do this work. The electrical cutting machine is clearly shown in the foreground above, on the right-hand table. The lower picture on page 372 shows a battery of sewing machines in the Upholstery Department. Forty-eight girls are employed in this department. Here, as in other parts of the factory, machines are arranged so that the work moves in logical sequence and is conveyed, by means of a belt conveyer, from end to end of the room.

Aerial Runway Down which the Wheels Travel to the Paint Shop
See pages 376 and 377

Elevator Lifting Wheels to Start Them on the Journey along the Aerial Track to the Paint Shop

THE TOP MACHINE DEPARTMENT

The tops are made in another department, where 148 girls and 12 men work from 7:30 a. m. to 4:15 p. m., turning out from 600 to 700 top covers every 8 hours. This work consists of four main operations: first, laying out and marking; second, cutting; third, creasing; and fourth, sewing. The cutting and creasing is done on a special automatic machine of Ford design. There are really six parts of the top made in this department: the deck and quarters which form the roof of the top, the curtains, the lights, the combination back curtain and back stays, the pads which fit on the curve of the bow, and the bow covers themselves.

Two of the Centrifugal Wheel-Painting Machines
The paint vats are mounted so that they can be raised and lowered for submerging the wheel. The construction of the wheel runway is plainly seen

How the Bows Are Made

The Bow Department, which has a capacity of about 75 sets per hour, also furnishes a very interesting example of compact assembly. The ten operations required are as follows: The bows are first broken open; second, inspected by gauge; third, sawed to size; fourth, ends

A Corner of the Wheel-Drying Room in the Wheel Paint Department
A tubular runway passes down the center, and the method of stacking prevents the wheels from rolling

shaped to fit bow sockets; fifth, a small strip is added to the top of the bow to keep the covering from sagging; sixth, the "stockings" are put on—that is, the bows are covered with cloth; seventh, the sockets are examined; eighth, bows are driven into sockets in pairs and then put

Putting on a Tire

onto a conveyer on which the straps and fasteners are added. The work is done at a point near the top-assembly line, so that no trucking is necessary.

Painting Ford Wheels

When you stop to think that the capacity of the Ford plant is 300,000 cars per year, and that each car is equipped with four wheels, you will get some idea of the number of wheels that must be painted and the difficulty which might be experienced in handling, painting, and "tireing" such an enormous quantity.

About 1,000 sets are run through every 8 hours, by a force of 27 men. It was formerly necessary to truck the wheels from the unloading dock to the paint shop. This, however, has been done away with by a new form of conveyer, the operation of which is simplicity itself.

The pictures on pages 374 and 375 show the manner in which the wheels are handled. They are put in a runway on the unloading dock and carried up by means of an elevator to a track slightly higher than the level of the third floor of building "H."

The wheels therefore run in under force of gravity, and finally reach a point where they are stopped in front of a centrifugal painting machine. These painting machines are unique. They consist, as will be seen by referring to the illustrations on page 375, of a circular paint vat, the revolving spindle being driven by means of a beveled gear mechanism from the shaft above. The wheels are picked out of the runway, placed in a horizontal position on this spindle, entirely submerged in the paint and then raised above the surface. The paint vat moves up and down— not the spindle. The power is turned on and the wheel is spun at the rate of about 720 revolutions per minute, which dries it sufficiently to be handled. It is then placed back in the rack runway, given a shove which sends it rolling down to the end of the storage room, and there picked out and piled for drying. Later, it is again put back in its track, and rolls around to a point where it is given its second coat of color varnish in the same manner, except that it is spun at a little slower speed— about 540 revolutions per minute. After the painting operations are

Enameling the Wind-Shield Frames, Showing Dipping Tanks and Draining Conveyer

Note how the parts are hung to ensure proper dripping—also opening in the wall (in the background) leading to the ovens

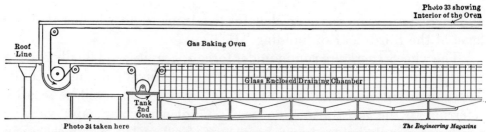

The Engineering Magazine

Sectional Diagram of Ford Fender-Enameling System. Half the Length is Shown above. The Section is Completed on the Opposite Page

finished the wheel is put back in its track and rolls to the tire room, by gravity.

Where the Tires Are Put On

The tires come up an incline to the third floor, pass over the body roller track and down to a flat belt conveyer, which carries them finally to the tire-storage room. Here the tires and wheels meet and are put together, after which they are sent down a chute to the chassis-assembly line in the machine shop.

How the Windshield Is Enameled

On page 377 is shown the method used for dipping and baking the enamel on the tube that surrounds the windshield glass. Two endless-chain conveyers, set side by side, with a dripping tank at one end and baking ovens at the other, are clearly shown. The irons are dipped and then hung in a slanting position by a short wire at one end and a long wire at the other. They travel in a westerly direction over a 14-foot drain, requiring 25 minutes to reach the other end, where they are removed by the oven operator and hung in pairs on the cross bars of a traveling chain which traverses one of the vertical baking ovens. These baking ovens are built on the outside of the building and therefore do not take up any of the floor space of the department proper. The ovens are about 30 feet high and contain four gas burners. The speed is so timed that it takes 25 minutes for the rods to make the trip. The temperature of the first oven is maintained at approximately 350 degrees F. After this baking operation, the parts are placed on a belt conveyer, which carries them back to the dipping end of the second endless-chain conveyer. In the photograph you will notice the man has just started to pick a part off the belt, preparatory to dipping it in the second time. After its second coat, it is hung again as before, travels the length of the second draining tank, and is taken off and hooked to the cross bars in the second oven. This runs at the same speed. The temperature is

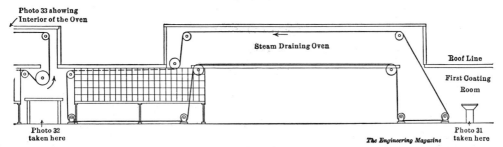

Photo 33 showing
Interior of the Oven

Steam Draining Oven

Roof Line

First Coating
Room

Photo 32
taken here

The Engineering Magazine

Photo 31
taken here

Sectional Diagram of Ford Fender-Enameling System. Completing the Section
of which the Other Half Appears on the Page Opposite

slightly higher—from 425 to 450 degrees. The capacity is 120 wind-
shield frames per hour.

How the Fenders Are Enameled

The enameling of the Ford fenders is a very interesting process and
one which requires some explanation on account of the unusual manner
in which the work is kept
in progress. Despite the
fact that, owing to the
bulkiness of this compo-
nent, a great amount of
room is ordinarily required,
by an ingenious system of
ovens mounted on the roof
very little actual floor
space in the shop itself is
needed under this improved
system.

The accompanying il-
lustrations will aid the
reader in understanding, in
a general way, how the
work is handled and the
process of baking made
almost continuous. On
this page the workmen are
seen dipping the fenders
for the first coat, after
which they are hung in sets
of four on the cross bars of

**Where Fenders are Dipped and Hung on the
Endless-Chain Conveyor Carrying Them
through the Steam-Heated Dripping
Oven on the Roof**

Where the Finished Fenders Are Taken Off

Fenders which have received their second coat and baking are removed from the line. Those which have
had but one coat are automatically dipped again and sent on a second journey through the
roof oven

Removing Fenders from the Draining Conveyor Traversing the Steam Drying Room, and Hanging Them on the Conveyor Which Carries Them Through the Gas-Heated Baking Oven on the Roof

Note glass enclosure to keep dust away from the freshly painted surface

an endless-chain conveyer, which carries them through a draining, steam-heated enclosure on the roof above. Page 380 shows the point at which they are taken off and hung on another endless-chain conveyer, which carries them up through another oven on the roof, heated to a temperature of about 400 degrees, by fourteen large gas burners. The illustration on this page is taken along the outside of this oven. Page 380 (top) is taken at a point after the fenders have come through the drying oven and are ready to pass on and be automatically dipped in the tank at the right. This is where they receive their second

Outside of the Gas-Heated Ovens, Built on the Roof, in Which the Fenders Are Baked

coat, passing on through a glass dripping chamber back to the oven on the roof again, receiving their second baking. They then return to the same point again, and are removed in a finished condition. The first conveyer can be run at a speed of either $2\frac{1}{2}$ or 5 feet per minute. The second conveyer running through the oven, travels 5 feet per minute.

The capacity of the fender oven is 480 front fenders or 240 rears per hour, first coats, and 240 front fenders or 120 rears, second coats.

Page 382 shows how the hoods are painted. They are simply dipped in the ordinary way, hung to dry, and afterwards baked. The picture is self-explanatory.

Dipping the Rear-Axle Assembly

Leading back from the dipping vats is the track down which the part goes to the elevator shown on page 383

Painting or Enameling the Hoods

Dipping and hanging to drain.   Capacity 700 hoods finished every 8 hours

Putting the Rear-Axle Assembly into the Elevator Carrying It to the Floor Above

How the Rear-Axle Assembly Is Painted

The illustrations on page 382 and above show how the rear-axle assembly is painted. In the foreground of the former view will be seen the tank filled with paint. Into this the entire rear-axle assembly is dipped, with the exception of the forward part, to which a set of rollers is attached. Immediately afterwards it is ended up so that these rollers fit on either side of an I-beam track. They roll by gravity down over a dripping tank, and arrive at a point shown in the cut just above, where they are removed and sent up, by means of an elevator, to a horizontal baking oven located just under the roof. Here they are carried on by an endless-chain conveyer through an oven about 110 feet long, the interior of which is heated to about 300 degrees. At the end of this 45-minute journey, they are lowered by another elevator and removed by the workman to await carriage to the assembly line.

South Side and East End of the New Buildings Looking Northwest along Manchester Avenue

Steam-heating plant installation at the middle right

CHAPTER XV

THE NEW FACTORY ADDITIONS

THE economic significance and effect of the general form and placing of work-shop floors is not yet so fully comprehended by industrial architects as to have evolved any one single form of factory building which has received widespread commendation and acceptance as the one and only best structure in points cf low first cost, durability, convenience, and perfection of floor arrangements for housing workers and materials for the production of comparatively light-weight machines.

For the production of heavy machines, in which individual gray-iron components may weigh, say, from 100 pounds to 100 tons, handling of components is the principal thing to be considered; but few pieces, comparatively speaking, are to be turned out, and there is little room for novel improvements in design of the plant buildings.

The forge and foundries are likely to have contiguous placing, and as the massive components leave the loam mould or the steam hammer they move in stately procession down a wide middle way, with huge machine tools on either side, to the place of launching or railway shipment, assisted by rollers, railways, and traveling cranes as best may be, with no sojourn of finished components in finished stores, no rush requisitions for rough stores, no army of truckers and counters and inspectors dealing with rough-stores consignments received. Under these conditions the factory buildings must fit the work, so that the architect has little or no choice as to the forms of shop structures which are best suited to the form of expected production, since the form and weight of the product itself determine the shape of the structures best suited to house the industrial agents to be employed.

With light work, like the Ford car, where the heaviest rough-component weight is only about a hundred pounds and that of the lightest piece produced may be only a few grains (as is the case in the Ford shops at Highland Park), and where the business demands the placing of thou-

Manchester Avenue Side of the Ford Plant, Looking Northeast from Woodward Avenue

Showing the total Manchester Avenue frontage of 1728 feet, with the new buildings at the extreme right

sands of workmen and very many workwomen, sexes separated, as closely together as possible on the factory floors—there is plenty of room for careful preliminary consideration and bold flights of invention in planning and designing the best possible factory building.

The Ford shop conditions when the Ford engineers began designing these new factory additions were highly satisfactory from a financial standpoint, but wholly unsatisfactory from the shop general-manager's position, as the factory production has been constantly below the product-purchasers' demands from the day that the small Ford car was first shown at Madison Square Garden. Every year saw the sales doubled or trebled, with the factory striving as best it might to meet the purchaser's demands by adding to the factory plant and to the number of workers employed, with no time whatever for studious consideration of factory betterments and labor economizing.

There was not floor space enough; machine tools and factory departments were not placed as the management knew they should be, and more than a thousand men worked as truckers, pushers, and draggers engaged in needless handlings of materials and work in progress.

There was no relief in sight. The Ford sales system, including branch buildings and agencies scattered broadcast, it might be said, over the entire habitable face of the world, created a demand for the best low-priced car ever offered for sale, which the Ford car certainly was, and no one knew the ultimate Ford-car purchase volume.

Under these commercial conditions the first essential was abundant floor space, and the second indispensable requirement was for mechanical transportation inside the factory walls, to do away, in so far as might be, with hand trucking and hauling.

The old buildings had been equipped with monorail tracks and electric locomotives, together with a crane-way opening to most of the departments; but these devices could not reach the entire inter-department traffic, which was a constant and costly feature of the Ford-shops routine. The ground plan of the works was already large, necessitating long lines of travel which must be very much increased by the length of the new additions; and because of the great floor-space needed it was decided to give the additional buildings six floors in each, to make each of the floors 60 feet wide, and to extend them 908 feet to the eastward of the John R Street wall of the old shops, on the south or Manchester Avenue side. This would bring the eastern line of the additions about even with the eastern end of the foundry, which is next the railway on the north side of the Ford Motor Company's premises, and leave space

Looking Southwest Down John R Street. Showing the Bridge from the Old Building at the Right to the New Building at the Left

for five more similar structures between the south line of the foundry and the north line of the two new buildings here under description— seven new buildings in all.

To meet the requirements of both rough-stores and finished-products handling, the plans included a railway track between each two of the new buildings, with two electric traveling cranes of 5-tons capacity each in each craneway, and they provided landing stages for each floor above the first, staggering the landings so that each one was fully open to crane service from overhead. The manufacturing departments were then so arranged that rough stores could be handled by the cranes directly to the top floors, and thence descend by gravity slides to floors below, so far as might be found feasible, so that the single product, the Ford motor car, might be finally assembled on a lower floor or floors, and be loaded directly on the railway freight cars, all with the least needless travel and handling that could be contrived.

At the date of this writing, August 25, 1914, two of the seven contemplated buildings are completed, the south building, on the Manchester Avenue north line, having a railway track on its north side only, and hence having crane service on the north side of its floors only; the next

North Side of New Buildings Showing North Wall Construction
Chute used in placing bodies on chassis in middle front

Hollow-Column Air Distribution System
West end of the fifth floor looking north. Craneway at the right end

building to the north has a railway on each side and crane service to each side of its floors, and the first floor of each building is placed at the railway car floor level, so that the first-floor continuous platforms need no crane service. The cranes are in place and working and the ventilating and "air-conditioning" units are installed, but are not yet in operation.

A very important feature of the ventilating system is the avoidance of all air-pipes, gained by making all the inside floor-supporting columns hollow, with either one or two openings in each hollow column near the ceiling of each room, each column air-opening being covered by an individual damper. The hollow columns take air at about 1¾-inches water-head pressure at the top, as supplied by eight "Sirocco" fan "air-conditioning" units (American Blower Company's ventilating, heating and cooling system), the volume of air forced into each column being regulated by an individual damper, this air being delivered to each room with damper regulation for each opening of each column, so that the delivery of ventilating air can be so directed and apportioned as to obtain satisfactory circulation of ventilating air throughout the entire space enclosed by the building walls.

This novel scheme of hollow-column air distribution was fully

Roof of the North Buildings Showing Skylights, Air Ducts, Pent Houses, and Craneway Glass Roof

The upper view is taken looking west between the craneways of the north building, the lower is looking easterly on the Manchester Avenue side of the south building roof

worked out and drawings were made for the seven new buildings about two years before the construction of these two Ford factory additional buildings was begun. In the meantime this hollow-column air-distribution had been fully tried out in the new building of the Ford plant at Ford, Ontario, where it was found to give satisfaction in every particular, as first designed by the Ford engineers and architects. As the inside floor-supporting columns are spaced 20 feet center to center, the use of hollow columns as air distributors, each column air-delivery opening being covered by dampers so that the volume of air delivered at that point could be regulated to suit the requirements of ventilation, heating, and cooling in the most suitable and satisfactory manner, ensured the air circulation in every part of the entire factory building at the lowest possible cost in money and with highest possible economy of enclosed space.

The value of this hollow-column air distribution cannot be over-estimated, since a separate system of air pipes capable of furnishing equivalent air-distribution facilities would entail such added cost, such waste of floor space, and such architectural disfigurement as to prohibit its installation. The only obvious alternative is the forming of air passages in the thickness of the floor and walls, entailing impossible requirements for the preservation of needful structural strength, so that this novel conception of hollow-pillar air passages seems to be really the only practicable method by which a large factory building can be ideally cooled, warmed and ventilated.

The details of this new Ford system of ventilation combined with the American Blower air-conditioning and Sirocco-fan circulating will be given in detail later in this chapter.

Ground was broken for the foundations of these Ford factory additions early in July, 1913, and the structures were completed about August 20, 1914.

Cost of buildings only	$1,039,793.89
Cost of elevators	23,500.00
Cost of cranes	11,950.00
Cost of ventilating system	51,873.41
Total Cost	$1,127,117.30

Floor area about 687,500 square feet.

Cost per square foot of floor	$1.64 nearly
Length on Manchester Avenue	842 feet
Width, over all	200 feet
Width of each craneway	40 feet
Width of floors in each building	60 feet
Main roof slab above Manchester Avenue	75 feet
Craneway peak, above sidewalk	89 feet

Six floors. From railway track to top line of first floor, 3 feet 6 inches; top surface of first floor to top surface of second floor, 14 feet 4 inches; top of second to top of third, 12 feet; top of third to top of fourth, 12 feet; top of fourth to top of fifth, 12 feet; top of fifth to top of sixth, 12 feet.

WALLS

Brick-work for all walls is carried on the concrete lintels over the windows. In general, the side walls are 8½ inches thick and 42 inches high from the floor to the bottom of the window sash. The brick walls of the elevator shafts and the toilets are also carried on concrete beams to each floor and are 8½ inches thick.

Craneway Door in East End of New Buildings Looking West

FLOOR CONSTRUCTION

Usual concrete flat slab, with mushroom-type pillars spaced 20 feet each way, floors reinforced with Cambria Steel Company's twisted square bars. The floor safe load is 200 pounds to the square foot, safety factor of 3.

COLUMNS

The soil is 36 inches loam, then blue clay to limestone.

The column footings are about 13 feet square, with reinforced - concrete base extending about 5 feet below first floor. There are 175 columns on each floor of each building, spaced 20 feet each way.

All interior columns are hollow and serve as air passages; they take air from the top (see the detailed description of the ventilation) and deliver air through rectangular openings covered by dampers, the bottom of the opening being about 9 feet above the floor.

All columns on the first, second, third and fourth floors are steel lattice work covered with concrete, rectangular in form, corners being taken off. On the fifth and sixth floors the columns are round, and have thin sheet-metal air pipes inside and reinforced concrete outside.

The column air-ways vary in diameter on each floor, being largest at the top, and smallest at the bottom. First-floor column air-ways are 12 inches in diameter; second floor, 13 inches; third floor, 14 inches; fourth floor; 16 inches; fifth floor, 17 inches, and the sixth-floor columns have air-ways 19 inches in diameter.

Roof

The flat roofs over the two buildings are reinforced-concrete, $8\frac{1}{2}$ inches thick, then cinders to obtain drainage slope, then $\frac{3}{4}$-inch thick-

Doors on Manchester Avenue with Skylight Canopy Above

ness of concrete, covered by tar and paper, all being of usual construction.

The craneways are covered by lantern roofs, the lantern sashes being hinged at the bottom to permit the tops of sashes to swing inward with fittings to retain sash positions. The craneway is roofed with wired glass so that in case of accident no glass can be dropped to craneway floor.

The roof has sky-lights next to the craneways, and each building has four pent-houses on the roof, housing the ventilating-system units. From the pent-houses the ventilating air goes to the middle air passages

Pivoted Window Sash

Hung on a vertical axis to suit wind in either direction, with retaining fixtures holding them in any desired position. Made by the Trussed Concrete Steel Co., Youngstown, Ohio

Elevator Shaft and Stairway, South Building

Note the excellent lighting of the entire interior

on the roof, from which oblique laterals open into the tops of the hollow columns, all as clearly shown in the two roof pictures.

Doors

The craneways have structural-steel doors vertically sliding in guides, at the railway-track exits, in the east wall of the buildings. These heavy doors are counter-balanced by weights moving up and down in the hollow columns which form the door posts, and are electric-motor raised and lowered.

The doors opening to Manchester Avenue are all alike, large double doors for goods entrance at the west, adjoined by six narrow doors for workmen's entrance to railed passages leading past the time clocks.

These doors are under sky-lighted canopies.

Windows

The steel window-sashes are pivoted top and bottom to swing either way and so take advantage of natural air-currents, and are provided with fittings to retain the sash positions. The north craneway on the north side is lighted by sashes pivoted to swing on a middle horizontal axis which can be opened and retained in any position from the ground.

Architectural Ornamentation

The Manchester Avenue side of the south building is relieved by brickwork pylons, carried above the eave line and capped with concrete. Otherwise the building has no decorations.

Elevators, Stairways and Closets

Seven elevators, supplied by the Haughton Elevator Company, Toledo, Ohio, are placed. One on John R Street is used for male passengers as well as freight, and one, with access from Manchester Avenue, past the time clocks, is used for female passengers (workwomen) and freight.

Brick-work shafts take the elevator at the best, the stairway in the middle, and form closets at the east. See illustration. The closets are suction-fan ventilated, with exit to roof.

The stairway entrances are fire-protected by metallic curtains, rolled overhead and retained in position by a fusible section, so as to drop automatically in case of heat enough to melt the fusible metal.

The elevator gates, supplied by the Quincy Company, are operated by a hydraulic vertical cylinder with a rack and pinion movement, connected with a motor-current switch, so that the elevator platform cannot be moved until the gates are fully closed. These gates are peculiar, having lazy-tongs-guided, automatically-lifted bars at the bottom, all so as to give a predetermined head-room with the least possible vertical travel of the gate. These gate-bottom closing-bars were added to the regular Quincy gates by the Haughton Elevator Company, to make the gate close down to the floor with the gate-travel head-room available. As the gates now are, they leave nothing to be desired, being fully auto-

Closets, with Vertical Window Sash and Suction-Fan Ventilation
Note the slate partitions, and the excellence of the fittings compared with ordinary factory practice.   Built
by L. Wolf Mfg. Co., Chicago

matic, closing down to the floor and giving abundant head-room in restricted vertical travel space, holding the current away from the elevator platform motors until the gate is fully closed and being prompt and smooth in action.

The elevator platforms are 113 inches wide by 198 inches long, and can handle 2½-ton loads. All elevator service is both costly and dangerous, at its very best. These Ford new-building elevators are smooth-running, speedy, and safe so far as an elevator can be made safe. The gates are in every way satisfactory in action, and interlocking the gate

Elevator-Shaft Door, South Building, with Gate Down and with Gate Raised

action with a motor-current switch of its own, so that no current can reach the motor until after the gate is fully closed, does all that can be done to avoid accident. The gate is notable as closing close down to the floor, where it is most needed. See illustrations.

The stairways have low risers, concrete treads, and substantial pipe-rail protection. The closets are as well fitted as in ordinary hotels, are ventilated by ample-capacity suction-fans, and the bowls are separated by slate partitions of good height, giving color enough of privacy to satisfy in some degree the demands of user's reasonable self-respect, being in this particular in strong contrast to the conditions commonly found in ordinary factory practice.

A Women's Rest Room

WOMEN WORKERS' ROOMS

The arrangement and fittings of the women workers' rooms are well shown in the illustrations. The rest room is open to any women at any time, with the forewomen's permission. The wash-room and clothes rack are reasonably convenient, all fully as good as the women workers are likely to have in their homes.

The women's workrooms (see illustration) are as good in points of light and ventilation as the best business offices in the best New York City office buildings. This photograph was taken before the white curtains, sliding on overhead rods, were in place. The wages of these women workers run from 32 to 62½ cents per hour, from \$2.66 to \$5.00 for an 8-hour day, and many of them are in the \$5.00 class. Such labor conditions as these should give the management untroubled slumbers and freedom from worry.

THE CRANES

The craneways and cranes are the dominating features of these new Ford plant buildings, and taken in connection with the staggered landing stages give this building the best installation of crane service within the writer's knowledge. The second, third, fourth and fifth floors have each thirty-seven landing stages, and the sixth floor has twenty-nine. The north building floors have twice as many landing stages as the south building, because the north building is served from both craneways while the south building is served from one craneway only. Landing stages are cantilever platforms of reinforced concrete, 10 feet long and projecting 6 feet into the craneway space, with pipe railing at ends and chain lengthwise in front. The landing stages are staggered so as to each have clear head-room up to the cranes.

Each craneway is served by two cranes, 5-tons capacity each, supplied by the Whiting Foundry Equipment Company, Harvey, Illinois.

The extreme lift of the crane-hook is about 75 feet, the crane track being placed 80 feet above the railway track. This 75-foot lift gives opportunity for undesirable sway of crane loads suspended by a single cable. To avoid load swaying, two cable drums are placed side by side in each crane unit, as long as the frame work

Stairway Next to the Elevator Shaft

Note the good lighting of the stairway. The rolling metal curtains on all stairway doors were made by the Variety Mfg. Co., Chicago

permits, and each cable drum or windlass is spiral-grooved right-hand at one end and left-hand at the other end; four lifting cables are used for each crane, the cable ends being fixed to the out ends of the right-hand and left-hand windlass spirals. This gives the crane load a four-cable suspension, with cables most widely sep-

Women's Toilet and Rest Rooms.   South Building

These are in the body tops department on the fourth floor.   One of the Childs wheeled fire extinguishers
is seen in the foreground

A Women's Wash Room

Fittings were obtained from the L. Wolf Manufacturing Co., Chicago

arated at low-load position, and approaching each other as the load is lifted, all so that sway of crane load becomes impossible. This converging four-cable load suspension is a new feature in traveling crane construction, original with the Ford engineers, and is of great working value, as sway of the crane load would lead to marked inconvenience and delay of the crane service. See page 403. The cranes are modern construction, electric of course, having all gears enclosed,

Women Workers, Body-Top-Making Department
The fourth floor of south building, Manchester Avenue side

all in most striking contrast to the mechanically operated traveling cranes which were once regarded as such triumphs of factory-equipment engineering.

ARTIFICIAL LIGHTING

The floors are lighted by about two thousand ceiling-placed reflectors and clusters, each cluster made up of four 60-watt tungsten lamps, having individual switches concealed in the pillars. Clusters supplied by the Western Electric Company.

Each craneway will have fourteen 5,000 candle-power quartz lamps, spaced 60 feet apart, placed in the roof peak, 76 feet above the ground, supplied by the Cooper Hewitt Company.

The South Craneway, Looking East

Cooper-Hewitt quartz lamps installed in craneway peak

FIRE PROTECTION

These buildings have no partition walls, being everywhere open and without hiding places. The concrete construction is non-inflammable so that the fire danger is from the contents, not from the containing structure.

The stairways and elevators, as already noted, have rolling metal curtains, fusible-metal retained in lifted positions, and automatically

Crane with Four-Cable Load Suspension and South Craneway
Note the floor lighting of the north building. Cranes are from the Whiting Foundry Equipment Co.,
Harvey, Ill.

dropped when surrounding temperature melts the fusible metal retention.

These buildings are equipped with fire-extinguishers supplied by Childs, of Utica, New York, four hundred and sixty-two extinguishers of 3-gallons capacity being distributed through the buildings, while seven of the Childs wheeled fire-extinguishers, 40-gallons capacity each, are stationed at suitable points on the floors.

These brief general specifications, sketchy and meager as space available compels them to be, will, nevertheless, when read in connection with the many illustrations given, enable the reader to obtain a fair idea

Looking East along the South Craneway, Showing Crane with Load

of these remarkable new factory buildings, which certainly appear to be the very best that can be done with a multifloored structure, up to the ventilation, heating and cooling requirements, which are so fully met that the ventilating system may deservedly be termed ideal.

Ford New Building Work-Shop Suitability

Beyond all question, these new Ford-factory additions give the workmen and workwomen therein housed ideal work-hour conditions. The lighting is, perhaps, the very best that can be obtained from the sun's rays in a multifloored building, floors 60 feet wide, and the night lighting is made as good as can be by placing of a great number of electric lamp clusters, each cluster provided with an individual switch so that lighting any one location need not waste current by turning on lamps where illumination is not needed. Light is the first essential of low labor-cost factory production. How the last generation of factory managers (previous to those of the present hour) could have ever accepted the bat-and-mole twilights of our first large American factory buildings is a question which no living person can answer, though perhaps we of today should keep our mouths shut about machine-shop lighting so long as we tolerate the present practice of overhead counter-shaft

Above: Looking Southeast along the North Craneway, Showing the Cranes in Front.
Below: The North Craneway, with Heavy Package Chute from the Shipping
Department (Second Floor of North Building) to Railway Track Platform

The chassis frames are seen in the lower picture on the platform along the south side

405

placing and belt-driving of machine tools—but that is another story. Certainly these new Ford shops are the best day-lighted of any shop floors within my observations. The heating, cooling, and ventilation are the best so far made public; pure, cool drinking-water is close at hand everywhere in these new buildings, the floors are swept continuously; the closets are sanitary and decent, and the stairways are well railed, easy rising, and have good fire-protection, double landings for each flight, and are as safe as any stairway can be made.

These conditions and provisions leave nothing but materials and work-in-progress handling and transportation to consider before these new buildings can be awarded first position among the multifloored factory structures of the whole world. The craneways, the staggered landing stages, and the seven elevators were placed to make electricity do as much of the lifting (inseparable from the multifloored factory) as is possible, and the absolutely novel feature of the four converging crane-load lifting cables was originated by the Ford engineers to prevent completely all swaying of crane loads, and also to locate the crane windlass pull infallibly in a truly vertical line above the load, so that no lengthwise dragging of the crane load need ever occur, and in practice never does occur. The chain hook is brought exactly to the load center, and the load is lifted in a vertical line and with absolute steadiness which is not affected by horizontal crane travel.

It is very doubtful if successful and altogether satisfactory use of a 70-foot traveling-crane-lift could have been had with free pendulum suspension of the crane load, while with the four-converging-cables load-suspension there is only the very short pendulum from the crane hook to the bottom of the load platform possible, so that load-sway consideration becomes negligible.

These Whiting Company cranes make a 70-foot lift in 35 seconds, and 800 feet of horizontal travel in 95 seconds, and travel in both vertical and horizontal directions can be made simultaneously after the load is above the freight-car tops.

MERCHANDISE PURCHASING AND RECEIVING

The Ford Company, when making 1,000 cars per day, purchases about $8,000,000 value of merchandise each month and receives and unloads about 100 railway freight cars daily, delivering merchandise from all points of the compass. Some of the shipments to the Ford Company are made by water. The Highland Park plant is about 6 miles north of Detroit city hall, and about 6½ miles north of the boat docks and the railway freight houses. The Detroit belt-line railway bounds the north side of the Highland Park realty, making this road the best line of city transit.

THE "TRAP" CARS

The Ford Company has five motor trucks of 3-tons capacity, four supplied by the Kelly Springfield Motor Truck Company and one by Grabrowski, all of which are giving satisfactory service, three being in use all the time. There are also three Ford motor-car chassis "haulers"—regular Ford chassis, save that a large rear-axle gear housing is fitted to take a strongly geared low speed, in use at the Highland Park plant. These little "haulers" have an astonishing road adhesion, without the use of rear-axle load-boxes, so that one of them pulls a freight car with 20 or 25 tons load along the Belt line tracks or takes a train of loaded monorail wheeled platforms to any accessible point on the shops' first floors.

To obtain omnibus transportation by Belt line, one 3-ton motor truck works downtown, taking Ford freight from the steamboat wharves and from other railway freight houses to the Michigan Central freight yards, where that road furnishes about three "trap" cars per day to the Ford Company, these trap cars being loaded with freight collected by motor truck from other transportation lines, and with the Ford city-purchased supplies, and sent to Highland Park via Belt line.

Merchandise to be delivered to the north and south craneway located midway of the old shop floors is unloaded at the "Dock" at that craneway north end. Foundry supplies are unloaded by a Shaw gantry crane working along the foundry north side, and by a flat-car crane working on the tracks east of the foundry. Supplies which go first to the smithy and the heat-treating buildings are unloaded on the platform of the first track south of those structures, and about thirty-five cars are unloaded daily from the new building craneway tracks.

SEQUENCE OF FREIGHT-CAR PLACING

It is of course needful that incoming freight cars should be placed in proper sequence on the tracks where they are to be unloaded. The Ford Company owns no switch engine; hence the received-cars switching and sequence placing is done by the Belt line, in the night time mainly, according to instructions given to the Highland Park yard-master by a Ford official, who first inspects the lading of cars as received and then gives written directions to the yard-master as to car placing for unloading.

Body Elevator East End of South Craneway, Showing Railway Track Door Lifted

The trap cars are always placed to enter craneways first, from the east, so as to stand for unloading at the craneways' west ends. Both the 3-ton motor trucks and the Ford haulers can enter the new buildings' ground floors from the John R Street level: About 90 per cent of the lading of the thirty-five cars daily unloaded in the craneways is delivered to various locations on the new buildings' twelve floors, the other tenth part being placed on the monorail wheeled platforms, which may be pulled, singly or made up in trains, by the Ford haulers, which are so small and handy that they can travel readily on the first floors of either the old or the new Ford buildings.

Floor Bridges

The new buildings extend 910 feet eastward of the John R Street east line. The railway tracks enter the craneways from the east end and extend westward on a sunken track, to bring the car floors level with the building first floor, for a length of 830 feet, to the buffers which stand 80 feet east of the new buildings' west end wall, thus making each floor west end 80 feet east and west by 200 feet north and south. Three elevators are placed along the south line of the north craneway, and three along the south line of the south craneway.

Bridges 20 feet wide connect the third, fourth, fifth and sixth north and south floors at the middle of the craneway length, while the eastern ends of the fourth, fifth and sixth floors are connected by bridges 10 feet wide, and an elevated bridge, 6 feet wide, is placed at the east ends of the third floors.

This arrangement gives about 2 miles length of floor 60 feet wide, all

Paint-Spraying Room with Exhaust-Fan Ventilation
Note the lighting of the sixth floor. The view is along the south side of the south craneway

this floor being paying-load surface, save the space taken by the elevator, stairway, and closet shafts.

ROUGH STORES TO TOP, FINISHED PRODUCT AT BOTTOM

The practice of taking rough stores to the top of a multifloored factory building and dropping finished components to the completed-product bottom-floor delivery is well known, though by no means commonly adopted, and is unquestionably the best possible procedure, as any other scheme must of necessity involve detail routing of lines both up and down. Hence, it is better to begin manufacture by transporting rough stores to the top floor, and routing the lines of descent so that components meet at convenient assembly points and the finished-product assembling ends at the shipping room.

PRESENT USE OF NEW BUILDING FLOORS

These new buildings have been available for work use since about August 20, 1914, and are now devoted mainly to body painting and top making, body and top assembling on a moving-assembly line 360 feet long, and to finished-components storage close to the boxing and shipping department, which loads all finished components, or "repairs" shipments, on freight cars in the north craneway.

It is not certain that the best arrangement for stock-received storing in the new building has yet been found, but the present department placing has effected a saving of about 200 men in merchandise-received handling. The body wood-working machinery is now being installed on the north-building top floor, and lumber dry-kilns are nearing completion east of the new building, where the craneway rail tracks (which are depressed inside the buildings) rise to the Belt line grade; this permits unloading of lumber directly into the dry kilns, and reloading it on freight cars after kiln drying, to go into the craneways to be lifted up to the top-floor body wood-shaping department.

These new buildings are so vastly better in every way than the old plant buildings that they are regarded by Ford officials as wholly above criticism in any direction, and will certainly appreciably lessen the labor cost of the yearly production of 300,000 cars, which is the figure now set by Henry Ford, who has very decidedly advanced his ideas since, in the not so very old Piquette Street days, he said he would rest satisfied when he could turn out 20 Ford cars per day, six days in the week.

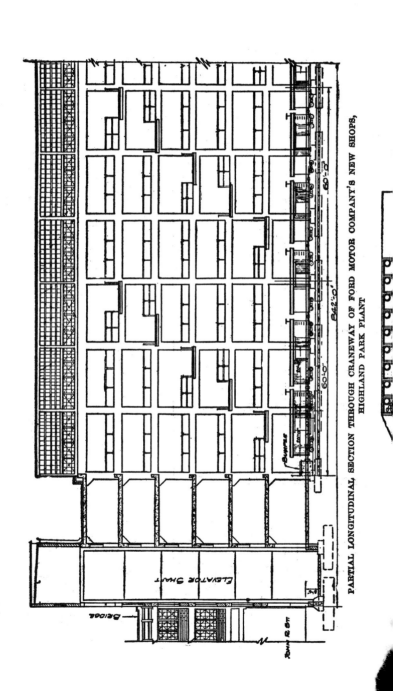

PARTIAL LONGITUDINAL, SECTION THROUGH CRANEWAY OF FORD MOTOR COMPANY'S NEW SHOPS, HIGHLAND PARK PLANT

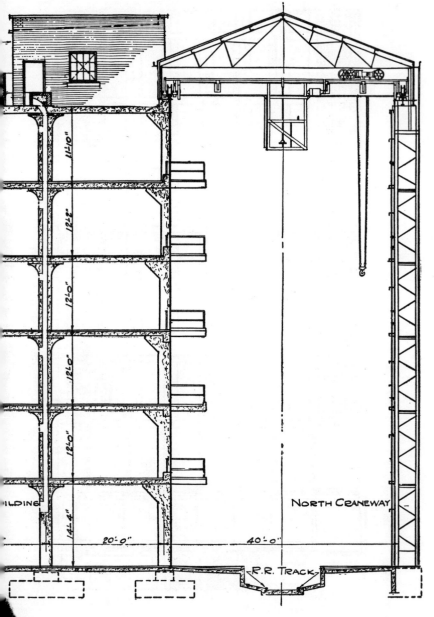

11'-0"

12'-4"

12'-0"

12'-0"

12'-0"

14'-4"

NORTH CRANEWAY

20'-0"

40'-0"

R.R. TRACK

'ILDING

X PLANT

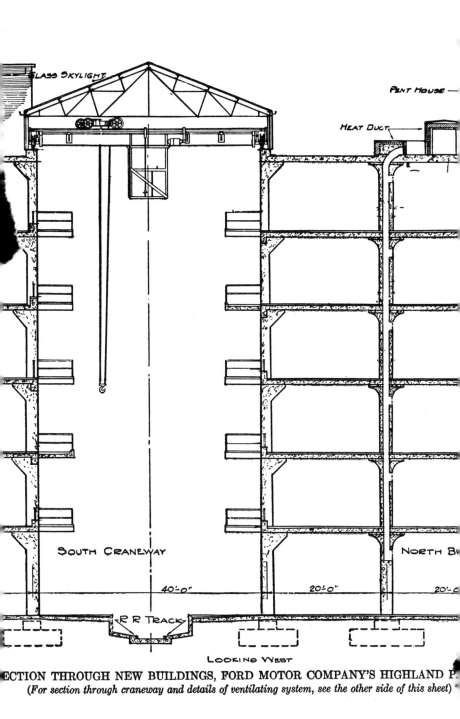

GLASS SKYLIGHT

PENT HOUSE ─

HEAT DUCT ─

SOUTH CRANEWAY

NORTH B

40′-0″

20′-0″

20′-0

R R TRACK

LOOKING WEST

ECTION THROUGH NEW BUILDINGS, FORD MOTOR COMPANY'S HIGHLAND P

(For section through craneway and details of ventilating system, see the other side of this sheet)

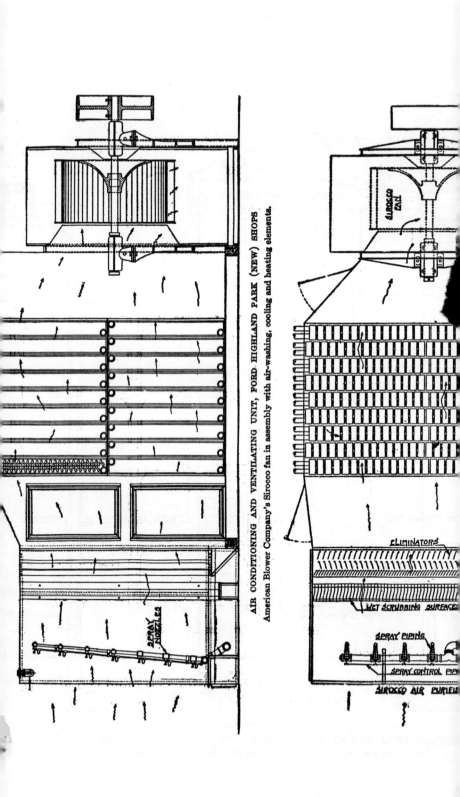

AIR CONDITIONING AND VENTILATING UNIT, FORD HIGHLAND PARK (NEW) SHOPS

American Blower Company's Sirocco fan in assembly with air-washing, cooling and heating elements.

SPRAY NOZZLES

SIROCCO FAN

ELIMINATORS

WET SCRUBBING SURFACE

SPRAY PIPING

SPRAY CONTROL PIP

SIROCCO AIR PURIFIE

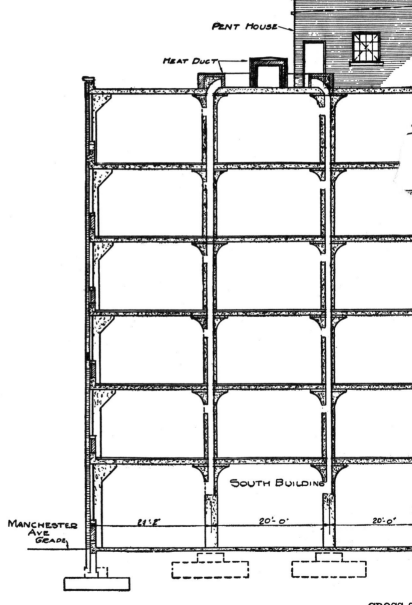

PENT HOUSE

HEAT DUCT

SOUTH BUILDING

MANCHESTER
AVE
GRADE

21'2"   20'-0"   20'-0"

CROSS S

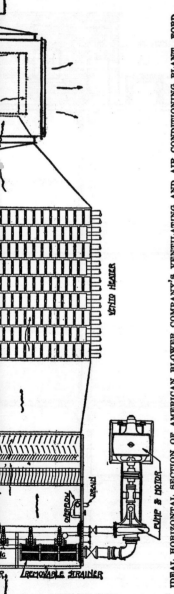

WATER HEATER

REMOVABLE STRAINER

OVERFLOW

DRAIN

PUMP & MOTOR

IDEAL HORIZONTAL SECTION OF AMERICAN BLOWER COMPANY'S VENTILATING AND AIR CONDITIONING PLANT, FORD HIGHLAND PARK (NEW) SHOPS

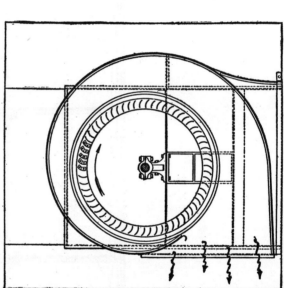

END ELEVATION OF AIR-CONDITIONING AND VENTILATING UNIT

Vertical section through Sirocco fan. Ford new buildings ventilating system.

EFFICIENCY REQUISITES OF FACTORY VENTILATION

Efficiency is the watch-word and war-cry of modern industrial equipment and organization. Our immediate predecessors in manufacturing were descendants of the blacksmiths, wagon-makers and the saw-mill men, and thought they did extremely well in the way of factory building when they placed a rain-proof roof over their workers and lighted the floors with few windows of small area, though the factory was inefficiently warmed and no attempt was made towards cooling, with no adequate sanitary provisions and wholly accidental ventilation.

Now we are fully aware that the factory building must be sanitary, must give the fullest possible admission of daylight, must have artificial lighting so good that the setting of the sun does not darken the factory, must give each and every worker ready access to pure drinking water, and, last and most important of all efficiency demands, must supply workrooms with an abundance of pure air, heated or cooled as the temperature of the changing seasons of the year may require; and that this abundant pure-air supply, warmed or cooled as may be needful, must be in constant circulation and must be always in process of purification and renewal, if the maximum efficiency of the factory workers is to be obtained—and without maximum labor efficiency, no factory of today can hope for marked commercial success.

To obtain pure air throughout large workrooms some means of effecting constant air circulation, constant admission of fresh air, and efficient washing of all air, together with needful heating or cooling of the air before sending it into the factory workrooms, must be provided. Where the factory is large a great volume of air must be in constant motion, in constant process of washing, heating or cooling, and must be so supplied as to circulate constantly through every portion of every room in the factory building.

One of the very best ventilation systems ever installed in any factory building is that placed by the American Blower Company in these two large new factory buildings of the Ford Motor Company, at their Highland Park plant, Michigan.

These buildings as already described are each 842 feet long by 60 feet wide, have six floors, are 77 feet high, have 687,500 square feet of working floor area, and enclose 11,200,000 cubic feet of space.

AIR VOLUME PER MINUTE

Eight "Sirocco" fans having rotors 72 inches diameter, 36 inches face and turned at 218 revolutions per minute, are placed, one in each of eight pent-houses, equally spaced on the roof of the new buildings. Each rotor has 64 blades and when driven at 218 turns will deliver 56,000 cubic feet of air at about 1¾-inches water-column pressure. Hence, if some method of air-piping can be found which will permit the distribution of air throughout the buildings without exceeding the air pressure specified, = 1¾ water-column inches, then, dividing 11,200,000 cubic feet of building enclosed space by 448,000 cubic feet of air delivered per minute gives about 25 minutes as the time demanded for an entire change of all the air within the factory walls, if the air supply to the fans is taken wholly from the outside.

Source of Air-Supply

Provisions are made for supplying air to the fans wholly from the outside or wholly from the craneways, or partly from each source. If air to the fans is taken from outside of the building only, then temperature modifications of the entire contained air volume must be made once in each 25 minutes; if the air to the fans is taken from the craneways only, then after the building interior is once warmed, only a comparatively small additional heating need thereafter be imparted to the fan air-supply to keep the factory temperature at, say, 65 to 70 degrees F., throughout the entire working day.

Air taken from above the roof would be almost perfectly pure, and it seems quite likely that labor efficiency would be so much increased by an entire change of air once in 25 minutes as to pay for the increased air-heating cost when the factory required heating. Of course, during the warmer months, when the factory demanded cooling effect, the air would be taken from the outside, and would be delivered to the factory at "wet-bulb" temperature, which is about 72 degrees F. for Detroit.

"Conditioning" the Air

By the ventilating methods employed the fan supply of air is first drawn past an assemblage of vertical pipes supplied with water at predetermined pressure, these pipes being fitted with a sufficient number of individual atomizers to maintain a heavy mist in the air which passes through the washing chamber. On the fan side of the washing chamber the air first meets closely spaced vertical plates set at a small angle to the direct line of air travel; these plates are constantly wet, and the inclination forces the air against them so that all dust particles contained by the passing air are certain to be collected on these many vertical plates, which do not, however, deprive the air of its surplus moisture.

To separate the air from its water carried in suspension, three sets of vertical metal plates, inclined to the direct line of air movement and hooked on their fan-ward vertical edges, are placed in the air-to-fan way; the first row is spaced much closer than the second row of these vertical "eliminators" (see sectional plan of "conditioning" elements) and the second row is closer spaced than the third row, while angles and hooksides are changed in each row of water detrainers, all so that the air is freed from water in suspension before it meets the "Vento" heating stacks in its way to the fan. These Vento heating stacks are composed of flat, hollow, gray-iron sections, each one carrying on its flat sides a great number of closely placed lozenge-shaped hollow projections; these studded and hollow flat sections are placed vertically, with their edges toward the air current, and are filled inside with hot water or steam to heat the air as it passes through the vast number of narrow and crooked passages before it reaches the fans. Each one of the eight Ford-buildings ventilating units has nine sections deep of 72-inch Vento heat-

Water Atomizer of the Air-Conditioning System

Showing the flushing water piston and automatic spring returning the atomizer to adjustment when the hydrant water is shut off

ers piled two stacks high, and presents a total heating surface of 10,250 square feet to the air passing to each fan.

It is the intention to use hot water supplied from the water-jackets of the gas-engine sides of the new "Gasteam" power units which are expected to drive the Ford shops in the near future, but for immediate use a battery of steam boilers is now being placed near the eastern end of these new buildings to supply heat until the "Gasteam" motors begin working.

From the fans the thoroughly washed and cooled or heated air goes to the hollow columns, as previously specified, past individual dampers which regulate the volume of air delivered to each air release opening throughout the entire heating, cooling, and ventilating system of the buildings. The roof air-passages have brick-work walls with 4-inch air spaces between walls and the enclosed sheet-metal air passages, and are covered with cinders, tar and gravel, making these roof-ducts nearly non-conductors of heat.

Each one of the eight fans is driven by a 40 horse-power electric motor, supplied by the Westinghouse Electric Company, but the actual driving of each rotor at 218 turns requires only about 28 horse-power. The Sirocco fan is capable of delivering air at the pressure of a 40-inch water column if desired, so that the air pressure specified, equal to that of a 1¾-inch water column, is easy work on the machine. It will be understood, of course, that greater pressures of delivered air require increased power, and increased stability of rotor construction.

It will be observed that the purity of the air depends entirely on the efficient action of the water atomizers fitted to the vertical water pipes which are shown herewith in section. Dirt contained in the water collects, of course, at the very narrow annular opening where the water leaves the pipes and strikes the concave surface of the atomizer head. This dirt can be instantly dislodged by increasing the discharge annulus area. To flush all of the atomizers of one unit instantly and at once, the atomizer-head stems are spring-pressed to close the annulus, and screw-adjusted to open the annulus to deliver water suitably, and each atomizing head stem has a small diameter piston fixed to it, the piston being so seated in its cylinder that pressure on one side of the piston will compress the stem spring and push the atomizer wide open.

These atomizer piston cylinders are piped to hydrant water-pressure, all so that by simply turning on the hydrant water all the atomizers of one unit are flushed at one time, and as soon as the hydrant water is shut off, the atomizers are automatically spring-returned to their original adjustments.

The heating efficiency of the Vento stack is obviously high, since all the heat delivered by the stack must be infallibly imparted to the passing air, as there is no other conductor by which it can be carried out of the system.

The entire water-washing system is placed over a water-tight pan; the air-washing system requires the circulation of 270 gallons of water per minute, at a pressure of 50 inches of water column. This water circulation is made automatically regulating by the water-piping arrangement, and the water circulation is effected by a centrifugal pump driven by a 10 horse-power electric motor.

This admirable ventilating and air purifying and heating and cooling system is illustrated by pictures prepared especially for this account, which show its extreme simplicity and ease of control, the clever atomizer-flushing device, which makes the air-cleansing and the air-cooling certain, being especially commendable, as a less ready and certain atomizer flushing and atomizer automatic return to original adjustment might easily lead to wholly unsatisfactory operation of the entire air-purifying system.

Taken as a whole, this combination of the air-conditioning and circulating system with the hollow-column circulation of the air throughout the entire factory seems to leave nothing whatever to be desired in the way of perfectly satisfactory heating, cooling, and ventilating, and this perfection of factory air-supply cannot possibly fail to affect most favorably factory labor-efficiency, both of officials and hand workers.

Chapter XVI

SAFEGUARDING THE WORKMEN

"FAMILIARITY breeds contempt." Nowhere is the truth of this old proverb more evident than in a manufacturing establishment; every man who has worked in a shop or factory knows this.

Electricians are proverbially careless. All too frequently they work in close proximity to high-tension currents without making use of their insulation gloves or taking pains to shield themselves from the deadly current. Railroad men crawl in and out under cars and squeeze through tight places, doing things that to the lay mind would seem to court certain death.

The everyday repetition of working motions soon makes them more or less automatic, capable of performance without thought. Like the Irishman sitting on a keg of powder smoking his pipe, there comes a time when a man gets used to his work and pays little attention to the danger.

Then, too, there is another element which must be taken into consideration—the steady hum of the lathe, the incessant tapping of the hammers, the dull thud of the presses, the click-clack of the shapers, the whirr of the drills, the groaning and creaking of the milling machines and reamers; all these things combine, in a machine shop, to produce a drowsy hum that has a tendency to dull the senses and induce a semi-hypnotic state from which the workman's mind emerges only at intervals—only when a definite action requiring his close attention must be performed. In the interim, his mind may wander to a nook in the woods, an old spot on the river, or possibly to a room where a dear one is suffering alone—then, crash! Something happens. A workman is hurt; possibly killed. The dreaded accident has come. Such things can happen easily and do happen frequently in shops where the most modern safety devices have been installed, even where men are cautious and careful, where machines are running perfectly, and surrounding conditions are in every way what they should be. What is the reason, then, that accidents happen? Cannot something be done to prevent them? The answer is "yes," and "no."

Accidents may be classed under two headings—those caused by things external; those caused by things internal. To explain: Those arising from the first cause are more or less due to unprotected or improperly protected machinery, to architectural shortcomings resulting in bad arrangements and insufficient light, and to other unnecessary and avoidable reasons that arise from a faulty provision for the safety of the working force in general.

The other class of accidents spring from deliberate disobedience of orders, rules or regulations, from unintentional or careless mishandling of tools or machines, or from the peculiar mental state induced by the conditions mentioned in the preceding paragraphs. This mental state may be influenced by many conditions, such as fatigue, lack of sleep, long working hours, the constant effort in a certain direction without sufficient resting period between operations, lack of understanding of the processes involved, worry, and a hundred other kindred causes.

If, then, one is to maintain an accidentless factory, the problem

One of the Many Forms of Fire Apparatus Found in the Ford Factory

Man with Whistle Preceding Crane

resolves itself into how to control all these various influences and reduce their effect to a minimum.

Protection against things external is comparatively easy. The things to be guarded against are physical. As known quantities, their form can be studied and suitable protective means designed and installed. The Ford factory contains hundreds of such protective devices, some of the most important of which will be illustrated and described here. The internal or mental side is not so easy to dispose of; hundreds of variations are met with and must be classified and handled. In the case of one man, it may be domestic trouble; in another it may be financial worry, in a third it may result from insufficient education or a meagre understanding of language and customs. The real causes, while falling under a few general heads, are really legion—one for each personality and individual condition. Active forces are at work in the Ford organization meeting these conditions and solving them as well as man can solve them. Remarkable progress is being made along these lines.

The problem of successfully providing for the safety of working forces is not only most perplexing, but one offering little possibility of

Above: A View Looking North Through the Main Craneway, Showing the Careful Manner in Which Stock is Piled. Note Light and Cleanliness of Shop. Below: General View Showing Close Machine Grouping

General Views of the Ford Machine Shop Showing the Exceptionally Close Grouping of Machines

Safety Pad on End of Press Lever   Red Flag on Hand Press

Monorail Aisle

ever being *entirely* solved. A few accidents are bound to happen in the best of regulated factories, but modern methods and the wide-spread "Safety First Movement" have done much to reduce their number and severity. Accidents in the Ford shop are comparatively few and of a less serious nature than would be expected in a metal-working establishment of its enormous size and complex character.

Students of "Safety First" methods class the principal causes of accidents under these twelve headings:

1. Defective structures
2. Defective machinery
3. Insufficient room
4. Absence of safeguards
5. Uncleanly conditions
6. Insufficient light
7. Lack of good air
8. Unsuitable clothing
9. Carelessness
10. Ignorance
11. Bad mental condition of workman
12. Lack of co-operation.

Defective structures, defective machinery, insufficient room, uncleanly conditions, insufficient light, lack of good air, bad mental condition of the workman, lack of co-operation, all these causes may be disposed of speedily; for these causes of accidents do not exist in the Ford plant. The factory structures, machinery and general arrangements are perfectly adapted to the work; everything is new and modern, scrupulously clean and sanitary. All parts of the shop are flooded with light; the air is clean and the temperature is kept at a proper point for efficient performance of work. The manner in which all this has been provided for has been explained in the preceding chapters.

The problem of placing suitable safeguards around the machinery, and in other ways providing against the carelessness and initial ignorance of workmen, has not been described, and is, therefore, the subject of a greater part of the following text.

In several of the chapters of this book attention has been called to the unusually close grouping of the machinery, especially in the main machine shop.

At first glance the lathes, milling machines, drill presses, with their accompanying belts, conveyers and work tables, appear to be so near to each other that there seems to be no room for operators; but upon close examination of the particular place in which the workman stands, it will be found that there is ample room for him to move about easily and without injury to himself.

This intensive grouping, however, has compelled the installation of a great many ingenious and well-worked out safeguards. On this page, for instance, can be clearly seen an iron fence partially surrounding a

Cast-Iron Gates around Belts

line of drill presses, shielding the workman who operates the drill on the left from the driving belts and pulleys of the machines on the right.

Page 424 shows the type of safeguards used for surrounding pieces of mechanism operating near the floor. The visitor will see many safeguards of this type scattered about the machine shop.

Endless belt conveyers are difficult things to protect. Page 425 shows how the ends are fenced in with a framed wire netting of substantial character. Bridges are placed at intervals along the conveyer so that it can be crossed with safety.

Wire Punch and Shaft on Drill Press Guard

Page 426 illustrates another type of wire-netting inclosure used to cover the driving pulley of an emery wheel; also note the shield partially surrounding the wheel and the goggles worn by the workman to prevent flying pieces of metal from striking his eyes.

In the Ford system of machine grouping it is very often necessary to put an annealing furnace, a brazing furnace, a cyanide bath, a baking oven, or some other form of heating or heat-treatment unit, amongst the

Cage around Endless Belt

other machines. Naturally such a furnace requires ample protection to prevent the operator or other workmen from coming in contact with hot metal or a naked flame. In such instances substantial railings are erected or iron fences like those shown on page 427.

Furthermore, the large number of visitors who go through the Ford plant makes it necessary for the aisles to be well defined, and machines into which clothing might be drawn well fenced off. The cast-iron gates shown in the upper picture on page 428, the tubular railings shown

Belt Guard on Double End Grinder

in the lower view on the same page and in the illustration on page 421, illustrate well how this is done. In passing it is also interesting to note how the monorail aisles are laid out, kept open, well lighted, and kept clean, so that danger from this source is reduced to a minimum.

The ends of shafts are protected by wire cages, such as are plainly shown on pages 429 and 430. The belt guard, of course, in this case is built integral with the machine, as modern designers recognize the need for such protection and incorporate it in their initial design. The lower cut on page 430 shows a Reed lathe with a belt and pulley guard of similar construction.

In turning up parts of large components like the crank case, there is danger that the large projecting part will catch on the clothing of the operator and draw him in. For this reason, and also to keep the liquid from splashing out onto neighboring machines, a form of cylindrical shield like that shown on page 431 is used. This can be easily opened when it is desired to take out the work, and closed when the machine is in operation.

A similar type of protective shield made of reinforced wire gauze is used to cover tumbler barrels and other revolving machines. This is illustrated on page 432.

The upper illustration on page 433 shows the form of guard used on low swing lathes.

The large revolving fly wheels on punch presses and high speed engines are covered in various ways. Page 433, lower picture, shows a form of sheet-metal protector placed around the large wheel.

The cut on page 434 illustrates how workmen are protected from high-speed engine fly-wheels. On page 435 is shown a railing around the

Protector and Furnace

Above: Cast-Iron Gates around Belts. Below: Railings around Machines

platform on one of the large drawing presses, also the way in which the faces of the large gears are protected.

Sometimes in the smaller presses a wire screen is placed in the center to cover the spokes and a metal band carried around the face of the wheel to protect the teeth. On page 435 are shown two styles of safe-guards; the large wheel being protected in the manner just described, the driving wheel by a semi-circular sheet metal trough together with a tubular railing.

Where it is necessary to carry a belt across an aisle between ma-chines, a form of safeguard shown on page 436 is used. In the nearer view of this same press, on the lower part of the page, will be seen clearly the form of gate by which such presses are protected; this gate rises and falls with the press.

Wire Cage around Belts in Machine Shop

Above: Belt Guard Built Integral with Machine, Showing Future Construction of Many Types of New Machines. Below: Reed Lathe Belt Guard

Substantial guards have been built for other large presses, and a number of small devices have been designed to prevent accidents on the smaller presses where there is a tendency for the workman to stick his hand between the dies at an inopportune time for the purpose of inserting or taking out a small piece. Page 437 shows an automatic gate on a small press, used for bending the body hinge to shape. Such

Above: Guard on Lathe Used for Turning End of Crank Case, Shown Closed.
Below: Same, Shown Open

devices in addition to assuring a reasonable degree of protection, also act as mental reminders, calling attention to the specific action, and momentarily, at least, acting as a warning signal.

Such devices as those already described, and also those which are striking in their color, direction, and suddenness of operation, have a peculiar psychological effect upon the workman and in most cases serve as sufficient warning of danger, effectually breaking the monotony which would otherwise result from a continuous series of more or less regu-

Guard on Tumbler Barrel

lar motions. Scattered throughout the shop are numerous "danger" warnings, notices, and cards, bearing the words, "To stop this machine pull plug." The starting switches for the draw presses are protected by large red metal tags which must be removed before the switch can be turned. This act serves as a mental reminder to see that everything is clear before setting this powerful machinery in motion.

The whistle sounded by the man who precedes the cranes, the clanging bel in the monorail cars, are examples of other protective measures

Guard on Low Swing Lathe

Tin Protector around Large Fly Wheel

along the same line, employed in the Ford factory, to render the lives of the men as safe as possible.

There are, of course, some places in the Ford factory where the element of great danger is ever present. In the foundry and heat-treatment departments where molten metal and high temperatures are found on every side, great precautions have been taken to prevent accidents and bad burns. The furnaces in the heat-treat department are all provided with fire shields like that shown on page 437. Saw-dust and sand

Wire Screen Over Fly-Wheel Spokes

boxes, with directions designed to instruct the men in the best way of preventing and putting out fires of various kinds, are distributed throughout all parts of these shops. (See page 439.) In the foundry plenty of room is allowed for pouring; the men are provided with long-handled ladles equipped with shields, and the work is done under a saw-tooth roof which, as shown in the illustration on page 439, admits plenty of light and renders the conditions under which the workmen must work as near ideal as possible.

Above: Railing around Platform on Big Drawing Press
Below: Press Forming Lamp Bracket

Bliss Crank-Case Forming Press

Upper left: Wire cage, overhead guard, and automatic gate.   Upper right: General view showing platform on top of press.   Below: Near view of automatic gate

Needless to say, the Ford foundry is well equipped as regards fire protection—hand grenades, reels of hose, sprinkler systems, and a practically fire-proof form of concrete and steel construction, make the fire danger a rather remote one. There are, however, places where a fire could start and attain considerable proportions if it were allowed to get beyond control. Some very ingenious methods of killing a fire under such circumstances are to be found in the fender baking system.

Paints and enameling liquids, due to their composition, are, of course, extremely combustible,

Automatic Gate on Ferracute Body Hinge Press

and were a fire to start in one of these large paint vats it would be very difficult to put out as long as the fuel lasted. In one tank alone, that used for giving the fenders a second coat, about 1,200 gallons of

Fire Shield in Front of each Furnace in Heat-Treat Department

enamel are kept constantly on hand. Should this inflammable liquid suddenly take fire it would be very hard to control were no provision made for emptying the vat. To point out how completely the Ford engineers have anticipated such a situation, I will explain what would happen if a fire of this nature broke out.

Each enameling tank throughout the factory is provided with a metal cover which, in most cases, is held up by a rope or wire cable provided with a fuse that melts quickly in the presence of a high temperature. In the case of the large tank, above mentioned, a cover cannot be used, so a fire door has been introduced between it and the dripping chamber beyond. The main problem is, of course, to empty the tank as rapidly as possible. For this purpose a large tank has been placed underground. outside the factory wall, connected to the overhead tank by a large pipe line of sufficient size to enable the entire contents to be withdrawn in three minutes. The enameling tank is on the fourth floor and the valve in the pipe on the third floor; therefore it is not necessary for the workman to approach the fire in order to empty the tank. A system of steam jets, easily reached, makes the extinguishing of the fire, caused from the remaining enamel in the tank, a matter of only a few minutes. This one example is given to show the thoroughness with which precautionary measures of all kinds are employed throughout the Ford factory.

The foregoing descriptions have shown, meagerly, how the Ford management is devising and installing every possible type of mechanical safeguard; trying to make all parts of the huge plant safe against foolhardiness. Of the twelve principal causes of accidents mentioned previously, we have seen that the only ones that may exist in the Ford plant are ignorance and unsuitable clothing. And of these, ignorance is the greater danger. From the polyglot nature of the workmen, and, in some instances, the low degree of mentality required in certain work, unusual care must necessarily follow the installation of new machinery or the hiring of new men. This attention is given by the foremen of each department. Danger signs of unmistakable character, easily read by the most ignorant, are everywhere in evidence and the specific dangers they prevent are pointed out. Constant warning is given, until it would seem that no accident by any remote chance could occur.

Obviously the workman himself should guard against unsuitable clothing. He should need no caution against loose clothing, for instance, among whirling shafts and speeding belts. A flowing tie, an open jacket, or torn sleeve, has been the cause of countless horrible accidents in ma-

Above: Saw-Dust and Sand Boxes in Heat-Treat Department
Below: Pouring in Foundry

chine shops from time immemorial. Shop tradition, it would seem, should long ago have stamped out that danger. On the contrary, unsuitable clothing of one sort or another exists wherever a machine shop or foundry exists. The management can only hope to minimize the danger by devising safeguards for every exposed moving part. Unsuspected sources can only be guarded after trouble has developed, of course, but the modern manufacturer leaves as little as possible to chance.

TECHNOLOGY AND SOCIETY

An Arno Press Collection

Ardrey, R[obert] L. **American Agricultural Implements.** In two parts. 1894

Arnold, Horace Lucien and Fay Leone Faurote. **Ford Methods and the Ford Shops.** 1915

Baron, Stanley [Wade]. **Brewed in America:** A History of Beer and Ale in the United States. 1962

Bathe, Greville and Dorothy. **Oliver Evans:** A Chronicle of Early American Engineering. 1935

Bendure, Zelma and Gladys Pfeiffer. **America's Fabrics:** Origin and History, Manufacture, Characteristics and Uses. 1946

Bichowsky, F. Russell. **Industrial Research.** 1942

Bigelow, Jacob. **The Useful Arts:** Considered in Connexion with the Applications of Science. 1840. Two volumes in one

Birkmire, William H. **Skeleton Construction in Buildings.** 1894

Boyd, T[homas] A[lvin]. **Professional Amateur:** The Biography of Charles Franklin Kettering. 1957

Bright, Arthur A[aron], Jr. **The Electric-Lamp Industry:** Technological Change and Economic Development from 1800 to 1947. 1949

Bruce, Alfred and Harold Sandbank. **The History of Prefabrication.** 1943

Carr, Charles C[arl]. **Alcoa, An American Enterprise.** 1952

Cooley, Mortimer E. **Scientific Blacksmith.** 1947

Davis, Charles Thomas. **The Manufacture of Paper.** 1886

Deane, Samuel. **The New-England Farmer,** or Georgical Dictionary. 1822

Dyer, Henry. **The Evolution of Industry.** 1895

Epstein, Ralph C. **The Automobile Industry:** Its Economic and Commercial Development. 1928

Ericsson, Henry. **Sixty Years a Builder:** The Autobiography of Henry Ericsson. 1942

Evans, Oliver. **The Young Mill-Wright and Miller's Guide.** 1850

Ewbank, Thomas. **A Descriptive and Historical Account of Hydraulic and Other Machines for Raising Water,** Ancient and Modern. 1842

Field, Henry M. **The Story of the Atlantic Telegraph.** 1893

Fleming, A. P. M. **Industrial Research in the United States of America.** 1917

Van Gelder, Arthur Pine and Hugo Schlatter. **History of the Explosives Industry in America.** 1927

Hall, Courtney Robert. **History of American Industrial Science.** 1954

Hungerford, Edward. **The Story of Public Utilities.** 1928

Hungerford, Edward. **The Story of the Baltimore and Ohio Railroad, 1827-1927.** 1928

Husband, Joseph. **The Story of the Pullman Car.** 1917

Ingels, Margaret. **Willis Haviland Carrier, Father of Air Conditioning.** 1952

Kingsbury, J[ohn] E. **The Telephone and Telephone Exchanges:** Their Invention and Development. 1915

Labatut, Jean and Wheaton J. Lane, eds. **Highways in Our National Life:** A Symposium. 1950

Lathrop, William G[ilbert]. **The Brass Industry in the United States.** 1926

Lesley, Robert W., John B. Lober and George S. Bartlett. **History of the Portland Cement Industry in the United States.** 1924

Marcosson, Isaac F. **Wherever Men Trade:** The Romance of the Cash Register. 1945

Miles, Henry A[dolphus]. **Lowell, As It Was, and As It Is**. 1845

Morison, George S. **The New Epoch:** As Developed by the Manufacture of Power. 1903

Olmsted, Denison. **Memoir of Eli Whitney, Esq.** 1846

Passer, Harold C. **The Electrical Manufacturers, 1875-1900.** 1953

Prescott, George B[artlett]. **Bell's Electric Speaking Telephone.** 1884

Prout, Henry G. **A Life of George Westinghouse.** 1921

Randall, Frank A. **History of the Development of Building Construction in Chicago.** 1949

Riley, John J. **A History of the American Soft Drink Industry:** Bottled Carbonated Beverages, 1807-1957. 1958

Salem, F[rederick] W[illiam]. **Beer, Its History and Its Economic Value as a National Beverage.** 1880

Smith, Edgar F. **Chemistry in America.** 1914

Steinman, D[avid] B[arnard]. **The Builders of the Bridge:** The Story of John Roebling and His Son. 1950

Taylor, F[rank] Sherwood. **A History of Industrial Chemistry.** 1957

Technological Trends and National Policy, Including the Social Implications of New Inventions. Report of the Subcommittee on Technology to the National Resources Committee. 1937

Thompson, John S. **History of Composing Machines.** 1904

Thompson, Robert Luther. **Wiring a Continent:** The History of the Telegraph Industry in the United States, 1832-1866. 1947

Tilley, Nannie May. **The Bright-Tobacco Industry, 1860-1929.** 1948

Tooker, Elva. **Nathan Trotter:** Philadelphia Merchant, 1787-1853. 1955

Turck, J. A. V. **Origin of Modern Calculating Machines.** 1921

Tyler, David Budlong. **Steam Conquers the Atlantic.** 1939

Wheeler, Gervase. **Homes for the People,** In Suburb and Country. 1855